BLACK WOMEN'S HEALTH
IN THE AGE OF HIP HOP AND HIV/AIDS

BLACK WOMEN'S HEALTH IN THE AGE OF HIP HOP AND HIV/AIDS

A NARRATIVE REMIX

Nghana tamu Lewis

THE OHIO STATE UNIVERSITY PRESS
COLUMBUS

Copyright © 2025 by The Ohio State University.
All rights reserved.

Library of Congress Cataloging-in-Publication data available online at https://catalog.loc.gov
LCCN: 2024039807

Identifiers: ISBN 978-0-8142-1580-7 (hardback); ISBN 978-0-8142-5934-4 (paperback); ISBN 978-0-8142-8383-7 (ebook)

Cover design by Susan Zucker
Text design by Juliet Williams
Type set in Adobe Minion Pro

♾ The paper used in this publication meets the minimum requirements of the American National Standard for Information Sciences—Permanence of Paper for Printed Library Materials. ANSI Z39.48-1992.

CONTENTS

Acknowledgments   *vii*

INTRODUCTION   A Tale of Three Influences: My Roots/Routes (in)to Black Women's Health, Hip Hop, and HIV/AIDS   1

CHAPTER 1   In Search of Our Mothers' Theories: Hip Hop Feminism in Praxis   15

CHAPTER 2   "Cunt Buckets" and "Bad Bitches": Black Girl Identity Formation and Sexual Health in *PUSH: A Novel* and *The Coldest Winter Ever*   27

CHAPTER 3   Transnational Flow(s): Staging Silence, Stigma, and Shame in *In the Continuum*   67

CHAPTER 4   "Prioritized": The Hip Hop (Re)Construction of Black Womanhood in *Girlfriends* and *The Game*   93

CHAPTER 5   In Memoriam—and in Life   123

Appendix   *Empirical Studies of Black Women, Silence, Shame, Stigma, and HIV/AIDS, 1986–2006*   *131*

Bibliography   *139*

Index   *161*

ACKNOWLEDGMENTS

This book was completed with generous financial support from the Newcomb College Institute at Tulane University, Tulane University's School of Liberal Arts, the Lavin-Bernick Faculty Grant Program, and the New Orleans Center for the Gulf South Monroe Fellows Research Grant Program.

To Ana Maria Jimenez-Moreno and the entire team at The Ohio State University Press: thank you for believing in this project.

I am always indebted to Sika Dagbovie-Mullins and Miyoshi Brown, for the professional community we share and for the support we have given one another, for the past twenty-five years, in our lives away from work.

Thank you, Mom and Dad, Kay, Fra, Scottie, Chi, Luke, Seth, Sasha, and Brock, for your unfailing love and encouragement; Corey, for being my best part; and Ciel and Cydney, for being my forever inspirations.

This book is dedicated to my cousin, Jason; my grandmother, Agnes; the activist Hydeia Broadbent; and all my ancestors guiding me from the spiritual world: I love you.

Portions of the introduction were originally published in Nghana Lewis, "Black Women's Health in the Age of Hip Hop & HIV/AIDS: A Model for Civic Engagement and Feminist Activism," *On Campus with Women* 38, no. 3

(Winter 2010). Reprinted with permission from the American Association of Colleges and Universities.

Excerpts of chapter 4 were originally published in Nghana Lewis, "Prioritized: The Hip Hop Reconstruction of Black Womanhood in *Girlfriends* and *The Game*," in *Watching While Black: Centering the Television of Black Audiences*, edited by Beretta Smith Shomade (New Brunswick: Rutgers University Press), 157–71. Reprinted with permission from Rutgers University Press.

INTRODUCTION

A Tale of Three Influences

My Roots/Routes (in)to Black Women's Health, Hip Hop, and HIV/AIDS

I do not see how colored women can be true to themselves unless they demand recognition for themselves and those they represent.
—Ida B. Wells-Barnett, *Crusade for Justice,* 364

You never know what is going to strike you, and you never know when it's going to strike you, but it's going to strike you, when you're open to receiving it.
—Byllye Avery, interview by Loretta Ross, 16

I don't plan on dying from anything, anytime soon.
—Jason Merrill Perry

Hindsight has clarifying force. Thus, it does not surprise me that HIV/AIDS entered my life at about the same time that novelists Sapphire and Sister Souljah; screenwriter, producer, and director Mara Brock Akil; and playwrights Nikkole Salter and Danai Gurira began summoning me and other black women and girls[1] in response to the impact of HIV/AIDS on our lives. Coming of age on hip hop throughout the 1980s and 1990s made it easy to recognize the language that these artists used to get my attention. Less easy was accepting that HIV/AIDS mattered to my existence, and thus, attending to the artists' consciousness-raising objectives. To paraphrase Byllye Avery, founder of the National Black Women's Health Project (known now as the Black Women's Health Imperative), and Ida B. Wells-Barnett, I was not open to receiving HIV/AIDS as relevant to my life, despite the pride I claimed to take in being a

---

1. Throughout, "black" refers to people of African origin or descent and people in the United States who socially and/or politically identify as "black." The existence of heterogeneity within African descent populations is undisputed. Studies reflective of this fact are vast and easy to locate.

black woman and advocating for black people. Change came about on August 13, 1995, the date my cousin, Jason, was shot five times in the line of duty: first in the chest, then in the spinal cord, left leg, left foot, and right leg.[2] He was twenty-three years old and had been an officer with Baton Rouge City Police for two weeks. Much of what transpired in the weeks that passed before Jason moved from the ICU to a private hospital room remains a blur. What I will never forget are the words Jason spoke, as the family gathered at his bedside for what we thought would be our first chance to talk about the shooting and his recovery: "I'm HIV-positive," he said. "I thought you should know, because I don't plan on dying from anything, anytime soon."

Until that moment, I never really thought about HIV, although I knew that, if left undetected or untreated in an infected person, the human immunodeficiency virus could lead to acquired immunodeficiency syndrome, the disease commonly referred to as AIDS.[3] My introduction came in 1991, when Earvin "Magic" Johnson announced his retirement from professional basketball because he had "attained" the virus. I remember finding the word "attained" oddly used but thought nothing more after Magic's announcement. Three years later, Chicago socialite and political organizer Rae Lewis Thornton became the first black woman living with AIDS to grace the cover of *Essence* magazine.[4] Seeing the cover, I thought, "What a pretty sister," but I did not read her story. Eazy-E, founder, president, and CEO of Ruthless Records and former member of NWA, died from AIDS-related complications a few months before Jason was shot. In a statement read by his attorney at a press conference the week before his passing, Eazy asked his fans to be vigilant, take precaution, and know that no one was immune.[5] I was a fan of Eazy, but did not give his plea a second thought. Until Jason announced his status, HIV and AIDS were nothing more than acronyms to me. They took on new meaning for me because Jason mattered to me. Making HIV/AIDS matter, regardless of our relationships with people living with HIV or AIDS, or who have died from AIDS-related complications, is this book's primary objective. Inextricably tied to this objective is examining how Sapphire, Souljah, Brock Akil, and Salter and Gurira imagined, embraced, and negotiated the specific challenges of making HIV/AIDS matter to black women and girls at the turn of

---

2. *State of Louisiana v. Ricky Fugler.*

3. June 5, 1981, marked the official onset of the HIV/AIDS epidemic, with the Centers for Disease Control and Prevention's (CDC's) report of five cases of *Pneumocystis carinii* pneumonia among previously healthy young men in Los Angeles. CDC, *Morbidity and Mortality.* As detailed in chapter 2, the earliest suspected cases of HIV/AIDS infection within black populations were in New York City in the late 1970s, and the mode of transmission is now widely believed to be IV-drug use.

4. Lewis-Thornton, "Facing AIDS."

5. Wild and Wiederhorn, "Eazy-E."

the twenty-first century. Their work equipped me to do the work of making HIV/AIDS matter to the masses.

That the lives of people who died from AIDS-related complications and are living with HIV or AIDS matter was a highly contested point at the onset of the epidemic, when high incidence and death rates, imprecise science, poor education, stigma, and politics controlled the narratives around HIV/AIDS. That the lives of people who died from AIDS-related complications and are living with HIV or AIDS matter remains a point too often obscured today, by poor education; politics; stigma; the exigencies of more recent global crises, such as COVID-19;[6] and advances in modern treatments and care management systems, which make it possible for people diagnosed with HIV to live long, healthy lives. The latter has even greater obfuscating effect when we consider numbers comparatively.

In 1995, the year HIV/AIDS entered my life, AIDS-related complications accounted for the deaths of approximately 870,000 adults and children worldwide. In 2022, AIDS-related complications accounted for the deaths of approximately 630,000 adults and children worldwide.[7] In 1995, 17.7 million adults and children were living with HIV and 3 million adults and children were newly infected with the virus worldwide.[8] In 2022, 39 million adults and children were living with HIV and approximately 1.3 million adults and children were newly infected with the virus worldwide.[9] While death and incidence rates have decreased over time, people continue to die from AIDS-related complications and become newly infected with HIV in sobering numbers.[10] Black women and girls have been consistently, disproportionately represented in these numbers.[11]

---

6. The effects of COVID-19 on viral overload in black women living with HIV is the subject of current trials. For preliminary findings, see Dale et al., "Daily Microaggressions and Related Distress."

7. UNAIDS, "HIV Estimates with Uncertainty Bounds."

8. UNAIDS, "HIV Estimates with Uncertainty Bounds"; and UNAIDS, *Path That Ends AIDS*.

9. UNAIDS, "HIV Estimates with Uncertainty Bounds"; and UNAIDS, *Path That Ends AIDS*.

10. HIV.gov, "Global HIV and AIDS Epidemic."

11. The earliest data released by the Centers for Disease Control and Prevention in response to physicians from metropolises across the United States reporting "cases of persistent, generalized lymphadenopathy—not attributable to previously identified causes—among homosexual males" were based on a sample size of fifty-seven males, 15 percent of whom were black. CDC, "Epidemiologic Notes and Reports." For the earliest epidemiological and environmental studies of HIV/AIDS among black women, see Ellerbrock et al., "Epidemiology of Women with AIDS"; Fullilove, Fullilove, et al., "Black Women and AIDS Prevention"; O'Leary and Jemmott, *Women at Risk*; DiClemente and Wingood, "Randomized Controlled Trial"; Rosenberg, "Scope of the AIDS Epidemic"; and Bedimo et al., "Understanding Barriers to Condom Usage."

According to the Centers for Disease Control and Prevention's most recent surveillance data, after black, white, and Latino men who have sex with men (MSM), heterosexual black women account for the largest group of people living with HIV or AIDS in the United States.[12] The Joint United Nations Programme on HIV/AIDS 2020 surveillance data reveal that in sub-Saharan Africa, women and girls accounted for 63 percent of all new HIV infections and six in seven new HIV infections among adolescents aged fifteen to nineteen.[13] Further, young women aged fifteen to twenty-four in sub-Saharan Africa were twice as likely as men to be living with HIV.[14] This study elaborates how Sapphire, Souljah, Brock Akil, and Salter and Gurira grappled with these numbers in service of a countervailing, collective voice, at a time when HIV/AIDS's striking impact on black women in the States and abroad was given short shrift in predominant medical, political, and popular cultural circles.

Building on the "intervention, challenge, change"[15] tenets of black feminist thought and black feminist activism, whose developments span multiple generations, Sapphire, Souljah, Brock Akil, and Salter and Gurira used the analytic and practical tools of hip hop feminism to foster a continuum of knowledge, between 1996 and 2006, in response to the most pressing public health issue affecting black women and girls during this historical period: HIV/AIDS. In the historical context of the HIV/AIDS epidemic, 1996 to 2006 is conventionally marked, on one end, by the availability of highly active anti-retroviral therapy to treat HIV infection[16] and, on the other end, by the first annual observance of National Women and Girls HIV/AIDS Awareness Day in the United States.[17] The span of 1996 to 2006 also marks the period of national and global reckoning with jarring incidence and prevalence rates of HIV/AIDS among black women and girls and the corresponding revelation that these data were foreseeable, but ignored, at the onset of the epidemic.[18]

---

12. The CDC provides a caveat regarding the accuracy of 2020 data because of the impact of COVID-19 on access to HIV testing, care surveillance, and care-related services. See CDC, "Diagnosis of HIV Infection."

13. These numbers trend higher in 2022 surveillance data, with girls and young women in sub-Saharan Africa accounting for 66 percent of new HIV infections among people aged fifteen years and above. However, 2022 surveillance data also show sharp declines in the total number of new HIV infections reported throughout most of sub-Saharan Africa. The impact of COVID-19 on these data is not yet known. UNAIDS, *Path That Ends AIDS*.

14. UNAIDS, "World AIDS Day 2023."

15. hooks, *Reel to Real*, 9.

16. Pau and George, "Antiretroviral Therapy."

17. "HIV/AIDS Education."

18. Hammonds, "Gendering the Epidemic."

In 1996, the Joint United Nations Programme on HIV/AIDS (UNAIDS) published the *Status and Trends of the Global HIV/AIDS Pandemic* from the Satellite Symposium of the 11th International Conference on AIDS, a report in which worldwide HIV/AIDS incidence rates for the previous year were documented.[19] While the data indicated an overall slowing in AIDS incidence in the United States, they also showed a "substantive shift in the populations affected," with incidence rates being 6.5 times greater for blacks than for whites.[20] The data also revealed that in 1995, 20 percent of new AIDS diagnoses in the United States were among women, 15 percent of whom were infected heterosexually.[21] In 2000, UNAIDS reported global estimates of the HIV/AIDS epidemic, indicating that women accounted for a little less than 50 percent of adults newly infected with HIV in 1999, 52 percent of AIDS-related deaths among adults for the same year, and 51 percent of AIDS-related deaths among adults since the beginning of the epidemic.[22] Two years later, the Centers for Disease Control and Prevention's *HIV/AIDS Surveillance Report* revealed that as of December 2001, black women accounted for 58 percent of cumulative AIDS cases among adolescent and adult women of all racial and ethnic groups in the United States, and AIDS incidence rates for black women were approximately 5 times the rate of the entire US population.[23] The neglect of these data was perhaps never more notoriously brought to light than during the 2004 vice presidential debate, when the late journalist Gwen Ifill attempted to engage then vice president Dick Cheney and vice presidential candidate John Edwards in a conversation about HIV/AIDS among black women in the United States.[24]

"I want to talk to you about health care," Ifill began, "but in particular, I want to talk to you about AIDS, and not AIDS in China or Africa, but AIDS

---

19. UNAIDS, *Status and Trends*. The two-day symposium on which the report was based took place July 5 and 6, 1996, in Vancouver, Canada, and was organized by the AIDS Control and Prevention (AIDSCAP) Project of Family Health International, the François-Xavier Bagnoud Center for Health and Human Rights of the Harvard School of Public Health, and UNAIDS.

20. UNAIDS, *Status and Trends*.

21. UNAIDS, *Status and Trends*. The report indicated that roughly 60 percent of the world's total HIV infections were located in sub-Saharan Africa, and in this region, "rates of newly acquired HIV infections were highest in the 15-to-24-year-old group among both females and males" (5).

22. UNAIDS, *Report*, 6.

23. CDC, "Cases of HIV Infection," 6–7.

24. "Transcript: Vice Presidential Debate"; see also Arledge, *Out of Control*. The late journalist Peter Jennings produced and narrated this ABC special, which aired August 24, 2006. Whitney Peoples alludes to the debate in her historiography of hip hop feminism and its relationship to other traditions of black feminist writing. See Peoples, "'Under Construction.'"

right here in [the United States] where black women between the ages of 25 and 44 are 13 times more likely to die from the disease than their counterparts. What should the government's role be in helping to end the growth of this epidemic?"[25] Unable to respond to Ifill's question because, as Cheney readily admitted, he had "not heard those numbers with respect to African American women," both Cheney and Edwards resorted to speaking in platitudes that acknowledged the global devastation caused by HIV/AIDS without addressing the specific impact of the epidemic among black women.[26] This study chronicles the work that Sapphire, Souljah, Brock Akil, and Salter and Gurira undertook to counteract the consequences of this obliviousness and related omissions and oversights, by marshaling a global will to change the social, political, and cultural conditions that place(d) black women and girls at disproportionate risk of becoming infected with HIV and dying from AIDS-related complications.[27]

If, as Foucault has argued, caring for one's self requires understanding immutable forces and conditions outside the realm of the personal that impact personal health,[28] then Sapphire, Souljah, Brock Akil, and Salter and Gurira are distinguished for the truths they collectively sought to tell about the life-altering role that HIV/AIDS played in the lives of black women and girls at the turn of the twenty-first century. This undertaking built upon the centuries-old work of black women artists who have always provided "the signs and symbols" of black women's "struggle for life," as social psychiatrist and veteran HIV/AIDS researcher Dr. Mindy Thompson Fullilove observes.[29] Indeed, the long history of black struggle for human rights, civil rights, and equal protection reveals that artists have always played indispensable roles in informing and mobilizing the masses.[30]

However, as Dorie Gilbert and Ednita Wright make clear in the introduction to the germinal essay collection *African American Women and HIV/AIDS: Critical Responses,* telling stories that have meaning to and for black

---

25. "Transcript: Vice Presidential Debate."

26. "Transcript: Vice Presidential Debate." Cheney's befuddlement was especially egregious, because four years prior, Congresswoman Barbara Lee, who represents California's 13th District, had worked with the Bush administration to draft and secure passage of the President's Emergency Plan for AIDS Relief (PEPFAR), while concurrently working with other members of the Congressional Black Caucus to compel the administration to declare an HIV/AIDS state of emergency in black communities throughout the United States.

27. Hammonds, "AIDS."

28. These tenets underlie much of Foucault's writing about human sexuality. See especially *The Use of Pleasure* and *The Care of the Self.*

29. Fullilove, foreword to *African American Women and HIV/AIDS,* x.

30. Studies reflective of this fact are voluminous and easy to locate.

women is not easy because of the "triple burdens" of race, gender, and class discrimination that have defined black women's lived experiences for centuries[31] and have historically marginalized their perspectives in mainstream artistic, political, and medical responses to public health crises.[32] Infant mortality and pregnancy-related complications and death, for example, have disproportionately impacted black women in the United States since the antebellum period, but these phenomena have only recently become focal points of well-funded clinical trials and biomedical research.[33] Married black women have higher allostatic loads in comparison to their white married and white and black unmarried counterparts,[34] and black women with low income and education are as likely to seek care for mental health disease as black women with middle-to-high incomes and education.[35] These facts and their implications are largely elided in empirical studies of morbidity, mortality, and black women's health.[36] In *Holding On: African American Women Surviving HIV/ AIDS*, Alyson O'Daniel imputes the specific neglect of day-to-day emotional, economic, environmental, and social factors shaping the conditions of black women living with HIV and AIDS to scientists' preoccupation with clinical measures that reduce black women to numbers associated with "length of time since diagnosis [. . .] blood quantification reporting, and programmatic service expenditures,"[37] but the marginalization and erasure of black women's lived experiences in discourses that implicate their health is not limited to scientific research. In their examinations of the history of AIDS activism, Paula Treichler and Sarah Schulman describe how power struggles within organizations that formed in the 1980s to lobby the government for more clinical drug trials resulted in the life experiences of middle-class gay white men controlling narratives around risk and thus, by extension, more resources being poured into middle-class gay white male communities to address the crisis.[38] In *The Normal Heart*, the late playwright and founder of the AIDS Coalition to Unleash Power (ACT-UP) Larry Kramer gestures toward the destructive effects of the politics of AIDS activism on black women in the early years

---

31. Gilbert and Wright, *African American Women and HIV/AIDS*, 6; Cohen, *Boundaries of Blackness*, 20–21; and Treichler, *How to Have Theory*, 12–14.

32. Gilbert and Wright, *African American Women and HIV/AIDS*, 5.

33. Kukura, "Better Birth"; Thompson, "Why We Need to Understand"; and Oribhabor et al., "Mother's Cry."

34. Tobin et al., "Does Marriage Matter?"

35. Copeland et al., "Major Depressive Disorder."

36. Klonoff et al., "Introduction"; and Mehra et al., "Black Pregnant Women."

37. O'Daniel, *Holding On*, 6.

38. Schulman, *Let the Record Show*; and Treichler, *How to Have Theory*. See also Shotwell, "'Women Don't Get AIDS.'"

of the epidemic, when the play's sole female character, Dr. Emma Brookner, bemoans the rejection of her funding proposal by the NIH: "We are enduring an epidemic of death. Women have been discovered to have it in Africa—where it is clearly transmitted heterosexually."[39] Persistent new incidence and stalling prevalence rates of HIV/AIDS among black women and girls in a contemporary moment suggest that the distinctive social and cultural experiences of this population continue to be marginalized and ignored in prevailing narratives of risk.

Marlon Bailey and Rodrigo Aguayo-Romero offer related accounts of why this is the case in pointing, on the one hand, to the failure of black studies "to delineate, in a cogent and coherent fashion, the co-constitutive nature of anti-Black racism and heteropatriarchy and HIV/AIDS-related stigma,"[40] and, on the other hand, the failure of mainstream medical and public health research to attend to the demands of intersectionality, which emphasize praxis as much as theory. "Intersectionality was designed to analyze interlocking systems of privilege and oppression and to develop strategies that challenge those systems," Aguayo-Romero observes. But "simply knowing my intersecting identities does not inform whether and to what extent I experienced oppression." He continues:

> Researchers must shift their practices and analyze social processes when conducting intersectional research. Social processes, such as experiences of discrimination, allow us to assess the effect of intersecting systems of privilege and oppression at the individual level and also to advance our understanding at the population level. [. . .] Assessing the structural-level effect of intersecting systems of privilege and oppression is central to intersectionality but more difficult to capture by assessing individual experiences. Although individuals can identify social processes, they might not necessarily identify the structures and institutions upholding those processes. For that reason, the analysis and discussion of individual-level results must address the structural level by providing the sociocultural context (laws, policies, norms, and interpersonal practices) of structural inequality on the research population.[41]

Before social media, streaming, and other digital platforms made it possible to target audiences, rapidly disseminate information, and correct misinformation,[42] and at a time when the exclusion of black women and girls

---

39. Kramer, *Normal Heart*, 81.
40. Bailey, "Whose Body Is It," 164.
41. Aguayo-Romero, "(Re)centering Black Feminism," 101–2.
42. B. Hill et al., "Leveraging Social Media."

as participants in empirical studies was not yet under direct indictment,[43] Sapphire, Souljah, Brock Akil, and Salter and Gurira used their platforms as artists to fill these discursive voids by confronting the effects of HIV/AIDS on black women and girls head-on.

Central to the methods that shaped and directed their artistic production are what I refer to throughout this study as Sapphire's, Souljah's, Brock Akil's, and Salter and Gurira's hip hop feminist states of mind, or what Gwendolyn Pough characterizes as the "oft-forgotten fifth element" of hip hop cultural production: "knowledge."[44] Knowledge consists of the "aesthetic, social, intellectual, and political identities, beliefs, behaviors, and values produced and embraced" by black women and girls for whom hip hop is a "way of life."[45] It is both product and process and reflects a conscious commitment to theory and praxis, as elaborated by Aguayo-Romero, in that black women's lived experiences are acknowledged, located, and examined in relation to social, historical, and cultural forces that shape these experiences. Knowledge is often fraught with tensions that can emerge at the sites of black women's intersecting subject positions, ways of knowing and experiencing the world, and complicity with systems that oppress them.[46] Rather than eschew these tensions, however, knowledge, as generated from within a hip hop feminist state of mind, embraces conflict, contradiction, and incongruence in order to amplify insight into the complexities of black women's lived experiences. While acknowledging that black women and girls are not a monolith, knowledge rooted in hip hop feminism nevertheless understands that black women's and girls' shared experiences with interlocked systems of oppression can inform and support collective, responsive action.[47]

Sami Shalk says that knowledge that seeks to improve the plights of people living with health challenges and directly impacted by disparities in access to quality health care services must resonate beyond the academy and filter into the day-to-day activities of people positioned to effect change.[48] Between 1996 and 2006, Sapphire, Souljah, Brock Akil, and Salter and Gurira intervened into prevailing knowledge systems around HIV/AIDS by centering

---

43. A literature review suggests that the earliest comprehensive examination of black women's exclusion from clinical trials and empirical studies involving the "problems that are most prevalent among and accountable for the poor health of Black women" was published in 1997. See the special issue of *Women's Health: Research on Gender, Behavior, and Policy* 3, no. 3–4 (Fall–Winter 1997).

44. Pough, "What It Do, Shorty?," 79.

45. M. Morgan and Bennett, "Hip-Hop and the Global Imprint," 177.

46. J. Morgan, *When Chickenheads Come Home*, 22.

47. Pough, "What It Do, Shorty?," 82.

48. Schalk, *Black Disability Politics*.

black women's and girls' lived experiences. These acts of creative-artistic disruption foregrounded the indispensable, yet underrepresented and underexamined, perspective that hip hop feminism brought—and continues to bring—to clarifying the personal, social, economic, and geopolitical ramifications of HIV/AIDS for black women and girls. Through rounded, complex character developments and layered narrative arcs, Sapphire, Souljah, Brock Akil, and Salter and Gurira elucidated and explored the politics of black girl identity formation and black female sexuality in direct relation to questions of self-care implicated by risk of and exposure to HIV as well as questions of self-care implicated by the expectations, benefits, and costs of black women caring for others. In this, the artists untangled and examined the network of factors—individual, social-contextual, and structural—that not only disproportionately increased risk for exposure to HIV/AIDS but also rendered black women and girls disproportionately vulnerable to a wider range of adverse health conditions, including stress, rape, unwanted pregnancy, domestic abuse battery, mental health disorders, and inadequate access to quality health care. They catalyzed thought and action in response to the particular circumstances of black women and girls and the will to change the conditions that put(s) black women and girls at disproportionate risk of becoming HIV infected and dying from AIDS-related complications. The five chapters that comprise this study flesh and substantiate these arguments by juxtaposing and cross-referencing close readings of creative works produced by Sapphire, Souljah, Brock Akil, and Salter and Gurira between 1996 and 2006 with epidemiological and empirical HIV/AIDS data from the same historical period. In this way, this study underscores the value of rigorous, sustained inquiry at the interplay among humanities, social science, and medical research.

Chapter 1 outlines the continuum of thought that anchors this project and draws from the vast literature on hip hop feminism to elaborate the common creative-disruptive ground that Sapphire, Souljah, Brock Akil, and Salter and Gurira staked out in response to HIV/AIDS. Emphasizing the praxis-focused tenets of hip hop feminism, I investigate how these artists' creative works are mutually constitutive of hip hop feminist–informed calls for black women and girls to heed the exigencies and circumstances of black women's health created by the HIV/AIDS epidemic. I also show how the intellectual and aesthetic roots of hip hop feminism shape and unsettle discourses of language use, silencing, visibility, protection, and preservation in Sapphire's, Souljah's, Brock Akil's, and Salter and Gurira's works.

In chapter 2, I match the aesthetics of hip hop feminism with temporal and spatial metaphors in Sapphire's *PUSH* and Souljah's *The Coldest Winter Ever* to show how interlocked questions of influence, image, and location impact black girl identity formation. I argue that Sapphire and Souljah advance knowledge of the workings of this process by accounting for the role of private family dynamics, specifically mother-daughter relationships, on the linguistic practices of the novels' black girl protagonists, Claireece "Precious" Jones and Winter Santiaga, and how these practices inform both Precious's and Winter's understandings of themselves as social agents and sexual subjects.[49] The authorities that Winter and Precious command as first-person narrators in *PUSH* and *The Coldest Winter Ever* are counterbalanced by the fact that the language that they use to communicate their desires and understanding of themselves as social agents is not completely their own but is, rather, a transference, or sampling, of their mothers' language. I show how Precious's and Winter's significations on their mothers' language constitute the central motif through which *PUSH* and *The Coldest Winter Ever* organize and interrogate the role that language plays in shaping Precious's and Winter's personal developments, interpersonal relationships, and social interactions and how these signifying practices bring HIV/AIDS risk and protective factors into sharp focus. This process, I contend, reveals how and why vulnerability to HIV/AIDS exposure among black girls results, in part, from the role language acquisition and use plays in fostering black girl identity and black girl sexual health.

In chapter 3, I consider questions of border crossing and globalization that Danai Gurira and Nikkole Salter raise in relation to larger issues of economic opportunity, geographic mobility, and social isolation confronting two HIV-infected black women of different nationalities in the critically acclaimed play *In the Continuum*. Gurira and Salter's inquiries are prompted by equally pressing consideration the play gives to elaborating how and why silence, shame, and stigma, and the particularities of their gendered and racial expressions, worked across geographic and cultural boundaries to exacerbate the HIV/AIDS crisis, as sponsored HIV/AIDS research studies were beginning to focus in earnest on women of African descent. Across geographies and cultures, the sexual histories of women of African descent are centuries-old by-products of living in white- and male-dominated societies and share themes of rape, assault, and other forms of physical violence; deprivation of basic rights of bodily protection and ownership; and forced repression of sexual desire. Yet as Deborah Gray White and other black women historians have long observed, mobilizing and sustaining the capacity of black women's sexual histories to give black women "a sense of identity, a feeling for who they are, and how far

---

49. Here, it should be noted that this study engages uncensored language uses, which explicitly implicate issues of race, gender, and sexuality. These uses may or may not offend readers. The goal is to affirm the lived experiences of black women and girls by examining and unpacking both the language as used and the complex cultural contexts that produce the language uses.

they have come" is complicated by the equal measure in which the reality of black women's sexual histories has been obscured and distorted by myth.[50] Rather than deconstruct these myths, I argue that Gurira and Salter locate and interrogate their reifying effects in the context of black women's struggle, throughout the diaspora, to break through silences and negotiate HIV/AIDS shame and stigma.

In chapter 4, I situate *Girlfriends* and *The Game* within the context of concurrent events that served as imaginative and rhetorical inspiration for Brock Akil to break silences, dispel myths, and prioritize black women's health issues over the course of each series' runs on UPN and the CW Network: the diminishing presence of black women in mainstream hip hop music and black women's movement to other sites of influence and authority within the entertainment industry. The thematic concerns of *Girlfriends* and *The Game* are mappable in story arcs that frequently reference HIV/AIDS protective and risk factors. The formal parallels to these thematic concerns are ensemble casts of female characters in each series, whose developments advance within storylines that balance consideration of each character's individual lifestyle and the effects of these lifestyle choices on the collective. From this dialectic emerges numerous commentaries that *Girlfriends* and *The Game* offer on the personal and social effects of sexual practices and the consideration that black women must give to these effects, while pursuing fulfilling, safe sexual relationships in the twenty-first century.

Chapter 5 concludes by drawing out the implications of this study for multiple disciplines that this project contributes to—medical humanities, public health, black cultural studies, HIV/AIDS studies, hip hop studies, social justice studies, media studies, crisis/disaster management studies—and for the current state of black women's health. As touchstones, I use contemporary policy debates over gender and sexuality identity as well as remarks that hip hop artist DaBaby made during his 2021 Rolling Loud Miami set to highlight the continuing need for the kind of interventions that this project argues Sapphire, Souljah, Brock Akil, and Salter and Gurira enacted at the start of the twenty-first century. Current debates over who can or should lay claim to the concept "woman," whether as a signifier of social or biological identity, not only obscure the historical record of performative trans identity and trans lived experiences,[51] they also deflect attention from the policy issues that have

---

50. White, *Ar'n't I a Woman*, 5.

51. C. Riley Snorton alludes to the 1897 publication of *Sexual Inversion* and argues that this book's concern with questions of sexual behavior necessarily implicates questions of "gendering practices and trans ways of being." Snorton, *Black on Both Sides*, 4. L. H. Stallings locates the origins of black expressive culture and identity in the African trickster figure, who, she argues, defies "binary models of gender and sexuality." Stallings, *Mutha' Is Half a Word*, 12.

historically aligned the interests of black cisgender and transgender communities, including access to affordable, quality housing and health care, gun and domestic violence, and HIV/AIDS.[52] Similarly, DaBaby's spontaneous invocation of an imagined—and desired—audience of people not living with HIV or AIDS or "any of them deadly sexually transmitted diseases that'll make you die in two to three weeks," and call out to women with vaginas that "smell like water"[53] speak to a positioning within mainstream hip hop culture that simultaneously traffics in misinformation about sexual risk and gynecological health and downplays the harrowing health disparity conditions that continue to impact the lives of too many cis- and transgender black women today. To underscore this point, I also briefly address how current HIV/AIDS advertising, nobly designed to draw audiences' attention to the cascade of care[54] that has enabled many people infected with HIV or living with AIDS to enjoy normal, healthy lives, ironically coextends with the narrowness of policy debates over the definition of "woman" and DaBaby's rant and perpetuates the erasure of black women's and girls' lived experiences within mainstream HIV/AIDS discourses.

This book is not about the misunderstanding, misreading, misuses, and abuses of hip hop. The value of hip hop, in all its expressed forms, has long been established,[55] and hip hop feminism's unwillingness to let misogyny, homophobia, and transphobia in mainstream hip hop music off the hook is well-settled and documented.[56] Throughout this study, I deliberately strive to bring hip hop and HIV/AIDS, as I have come to live and experience them, to bear upon my analyses. By consciously deploying the techniques and values of hip hop feminism in their writing, Sapphire, Souljah, Brock Akil, and Salter and Gurira pushed the discursive practices of hip hop to levels that were only beginning to be contemplated at the turn of the twenty-first century. My hope is that this book's response to these artists' calls to action will encourage others to see the relevance of HIV/AIDS to their lives, regardless of status. As well, I

---

52. Laverne Cox, quoted in Snorton, *Black on Both Sides*, vii.

53. DaBaby, "DaBaby's Message"; DaBaby, Rolling Loud Concert. See also "DaBaby Goes On Homophobic Rant."

54. The cascade of care is knowing one's status, seeking care, sustaining care, and achieving viral suppression, where HIV is less than 200 copies per milliliter of blood. Early detection and diagnosis is key, because current antiretroviral therapies enable most HIV-infected people brought into care and sustaining care for a period of six consecutive months to achieve undetectable HIV viral loads.

55. This body of research is vast and easy to find. For representative works, see Rose, *Black Noise*; Kitwana, *Hip Hop Generation*; Perry, *Prophets of the Hood*; Chang, *Can't Stop, Won't Stop*; and Jeffries, *Thug Life*.

56. See, for example, Sharpley-Whiting, *Pimps Up, Ho's Down*; Rose, *Hip Hop Wars*; and Kumpf, "From Queering to TransImagining."

hope to move the needle in making HIV/AIDS matter to the masses and, by extension, bringing the HIV/AIDS epidemic to a sustainable end. Fundamentally, I want this book to serve as a guide for the next generation of hip hop feminist scholars and practitioners committed to fostering health and wellness for all people.

CHAPTER 1

In Search of Our Mothers' Theories

Hip Hop Feminism in Praxis

Black women writers, in their efforts to tell the truth about our lives, necessarily deal with health.

—Beverly Smith, "Black Women's Health," 103

I started doing research. I got all the books and I was shocked at what I saw. I was angry—angry that the people who wrote these books didn't put it into a format that made sense to us, angry that nobody was saying anything to black women.

—Byllye Avery, "Breathing Life into Ourselves," 149

The shit black women don't have time for [. . .] is dying and suffering from exorbitant rates of sole parenting, domestic violence, drug abuse, incarceration, AIDS, and cancer.

—Joan Morgan, *When Chickenheads Come Home to Roost*, 53

Critics generally agree that the cultural phenomenon known as hip hop originated in the Bronx, New York, but you'd be hard-pressed to convince me and my B-Girls growing up in Breaux Bridge, Louisiana, throughout the 1980s and early 1990s that our pops, locks, and drops were not the most skillful, most innovative, and most daring expressions of hip hop dance worldwide.[1] Our battle routines regularly opened with a highly anticipated, crowd-pleasing a cappella signification on Man Parrish's classic "Boogie Down Bronx" (1984):

---

1. Breaux Bridge is perhaps best known for being the "Crawfish Capital of the World" and original home of the internationally renowned Cajun food and line dance restaurant Mulate's. My birthplace, and another Louisiana town that I claim as home, is Lafayette. Lafayette is located approximately ten miles from Breaux Bridge. I spent my formative years with immediate and extended family and friends who resided in both locations.

16 • CHAPTER 1

> We came here to do a def dance for you
> In the Boogie Down Breaux Bridge it's the SK-3 Crew[2]
> Breaux Bridge is the place to be, no doubt
> So clear the floor party people as we rock the house.

In preparing to write this book, I returned to Strawberry's (see figure 1),[3] the bi-level barnyard-turned-hip-hop-dance club, where I spent just about every Saturday night of my teenage years, earning the dance moniker that defined my earliest relationship with hip hop. Looking back and critically engaging the past enabled me to come to terms with the limitations of my geographic location (and lyrical flow). But it also occasioned an opportunity for me to reflect on how my relationship with the culture of my youth has evolved over time and, moreover, prepared me to do the work of this project. *Black Women's Health in the Age of Hip Hop and HIV/AIDS: A Narrative Remix* arose out of the imperative duty that I share with other public health advocates, social justice stakeholders, and humanities scholars to listen, to contextualize, to analyze, to agitate, and to act in ways that promote quality health and wellness outcomes for all people. Inextricably tied to this duty is clarifying the indispensable, yet underrepresented, perspectives that hip hop feminism, as knowledge production, can bring to bear upon fighting HIV/AIDS among black women and girls specifically. As a progeny of black feminist thought and womanism, the term Alice Walker coined to refer to black women's contributions to advancing the political, social, and spiritual needs and interests of black people, hip hop feminism's primary subjects are black women and girls, and her primary objective is consciousness-raising within this demographic. Like her intellectual forebearers, hip hop feminism wrestles with the long history of systemic injustices to which black women have been subjected while acknowledging that black women's diverse relationships to power, based on education, sexuality, class, age, and ability, situate and inform their lived experiences. In this, hip hop feminism especially endeavors to equip black women and girls to see, confront, negotiate, and, at times, accept contradiction as part of their lived experience. My use of hip hop feminism as an intellectual anchor brings this project into conversation with a number of recent studies that draw from the range of intellectual thought that black women have

---

2. At different times, the SK-3 Crew consisted of myself, Katina Duhon, Melissa Jean-Baptiste (Dixon), Andrea Dennis, and Erica Thompson (Brown).

3. Before acquiring the moniker Strawberry's, this club, famous for not opening until 2:00 a.m., was known widely throughout the Southeast as the Kingfish. See Fuselier, "Party until Sunrise."

FIGURE 1. Strawberry's dance hall in Breaux Bridge, Louisiana. Photograph by the author, November 12, 2012.

produced to offer innovative ways of thinking about and understanding black women's health.

In *Carrying On: Another School of Thought on Pregnancy and Health* (2022), for example, independent scholar Brittany Clair considers what history and normative discourses around pregnancy teach us about related health disparity issues that disproportionately affect black women, including maternal mortality and sudden infant death syndrome. Dana Ain Davis, in *Reproductive Injustice: Racism, Pregnancy, and Premature Birth,* traces the origins of predominant ideas about reproduction to the legacy of slavery to explain high rates of infant mortality and premature births among black women and to argue in favor of alternative forms of labor assistance for black women, including midwives and doulas. In shared spirit, this book centers work produced by Sapphire, Sister Souljah, Mara Brock Akil, Nikkole Salter, and Danai Gurira between 1996 and 2006 to mine issues at the intersection of black expressive culture, black female identity politics, black women's health, public health policy, and HIV/AIDS. Of concern to this book project is answering two central questions prompted by these artists' collective industry: What practical understanding did Sapphire, Souljah, Brock Akil, and Salter and Gurira bring to the most pressing public health issue confronting black women and girls at the turn of the twenty-first century? And how did they foster this understanding for the masses? These parallel inquiries rely upon a definition of hip hop feminism, stressed continually throughout this study, that emphasizes its functionality as theory and praxis, as philosophical concept and tool for political action and social justice, and underscores hip hop feminism's commitment to fundamentally altering the material conditions that have historically silenced, marginalized, and oppressed black women and girls. By centering Sapphire, Souljah, Brock Akil, and Salter and Gurira's collective work in response to HIV/AIDS, this study puts hip hop feminism into practice by decentering predominant knowledge systems and discursive frameworks for understanding the epidemic and the wide range of associated psychosocial and environmental factors impacting black women's health and well-being. Decades ago, Dorothy Roberts said it best, when calling out "the dominant notion of reproductive liberty": for too long, she opined, black women's stories have been "inserted as an aside in deliberations," rather than being at the center of discourses, that determine policy.[4] This has no less been the case in prevailing discourses about the disease spectrum known as HIV/AIDS.

According to the Joint United Nations Programme on HIV/AIDS (UNAIDS), the organization established in 1994 by the United Nations Economic and Social Council for the purpose of ending HIV/AIDS as a public health threat, forty years into the epidemic, AIDS-related complications remain the "leading cause of death of women of reproductive age" and mortality rates are most prevalent among women in sub-Saharan Africa.[5] In the United States, where overall incidence rates decreased between 2015 and 2019, the annual number of new HIV infections in 2019 nevertheless remained highest among black people,[6] and black women accounted for nearly 60 percent of new HIV infections among all US women, despite their comprising less than 15 percent of the country's total female population.[7] This book reframes these unsettling data within the long history of the HIV/AIDS epidemic to chronicle the work that Sapphire, Souljah, Brock Akil, and Salter and Gurira undertook to clarify challenges to combating HIV/AIDS among black women and girls, while simultaneously cultivating spaces, both actual and imaginary, for affirming, valuing, and sustaining black women's health. While the genealogy and theoretical tenets of the methodological framework within which Sapphire, Souljah, Brock Akil, and Salter and Gurira labored have been the focus of numerous studies, hip hop feminism in praxis, specifically at the intersections of cultural and artistic production, HIV/AIDS, and black women's health, has not been the subject of sustained, rigorous inquiry. Katie Hogan's examination of *PUSH*, Pearl Cleage's *What Looks Like Crazy on an Ordinary Day* (1997), and Charlotte Watson Sherman's *touch* (1995) too narrowly centers respectability politics and thus misses much of the sophistication and nuance of how HIV/AIDS literature authored by black women grapples with related questions of black female identity, black female sexuality, black women's bodies, sexually transmitted disease (STD), and health.[8] Sociologist and hip hop

---

4. D. Roberts, *Killing the Black Body*, 6.
5. UNAIDS, "Forty Years."
6. CDC, "Estimated HIV Incidence."
7. CDC, "Diagnoses of HIV Infection."
8. Hogan, "Gendered Visibilities," 177; and Hogan, *Women Take Care*.

feminist foremother Tricia Rose only cursorily addresses HIV/AIDS in her otherwise searching examination of black women's sexual storytelling in *Longing to Tell: Black Women Talk about Sexuality and Intimacy* (2003).[9] Brittney Cooper deftly maps how "breaks" and "sampling," tools of the hip hop feminist aesthetic, work in *PUSH* to call "a new generation of black women's stories" into existence in the context of hip hop culture, which, Cooper notes, is defined by "the AIDS epidemic, the conservative backlash of the 1980s, and the deindustrialized city confronting urban blight."[10] However, Cooper's insights orient more toward the academic process of "grounding characters in their proper aesthetic context" than clarifying how *PUSH* and other "hip-hop generation truth telling"[11] stories about black women's and girls' lived experiences with HIV/AIDS facilitate measurable, affirmative change in black women's health outcomes. This study operates on the premise that Sapphire, Souljah, Brock Akil, and Salter and Gurira consciously operationalized hip hop feminism's change-agent-building capacities not only to tell black women's stories but also to build knowledge and cultivate action aimed at disrupting the status quo and improving black women's health in the age of hip hop and HIV/AIDS.

To be certain, when Joan Morgan coined the term "hip hop feminist" in 1999 to define her "generation of black women's precarious relationship with feminism" and to call for "the development of a new black feminist movement" that "claimed the powerful richness and delicious complexities of being black girls [. . .] of the post-Civil Rights, post-feminist, post soul, hip-hop generation,"[12] the devastating impact of HIV/AIDS, among a host of related health disparities confronting black women and girls, was on her mind. "*The shit* black women don't have time for," Morgan maintained, "is dying and suffering from exorbitant rates of sole parenting, domestic violence, drug abuse, incarceration, AIDS, and cancer."[13] Eight years later, Kimala Price was also thinking about black women's health in the age of hip hop and HIV/AIDS

---

9. Tricia Rose's *Black Noise: Rap Music and Black Culture in Contemporary America* is among the earliest sociological studies of hip hop culture. In *The Hip Hop Wars: What We Talk about When We Talk about Hip Hop—and Why It Matters,* Rose tenuously links the concurrent rise of hip hop culture and the crack cocaine epidemic to the spread of HIV/AIDS in black communities. Chapter 2 examines these related phenomena in depth. An earlier model for the work Rose does in *Longing to Tell: Black Women Talk about Sexuality and Intimacy* is Barbara Ogur's collection of stories diverse women living with HIV or AIDS told about their experiences as patients of an HIV clinic at the Cambridge Hospital throughout the early 1990s. See Ogur, "Smothering in Stereotypes."

10. B. Cooper, "'Maybe I'll be a Poet,'" 55.

11. B. Cooper, "'Maybe I'll be a Poet,'" 61, 63.

12. Morgan, *When Chickenheads Come Home,* 52, 56–57.

13. Morgan, *When Chickenheads Come Home,* 53.

when she outlined ways that hip hop feminism, which she described as "a feminist curiosity that is infused with a hip-hop sensibility," could inform reproductive justice and sex education policy and political platforms that target, organize, and mobilize young people.[14]

> HIV/AIDS has reached epidemic proportions within the African-American community with African-American women having especially been hard hit. We constitute the highest proportion of new cases. In 2001, HIV was the number one cause of death for African-American women between the ages of twenty-five and thirty-four (Kates and Leggoe 2005). Moreover, many middle- and high-school girls are subjected to federally funded abstinence-only-until-marriage programs instead of comprehensive sex education programs, where they can learn about developing a healthy sexuality (US House of Representatives 2004). [. . .] The question becomes: What should we do then?[15]

In fact, a cursory review of representative scholarship reveals that HIV/ AIDS has consistently been acknowledged as a continuing problem for black women and girls[16] over the roughly twenty-five years that hip hop feminism has served as an expressive framework for people to engage with, critique, and build upon their self-identified cultural and philosophical ties to hip hop, womanist, and black feminist thought.[17] But if it is the case, as Aisha Durham contended roughly fifteen years ago, that hip hop feminism is concerned both to spotlight black women's conditions and to dismantle the systems that oppress them, why do black women continue to be disproportionately impacted by HIV/AIDS, with new diagnosis rates annually running close to

---

14. K. Price, "Hip Hop Feminism," 392.

15. K. Price, "Hip Hop Feminism," 402–3.

16. In their expansive study of hip hop feminism's rootedness in "the pioneering work of multiple generations of black feminists based in the United States and elsewhere in the diaspora but focused on questions and issues that grow out of the aesthetic and political prerogatives of hip-hop culture," Aisha Durham, Brittany C. Cooper, and Susana M. Morris count "the global AIDS epidemic, which disproportionately affects women (in the United States, Africa, and across the African diaspora)" among the issues with which hip hop feminism is concerned. Durham et al., "Stage Hip-Hop Feminism Built," 722. Treva Lindsey alludes to the Gay and Lesbian Latino AIDS Education Initiative (GALAEI) as among a cohort of notable organizations doing hip hop feminist work. Lindsey, "Let Me Blow Your Mind." Noteworthily, Lindsey's discussion highlights several urban community–based organizations with missions founded on hip hop feminist principles and whose work centers around improving education outcomes for brown and black children.

17. Pough, "What It Do, Shorty?," 79.

3 times that of their white and Hispanic counterparts?[18] Why are black girls aged thirteen to twenty-four, who make up roughly 15 percent of the United States' total female adolescent population, diagnosed with HIV at rates that are 3.8 times those of their white counterparts,[19] and diagnosed with chlamydia and gonorrhea—sexually transmitted infections (STIs) that often manifest as comorbidities with HIV[20]—at rates that are 5 and 11.3 times those of their white counterparts?[21] Why does HIV-related stigma continue to present barriers to care, particularly among midlife black women living with HIV?[22] While I do not share in Michael Jeffries's belief that maintaining "the insurrectionary ethos" of hip hop feminism has become more challenging with the increased institutionalization of hip hop studies in the academy,[23] I do believe that these data warrant inquiry into the work hip hop feminism has actually done to unsettle, shift, and change the material conditions that inform the statistics and sustain HIV/AIDS as a threat to the health and wellness of black women and girls. What metrics has hip hop feminism provided for measuring its effectiveness in fostering black women's health and wellness? How has hip hop feminism guided strategies for stymieing new incidence rates of HIV infection among black women and girls, encouraged them to know their status, brought them into care, and sustained them in care? How has hip hop feminism facilitated understanding of the often tenuous relationship between HIV/AIDS risk-tolerant and risk-averse behavior and black women's health? What barriers to health and wellness has hip hop feminism exposed in the continuing fight to lessen AIDS-related death and new HIV infection rates among black women and girls? This book's examination of work generated by five black women artists between 1996 and 2006 clarifies efforts undertaken to put hip hop feminism into practice in furtherance of these solutions-driven inquiries and outcomes. By structuring narratives centered on black women's lived experiences with HIV/AIDS, Sapphire, Souljah, Brock Akil, and Salter and Gurira underscored hip hop feminism's utility in cultivating transformative knowledge directed simultaneously toward heightening awareness of HIV/AIDS and combating its devastating impact on black women and girls. Recent reflections hint at why this impetus was a common creative force for these artists, at the turn of the twenty-first century.

---

18. Ojikutu and Mayer, "HIV Prevention among Black Women."
19. Brawner et al., "Project GOLD."
20. S. Aziz and Sweat, "Subsequent HIV Diagnosis Risk."
21. Diesel et al., "Reported Chlamydia and Gonorrhea."
22. Sangaramoorthy et al., "Intersectional Stigma."
23. Jeffries, "Hip Hop Feminism and Failure."

22 • CHAPTER 1

While promoting *Life after Death*, the 2021 sequel to *The Coldest Winter Ever*, Souljah recalled creating Winter Santiaga for the purpose of helping the community to understand what it feels like "when somebody you love, whose presence you enjoy," she insisted, "gets removed from your social and cultural existence [. . .]. If it was going to be a genuine cautionary tale," Souljah explained, "it was very important for the whole 'hood to feel the absence of Winter Santiaga."[24] At the 2016 Global Citizen Festival, Gurira praised the work of Nyumbani Village, a community in Kenya, founded in 2006, to provide sustainable housing and services for HIV/AIDS-infected and -affected elders and children by remembering her upbringing in Zimbabwe in the 1980s and 1990s: "I witnessed firsthand the ways HIV and AIDS hit communities, families, and the very fabric of life."[25] While a guest on *The Breakfast Club* in 2020, Brock Akil acknowledged her intent to make *Girlfriends* "appointment television for black women" and explained why it was important for her to "have a conversation with her audience" about HIV/AIDS specifically:

I took that to the writer's room, they were like, "What?" I remember Kenya Barris[26] was one of the first one's like, "Guys this is a comedy." And I'm like, "Yeh, and we are going to figure this out, because this is what's real, and this is what's happening, yet we are surviving it, yet we are dealing with it [. . .]. How do we take ownership of a story that is hurting black women?[27]

In the afterword to the twenty-fifth anniversary edition of *PUSH*, published in 2021, Sapphire describes being in a classroom in 1987 and listening to one of her students, a "beautiful young black woman," lament the trouble she was having getting AZT.[28] "It wasn't the first time a student had put her life at center stage for us to see," she remembers, "braving stigma to shatter walls of silence and shame." Sapphire goes on to characterize the social, political, and economic climate of the 1980s, which, she says, "stunted" the lives of black women, much like those characterized in *PUSH*. "What I saw," she recalls,

---

24. Sister Souljah, "Sister Souljah Releases Sequel."

25. Gurira, "HIV/AIDS in Africa."

26. Perhaps best known as the creator of the hit sitcom *black-ish*, Barris wrote for both *Girlfriends* and *The Game*.

27. Brock Akil, "Mara Brock Akil."

28. AZT, or azidothymidine, is an antiviral drug originally developed to fight cancer. Despite controversy surrounding clinical trial testing and serious side effects associated with its use, the FDA fast-tracked approval of AZT, and on March 19, 1987, it became the first FDA-approved medication for treating HIV and AIDS. For an examination of the controversies surrounding AZT approval and contemporary care practices of black and Hispanic persons living with HIV, see Freeman et al., "Critical Race Theory."

"was that black women were part of an underserved, devalued population from whom resources that could have saved [their] lives were being shunted."[29]

In their genealogy of hip hop feminism, Aisha Durham, Brittney Cooper, and Susan Morgan, like Sapphire, characterize the Reagan era and its aftermath as distinctively challenging for black women.[30] The long record of black feminist thought and writing, which Durham, Cooper, and Morgan adeptly demonstrate hip hop feminism builds upon, evidences black women's chronic struggles with, and within, situations that have historically sustained disparities in black women's health, health care, and health outcomes.[31] Sapphire, Souljah, Brock Akil, and Salter and Gurira's use of narrative to build practical knowledge about black women's health in the age of hip hop and HIV/AIDS underscores these artists' indebtedness to black women creators whose age-old demands at the crosscurrents of artistic production, literary and cultural criticism, and intellectual thought have consistently given voice and validation to black women's lived experiences. As Barbara Christian reminded us long ago, black women "have always theorized [. . .] often in narrative forms" and through "pithy language" to provide "necessary nourishment for [black] people."[32] In this way, Beverly Smith tells us, black women "necessarily deal with health."

Despite health being part of the experience terrain that black women artists have always crossed to tell their stories, biomedical and public health research focused on black women and girls rarely draws insight from what black women artists have to say about black women's health. In her introduction to the classic anthology *The Black Woman* (1970), Toni Cade Bambara called out this oversight in her critique of what "the experts" in psychiatry, psychology, biology, and biochemistry tell us when their attention turns to black women: "The reports get murky, for they usually clump the men and women together and focus so heavily on what white people have done to the psyches of Blacks, that what Blacks have done to and for themselves is overlooked,

---

29. Sapphire, *PUSH*, 183.

30. Durham et al., "Stage Hip-Hop Feminism Built," 722–23.

31. See Heckler, *Report of the Secretary's Task Force,* which maps rising disparities in rates of morbidity and mortality and quality of life for black Americans closer to the start of Reagan's administration, despite overall improvements in the health of nonminority Americans; Ula Taylor's copious historiography of "episodical turning points in black women's history" in "Historical Evolution"; Juanita Chinn, Iman Martin, and Nicole Redmond's review of the historical contexts informing issues of access to quality health care in a contemporary moment for black women in "Health Equity"; Nina Banks's germinal examination of black women's community activism as a locus of unpaid labor in "Black Women in the United States"; and Mariola Espinosa's correction of the historical record regarding yellow fever and morbidity and mortality rates among people of African descent in "Question of Racial Immunity."

32. Christian, "Race for Theory," 52–53.

24 • CHAPTER 1

and what distinguishes the men from the women forgotten."[33] Byllye Avery echoes Bambara when describing the impetus for founding the National Black Women's Health Project (now the Black Women's Health Imperative) in 1984, to advocate for black women's health and reproductive rights and to break the "conspiracy of silence" in research that purported to address the health needs of black women. "I got all the books," Avery observes, "and I was shocked at what I saw. I was angry—angry that the people who wrote these books didn't put [the research] into a format that made sense to us, angry that nobody was saying anything to black women."[34] This felt sense of exclusion, of being left out, kept out, silenced, banished, misrepresented, and ignored in medical research has provided fodder for black women creatives and, over time, resulted in black women's writing serving as, paradoxically, the most reliable, undervalued, and underutilized guide to black women's health. Consider what Zora Neale Hurston tells us about her experience with a health care provider in 1931:

> The doctor appeared in the door all in white, looking very important, and also very unhappy from behind his rotund stomach. He did not approach me at all, but told one of his nurses to take me into a private examination room. The room was private all right, but I would not rate it highly as an examination room. Under any other circumstances, I would have sworn it was a closet where the soiled towels and uniforms were tossed until called for by the laundry.[35]

How much further might science be in addressing high incidence rates of maternal morbidity and mortality among black women today[36] had the racism Hurston was subjected to been a focal point in training medical researchers and providers nearly a century ago? What would indicators of life expectancy, chronic health conditions, and overall quality of life look like for black women if prevailing medical research consistently drew insight from stories about black women's and girls' experiences with stress, obesity, domestic violence, sexual violence, substance addiction, and suicide ideation, which inform the themes, tensions, and plots of such time-honored novels as *The Bluest Eye, Corrigadora, The Color Purple, The Salt-Eaters,* and *Sugar*? How better rounded might discourses centered on adolescence and eating disorders be

---

33. Bambara, preface to *The Black Woman*, 8.
34. Avery, "Breathing Life into Ourselves," 149.
35. Hurston, "My Most Humiliating," 163.
36. Black women are 3.3 times more likely to die from pregnancy-related causes in comparison to their white and Hispanic counterparts. Oribhabor et al., "Mother's Cry."

if Anissa Gray's *The Care and Feeding of Ravenously Hungry Girls* (2019) was required reading for medical and public health students?[37] And what of Naomi Osaka's refusal to speak with the press and withdrawal from the French Open in 2021: would the outcry have been as resounding if the effects of living up to the demands of the strongblackwoman on black women's mental and physical health and wellness were as well documented, explored, and untangled in medical literature as they are in the lyrics of Ntozake Shange, Nikki Giovanni, and Lucille Clifton; the memoirs of Audre Lorde, Maya Angelou, and Alice Walker; the short stories of Zora Neale Hurston and Ann Petry; the plays of Lorraine Hansberry and Alice Childress; and the speculative fiction of Octavia Butler, N. K. Jemisin, and Tracy Cross? In *Men We Reaped,* Jesmyn Ward chronicles her experiences with alcohol abuse, depression, and post-traumatic stress disorder after losing family members and friends to drugs, suicide, and drunk driving. In her "search for words" to tell her haunting, beautiful story of love and loss, Ward informs us, she found "more statistics about what it means to be Black and poor in the South" and concluded that "by the numbers, by all the official records, [. . .] this is what our lives are worth: nothing."[38] These numbers are devoid of what Karla Holloway, in *Private Bodies, Public Texts: Race Gender, and a Cultural Bioethics* (2011) characterizes as the indispensable, "constitutive weight" of black women's "cultural and historical context."[39] As a consequence, explains Evelyn White in the introduction to *The Black Women's Health Book: Speaking for Ourselves* (1990), black women have always had to be the primary torchbearers in looking beyond statistics to understand what ails them and decide how to "get better."[40]

The will to help black women and girls "get better," or, as Salamishah Tillet and Scheherazade Tillet, put it, to "be well,"[41] drives the inquiries and industry of *Black Women's Health in the Age of Hip Hop and HIV/AIDS.* In this, the chapters that comprise this study necessarily grapple with concepts,

---

37. While doctors' interests in the relationship between body mass index (BMI) and obesity in black girls is extensively documented, the body of research on associations between race and disordered eating among adolescents, including dieting, bulimia, and anorexia nervosa, is scant and even less existent on the etiology of disordered eating among black girls specifically. Ballom, "Prevention of Overweight."

38. Ward, *Men We Reaped,* 236, 237.

39. Holloway, *Private Bodies, Public Texts,* xvii.

40. E. White, *Black Women's Health Book,* xv.

41. In 2003, the Tillet sisters founded A Long Walk Home, a Chicago-based not-for-profit organization, using blended theories of black feminism, art therapy, social justice, and grassroots community organizing, to prepare young girls to be change agents in their communities, especially, though not exclusively, in the context of fighting violent crimes against women and girls. For insight into some of the organization's successes, see Tillet and Tillet, "'You Want to Be Well?'"

themes, and issues that have historically marginalized, silenced, and killed black women and girls. But, as Ruth Nicole Brown unforgettably reminds us, "the purposeful action of creating new knowledge" about the lived experiences of black women and girls starts with us.[42] Kyra D. Gaunt instructs us on the importance of listening to the "repertoire of chants and embodied rhythms" of black girls' play to understand how black girls simultaneously learn from established oral-kinetic practices and adapt and reshape these practices toward both transgressive and transformative ends.[43] By listening to the ways that Sapphire, Souljah, Brock Akil, and Salter and Gurira made black women and girls visible and heard, made their silences intelligible, and made their stories part of the understanding of HIV/AIDS at the turn of the twenty-first century, this book centers the voices of black women and girls at the cross-currents of research and activism. Without doubt the completion of this book is also motivated by memories of barnyard nights long past, where the music played 'til "6'n the mornin'" and the SK-3 Crew dominated the floor. These memories, and the chapters that follow, teach me about me and my culture. They underlie my unflagging determination to advance thought and action that foster sustainable health and well-being for black women and girls.

---

42. Brown, *Black Girlhood Celebration*.

43. Gaunt, *Games Black Girls Play*.

CHAPTER 2

"Cunt Buckets" and "Bad Bitches"

Black Girl Identity Formation and Sexual Health in *PUSH: A Novel* and *The Coldest Winter Ever*

What's with that cunt bucket? (That's what my muver call women she don't like, cunt buckets. I kinda get it and I kinda don't get it, but I like the way it sounds so I say it too.)

—Claireece Precious Jones in Sapphire's *PUSH*, 3–4

Momma didn't work 'cause beauty, she said, was a full-time occupation that left no room for anything else [. . .]. She made it clear to me that beautiful women are supposed to be taken care of. She would whisper in my ear, "I'm just a bad bitch!"

—Winter Santiaga in Sister Souljah's *The Coldest Winter Ever*, 1

Sticks and bricks might break our bones, but words will most definitely kill us.

—Hortense Spillers, "Mama's Baby, Papa's Maybe," 68

When asked about the impact of childhood experiences on her imagination, the late Toni Morrison responded that her work is "completely informed" by "the language" of her upbringing. "I woke up to the sound of my mother's voice," she explains, "and it was information. I knew her mood, and it was a support system for us. It wasn't something where you went in order to feel good and then come back; it was real information."[1] In the classic hip hop social study *Yo' Mama's Disfunktional* (1997), historian Robin D. G. Kelley discusses growing up "in a world in which talking about somebody's mama was a way of life" and, like Morrison, elaborates how language acquisition and use constitutes an intimate, maternal-centric process and source

---

1. Toni Morrison, "Toni Morrison Interview."

of knowledge-building and socialization for coming-of-age black youth.[2] The refrain to "Mamma Got Ass," the chart-topping dance hit off rapper Juvenile's platinum-certified fifth studio album, *Project English* (2001), exemplifies both the socially situated and cognitive function of language acquisition and use that Morrison and Kelley describe, through imagery that takes the form of a young female, whose physical and behavioral attributes derive from her mother:

> But where she get that ass from? She get it from her mamma
> But where she get her class from? She get it from her mamma
> Oh where she get that chest from? She get it from her mamma
> Where she learn how to dress from? She get it from her mamma.[3]

The passages from the novels *PUSH,* by Sapphire, and *The Coldest Winter Ever,* by Sister Souljah, which open this chapter, construct the mother as a shaping presence and information source for Claireece Precious Jones and Winter Santiaga, the novels' black girl protagonists, and, in this way, advance ideals about the relationship among black mothering, black girl linguistic practices, and black girl identity formation, that echo Morrison, Kelly, and Juvenile. Indeed, the passages reflect what might be called moments of language acquisition for Precious and Winter, because they contemplate intersecting issues of mothering, childhood and adolescent development, and identity formation that underlie these characters' growths. The crudeness of the imagery through which Mary Johnston and Mrs. Santiaga encourage their daughters to see themselves and other women resonates in the language Precious and Winter use to introduce themselves to readers at the novels' openings: "Brooklyn-born I don't have no sob stories for you about rats and roaches and pissy-pew hallways," announces Winter. "I came busting out of my momma's big coochie on January 28, 1977. So my mother named me Winter" (1). With similarly raw inflection, Precious declares:

> My name is Claireece Precious Jones. I don't know why I'm telling you that. Guess 'cause I don't know how far I'm gonna go with this story, or whether it's even a story or why I'm talkin'. [. . .] Some people tell a story 'n it don't make no sense or be true. But I'm gonna try to make sense and tell the truth, else what's the fuckin' use? Ain' enough lies and shit out there already? So, OK, it's Thursday, September twenty-four, 1987 and I'm walking down the hall. I look good, smell good—fresh, clean. (3–4)

---

2. R. Kelley, *Yo' Mama's Disfunktional,* 1.
3. Juvenile, "Mamma Got Ass."

In these passages, words, intonation, and imagery converge to tell of Precious's and Winter's origins, both as characters and as storytellers. Their language constellates around a set of images and themes that are common to the black female imaginary and communicate messages and feelings through metaphors associated with contested notions of black female subjectivity and sexuality. While hip hop feminist interrogation of this type of language is nothing new,[4] the insight that this chapter offers into the role that language plays in shaping black girl identity and sexual health is distinctive. Because there is no mistaking the content of Precious's and Winter's language as at once sexually and maternally framed, this chapter argues that *PUSH* and *The Coldest Winter Ever* compel consideration of how the mother-daughter relationships giving rise to Precious's and Winters' acquisition and use of language inform values, beliefs, and decision-making around sexual health that interact with risk of exposure to HIV/AIDS. Put another way, by roughly paraphrasing the quote from Hortense Spillers's classic essay "Mama's Baby, Papa's Maybe," which also opens this chapter, because the language that Precious and Winter learn from their mothers and use, both to establish and claim their identities, could very well kill them, *PUSH* and *The Coldest Winter Ever* direct attention to how mothering and language acquisition and use operate as co-constitutive components of black girl development[5] that inform issues of sexual health, wellness, and risk for black girls. This insight is indispensable for building knowledge about black women's health at a time when HIV/AIDS incidence and prevalence rates literally rendered healthy identity formation a matter of life and death for black girls coming of age in the United States.

This chapter builds on the premise that Sapphire and Sister Souljah used the knowledge-building capacities of hip hop feminism to advance understanding of the interrelations among mothering, language acquisition and use, sexual health, and black girl identity formation. Drawing on Morrison's, Kelly's, and Juvenile's logic of everyday blacklife existence, education, and performance through language use, and harking back to Spillers's classic analysis

---

4. For example, Cherise Pollard examines language in both *PUSH* and *The Coldest Winter Ever* within the familiar framework of "negative and dehumanizing representations of black women" in hip hop music. See Pollard, "P-Word Exchange," 113. In her examination of Megan Thee Stallion's reclamation of "hot girl" and invocation of the term as a source of sexual empowerment for black women and girls, Ebony L. Perro also points to the "lineage of cultural work" that women in hip hop have generated around and through language use as a means of "problematizing one-dimensional readings of Black womanhood." See Perro, "Thee Megan Movement."

5. The World Health Organization defines adolescence as the period of life "between childhood and adulthood, from ages 10–19," when people experience "rapid physical, cognitive, and psychosocial growth," which impacts how they "feel, think, make decisions, and interact with the world around them." World Health Organization, "Adolescent Health."

30 • CHAPTER 2

of language as a symbolic system that has historically marked black women's flesh (and bones) as sites of complex, contested meanings, I contend that Sapphire and Souljah used the "lexical and living"[6] aspects of black girl identity formation to show how the interplay between mothering and language acquisition and use shaped crucial questions of health and wellness for black girls throughout the 1980s and early 1990s, the historical period that marked the height of AIDS complications–related deaths in the United States.[7] While a number of scholars have examined Precious's struggle to learn to read and write in relation to the theme of agency, little attention has been given to the characteristics and functions of the language that Precious possesses—her articulateness, as Lydia Kokkola puts it[8]—prior to her introduction to Ms. Rain and Each One Teach One.[9] Critical commentary on Winter's language use has largely served to disparage the quality of Souljah's writing, or to relegate *The Coldest Winter Ever* to "streetlit" or "urban fiction,"[10] labels Souljah

---

6. R. Kelley, *Yo' Mama's Disfunktional,* 32, 37.

7. Spillers, "Mama's Baby, Papa's Maybe," 68. See also CDC, "Current Trends."

8. Kokkola, "Learning to Read Politically," 394.

9. Sathyaraj Venkatasan, for example, locates the origins of Precious coming to terms with her HIV-positive diagnosis in the scriptotherapy she undertakes at Ms. Rain's urging. Venkatasan, "'Telling Your Story,'" 113. This analysis does not account for the interplay between Precious's preliterate uses of language and existential ruminations, both before and after she learns that she is HIV-positive. Similarly, Silvia Pilar Castro Borrego's claim that Precious "lacks the vocabulary to understand the context of the violence" she endures at the hands of her mother and father is inconsistent with extensive textual evidence of Precious's use of speech to decry the effects of violence on her, notwithstanding her delayed ability to name these acts of violence in conventional terms, that is, rape, incest, and abuse. Borrego, "Re(Claiming) Subjectivity," 150. Like Venkatasan, Marlo David emphasizes the written word in her examination of Precious as the embodiment of a counternarrative to "dysfunctional black motherhood," as represented in popular cultural and political discourses of the 1980s and 1990s. David, "'I Got Self,'" 173. Nels Highberg is among the handful of scholars who acknowledge that, though she lacks the ability to read and write standard English, Precious is not without a language, and, as Highberg notes, Sapphire's stylistic choice to weave Precious's "illiterate speech patterns and errors intact," into the narrative, as her traditional literacy skills build, "validates Precious' perspective" and maintains the integrity of her "voice." See Highberg, "(Missing) Faces," 11. Similarly, Mary Thompson acknowledges that "the narrative challenges any readerly assumptions that Precious is deficient in self-knowledge and broader cultural wisdom," despite her inability to read and write. Thompson, "Third Wave Feminism." See also Laurie Stapleton, who uses Freirean theories of agency and education to examine the "lexicon and linguistic rhythms" of Precious's "oral voice." Stapleton, "Toward a New Learning System."

10. See Pollard, "P-Word Exchange"; M. Hill et al., "Street Fiction"; Dunn, "Hip Hop Afro-Feminist Aesthetic"; Steinberg, "[Review of] *The Coldest Winter Ever*"; and Pearl, "[Review of] *The Coldest Winter Ever.*" Brittney Cooper's analysis of *PUSH* ultimately invokes this binary by arguing that the novel "acts as a bridge text between earlier generations of black women's writing and the urban street dramas that predominate today." See B. Cooper, "'Maybe I'll Be a Poet.'"

summarily rejects, because they (re)inscribe false binaries between "high" and "low" literature.[11] My interest in the family-level sociocontextual correlates of Precious's and Winter's acquisition and use of language builds on classic black feminist thought, which has long held that filial connection between black mothers and black daughters is both a "fundamental relationship among black women" and the primary means through which black mothers have "empowered their daughters," as sociologist Patricia Hill Collins writes, "by passing on the everyday knowledge essential to survival" for black women.[12] I also draw from established tenets of early childhood education, which recognize language acquisition, cognitive development, and social functioning as dynamic, interactive processes that commence in children from birth[13] and correlate the formative years of children's emotional, physical, and cognitive developments with adolescent health-averse conditions, ranging from anxiety and depression to obesity,[14] and health-affirming attributes, including executive functioning; the ability to concentrate, recall, and reason; regular exercise; and balanced nutrition.[15] These basic scientific principles guide my analysis of how the trope of black mothering in *PUSH* and *The Coldest Winter Ever* evokes what sociologist and civil rights activist Joyce Ladner, writing at the turn of the twenty-first century, identified as the "problems facing black females in the United States."[16] Among these problems were gross disparities in black and white income and education, rising rates of black single-female-headed households, black teenaged pregnancy, black infant mortality, black high school dropout, and HIV/AIDS.[17] In probing these issues, I argue that Sapphire and Souljah, like Ladner, endeavored to shift debates about black

---

11. Ofori-Atta, "Sister Souljah."

12. Collins, *Black Feminist Thought*, 96.

13. The body of research that addresses these interactive processes is vast and spans several decades. For more recent studies, see Gomez and Strasser, "Language and Socioemotional Development"; G. Price et al., "Sorting Out Emotions"; and Ren et al., "Fathers' and Mothers' Praise."

14. See, for example, Godleski et al., "Parent Socialization of Emotion"; Barch et al., "Early Childhood Depression"; Gueron-Sela et al., "Maternal Depressive Symptoms"; and Bodell et al., "Longitudinal Association." In "From Living to Eat to Writing to Live," Sika Dagbovie charts parallels in Precious's cognitive and personal growths and links these to her evolving relationship to food.

15. See, for example, Willoughby et al., "Improvements"; Vicari et al., "Spatial Working Memory"; Liang et al., "Early Home Learning Environment"; and Staiano and Abraham, "Competitive v. Cooperative."

16. Ladner, "Black Women."

17. Ladner, "Black Women," 13.

32 • CHAPTER 2

mothering from the politics of representation,[18] as bolstered by the notorious 1965 publication of *The Negro Family: The Case for National Action,* more widely known as the *Moynihan Report,* to an examination of the ramifications of what Ladner calls the muting of public discussion of the challenges confronting black mothers and their daughters at the turn of the twenty-first century because of "negative labels and stereotypes of the past."[19] As Ladner explains:

> For almost 20 years following the publication of the Moynihan Report, black scholars devoted considerable time to producing an alternative body of scholarship which sought to depict the strength, coping skills and overall positive aspects of black family life. Notably, many black scholars used the Moynihan controversy to launch alternative analyses and perspectives on family scholarship. There was also a noticeable "closing of the ranks" among some scholars who chose not to dwell on the negative aspects of black family life.[20]

"Negative aspects of black family life," which Ladner explicitly links to the "transformation of the economy and conservative social policies leading to a dismantling of the welfare state" under the Reagan administration, pervade the pages of *PUSH* and *The Coldest Winter Ever.* Along with the welfare state, the novels lay bare the interlockings of oppressive mass media and government-structured education, criminal legal, and health care systems[21] and, accordingly, place *PUSH* and *The Coldest Winter Ever* in conversation with the coming-of-age black girl storytelling traditions of Toni Morrison, Alice Walker, Maya Angelou, and a host of other black women writers of the late twentieth century, concerned about what the late Cheryl Wall rightly characterizes as the "profound and multifaceted impact of racism," sexism, and

---

18. David intimates that the body of extant scholarship on *PUSH* is relatively small because the novel's "disturbing language and imagery" are incompatible with "dominant (white) domestic ideologies or black communities' expectations of respectability." See David, "'I Got Self,'" 174. In contrast, Susana Morris in *Close Kin and Distant Relatives* argues that *PUSH* deliberately takes aim at "respectability politics" as a means of "advocating for more transgressive expressions of family." See, Morris, *Close Kin,* 104.

19. Ladner, "Black Women," 13.

20. Ladner, "Black Women," 13.

21. Christine Pappas makes a compelling case for reading *PUSH* in the framework of civics education and experiential learning advocacy and posits that the novel should be required reading for political science students, many of whom, she notes, "view their education as a means to an end, typically training to work in service-oriented careers." Pappas, "'You Hafta Push,'" 40.

classism on the lived experiences of black girls.[22] The novels also deconstruct the heteronormalizing, hegemonic masculinity of the English language, and, to this end, cultivate a sensibility around black girl identity formation that is tempered by the erotic, a narrative process, which Lamonda Horten Stallings marks as the undoing of conventional wisdom about sexuality that teaches black women and girls that they are not desired, cannot desire, cannot act on desire, and cannot reject the desires of others that are inconsistent with their own.[23] Absent from Stallings's theorization of erotic literacy as an indispensable element in the "formation of black girl sexual agency"[24] is consideration of the multiple ways in which risk of exposure to HIV, and dying from AIDS-related complications, heightened scrutiny around notions of individual choice, sexual agency, and bodily autonomy for black girls coming of age throughout the 1980s and early 1990s. These historical periods compelled scientists and artist-activists alike to come to grips with "the severity of the impact of AIDS on adolescents,"[25] especially those living throughout America's urban centers. This reckoning is traceable across the nascent body of scientific studies of the HIV/AIDS epidemic among adolescents in the United States that emerged during the same historical periods as the settings and publications of *PUSH* and *The Coldest Winter Ever*.

For example, in a 1993 study titled "HIV and Adolescents," pediatrics researchers Martin Anderson and Robert Morris observed substantial differences in confirmed AIDS cases among persons aged thirteen to nineteen and persons aged twenty to twenty-nine. "As of December 1992," they noted, "less than 1% (946) of AIDS cases were in 13 to 19 year olds, while 20% (48295) of cases occurred in 20 to 29 year olds." From these data, Martin and Morris concluded that "many of the 20 to 29 year olds who developed AIDS" were infected with HIV as adolescents. This deduction, supported by the virus's medium ten-year incubation period,[26] corroborated the building consensus that AIDS was primarily "a young person's disease," and that detection, intervention, and prevention methods needed to focus on curtailing the "risk of silent spread through an asymptomatic adolescent (12–20 y. o.)

---

22. Cheryl Wall identifies these luminaries as "three of the most influential writers of the late twentieth century." Wall, "On Dolls." To these names, I would add Paule Marshall, Gayl Jones, and Gloria Naylor for the thematic and stylistic resonances between their works—*Brown Girl, Brownstones* (1959); *Corregidora* (1975); and *The Women of Brewster Place* (1982)—and *PUSH* and *The Coldest Winter Ever*.

23. Stallings, "Erotic Literacy," 119.

24. Stallings, "Erotic Literacy," 114.

25. Greig and Raphael, "AIDS Prevention and Adolescents."

26. Anderson and Morris, "HIV and Adolescents."

community."[27] In their 1994 study of AIDS and female minority adolescents, pediatrics researchers Kim Overby and Susan Kegeles found that "inner city minority youth" were "overrepresented among both AIDS cases and asymptomatic seropositive individuals" and that "young, sexually active, minority women" living in urban regions were "at greatest risk of heterosexual HIV exposure."[28] A retrospective medical chart review of ninety-one HIV-infected adolescents visiting the same comprehensive adolescent clinic between 1992 and 2003 revealed that 95 percent of the adolescents treated were black and 64 percent were females.[29] A longitudinal study of persons aged thirteen to twenty-four diagnosed with HIV and AIDS between 1985 and 2003, from the fifty states, the District of Columbia, and the US trusts and territories, found that by the end of 2003, 7,074 adolescents were living with AIDS in the United States, and adolescent AIDS rates were highest among black adolescents.[30] While this study identified an overall greater proportion of HIV-positive diagnoses in males, the study also indicated that among adolescents aged thirteen to fifteen, "the highest proportion of HIV infections (77%) was diagnosed among females."[31] A 1992 analysis of national vital statistics data found that "women 15 through 44 years of age account[ed] for more than 80% of reported AIDS cases among adolescent and adult women in the United States."[32] As of December 1992, AIDS-related complications was the sixth leading cause of death for all persons in the United States aged fifteen to twenty-four.[33] In 1995, AIDS-related complications was the third leading cause of death among all women in the United States aged twenty-five to forty-four. A year later, AIDS-related complications was the second leading cause of death for black women in the United States aged twenty-five to forty-four.[34] Surveillance data covering the 1990s consistently show that black women and girls were at substantially increased risk of exposure to HIV infection and dying from AIDS-related complications in comparison to their white counterparts.[35] While scant in proportion to the number of studies and volume of clinical trials focused on gay white and black men, scientific research generated throughout the 1990s that addressed the impact of the HIV/AIDS epidemic among

---

27. Greig and Raphael, "AIDS Prevention and Adolescents," 211.

28. Overby and Kegeles, "Impact of AIDS."

29. Kadivar et al., "Psychosocial Profile."

30. Rangel et al., "Epidemiology of HIV."

31. Among people aged sixteen to nineteen, HIV-positive diagnoses were approximately equal for cisgender males and cisgender females. Rangel et al., "Epidemiology of HIV," 159.

32. Buehler et al., "Reporting of HIV/AIDS Deaths."

33. Anderson and Morris, "HIV and Adolescents," 436.

34. Polacsek et al., "Correlates of Condom Use."

35. See, for example, CDC, "Mortality Attributable."

black women and girls in America[36] repeatedly cited patterns in information, beliefs, and behaviors to explain these disparities.[37]

For instance, in her investigation of the "subjective meanings" that a focus group of black adolescents aged eleven to thirteen assigned to black women's sexuality based on their beliefs about eight sexualized images associated with black women—the Diva, the Gold Digger, the Freak, the Gangsta Bitch, the Dyke, the Baby Mama, the Earth Mother, and the Sister Savior—psychology professor Dionne Stephens found that the images "provided cues regarding values given to African American female physical attractiveness."[38] These visual cues in turn informed the norms associated with appropriate sexual beliefs and behaviors, and for black girls especially, the images were closely associated with perceptions of "what it means to be a sexual being."[39] Baseline data from a study of black youth aged twelve to eighteen, recruited to plan and organize an after-school program designed to reduce teenage pregnancy and adolescent premarital sex among black youth, established that most of the study participants believed that their peers were already sexually active or "felt intense social pressure to have sex."[40] The results of this study, based on focus group and survey data, revealed that providing a sustainable "evidence-base in HIV risk reduction" and tailoring health education programs to black youth needs mandate consideration of black youth "cultural norms [. . .], *linguistic abilities,* developmental stage, [and] popular culture" (emphasis added).[41] Survey data from a study of "the knowledge, attitudes, beliefs, and behaviors" concerning AIDS within a group of 196 minority adolescents in New York City indicated that among black female participants, 71 percent reported being sexually active. While roughly one-third of all participants surveyed reported not using condoms during their most recent sexual encounter, 73 percent of sexually active female participants reported not using a condom, or any other form of pregnancy prevention, during their most recent sexual encounter.[42] In one of the earliest, among many, studies in which veteran

---

36. Chapter 3 offers an in-depth review of HIV/AIDS research and clinical trials focused on black women during the 1990s and 2000s.

37. Stuntzner-Gibson, "Women and HIV Disease"; Jemmott and Jemmott, "Increasing Condom-Use Intentions"; Walter et al., "Prevalence and Correlates."

38. Stephens, "Effects of Images," 252, 255. The focus group, comprising fifteen total participants, included seven black boys and eight black girls recruited from a federally funded after-school program. This study is noteworthy for pointing to the need for increased analysis of the roles that both the mother-daughter and father-daughter dyads play in informing black girl sexual health and wellness.

39. Stephens, "Effects of Images," 260.

40. Akintobi et al., "Applications in Bridging the Gap."

41. Akintobi et al., "Applications in Bridging the Gap."

42. Goodman and Cohall, "Acquired Immunodeficiency Syndrome," 38.

HIV/AIDS prevention researchers Drs. Loretta Sweet Jemmott and John Jemmott surveilled condom-use intentions among sexually active black female adolescents, preintervention data showed that the average onset age of sexual intercourse was 14.41 years and the "chief risky sexual behavior" among sexually active black female adolescents was the "failure to use condoms."[43] Sapphire's and Souljah's efforts to uproot, examine, and disrupt the implications of these data for black women's health are made apparent by the numerous narrative elements in *PUSH* and *The Coldest Winter Ever* that weave HIV and risk of exposure to the virus into Precious's and Winter's stories.

Flashbacks mark Precious's and Winter's birth years in 1970 and 1977, the historical period that marks the onset of the HIV/AIDS crisis in black America.[44] These flashbacks recount pivotal events from Precious's and Winter's early childhood and adolescence that intersect with key points on the timeline of the HIV/AIDS epidemic and pathways to HIV infection. For example, the year 1982, one year before Precious has her first child by her father, and five years after Winter's birth, is the same year that the Centers for Disease Control and Prevention officially identified the term "acquired immune deficiency syndrome," and its acronym AIDS, to describe the transmission of an infectious agent, through blood, semen, and vaginal secretions, that "produces a suppression of the body's natural defenses and sets the stage for the intrusion of severely deadly afflictions, including a rare form of cancer called Kaposi's sarcoma and a rare pneumonia."[45] Two years after naming the disease, the CDC reported that black babies accounted for 50 percent of pediatric AIDS cases in the United States.[46] Celia W. Dugger mapped HIV incidence rates among women having babies in New York City specifically, and found that "the rate of infection for non-Hispanic black women who gave birth jumped 12 percent" throughout the 1980s and into the early 1990s, despite rates of HIV infection dropping among white and Hispanic mothers for the same historical period.[47]

The psychophysiological consequences of pediatric AIDS, adolescent childbearing, and childhood sexual abuse are brought to the fore for Precious

---

43. The focus group for this study was comprised of 109 black female adolescents enrolled in an Urban League–sponsored AIDS-prevention program. Jemmott and Jemmott, "Increasing Condom-Use Intentions," 274, 276.

44. Cohen, *Boundaries of Blackness*, 126. Cohen cites the findings of Des Jarlais et al., "First City."

45. Herman, "Disease's Spread," 31.

46. Curran et al., "Epidemiology of HIV Infection." The authors concede that the disproportionality in black-white AIDS rates among infants, women, and men may result from higher rates of self-reporting and disclosure.

47. Dugger, "HIV Incidence Rises," B3.

when Mary tells her that "Carl had the AIDS virus" (85). This revelation exacerbates the existential crisis Precious experiences as a result of wanting Abdul, despite the violative circumstances of his conception, not only because of the burgeoning awareness that her father may have transmitted HIV to her but also because of the fear that she may have perinatally transmitted HIV to Abdul: "Abdul could be—oh no, I can't even say nuffin'" (85). Despite words escaping her, Precious nevertheless uses imagery to make meaning of the revelation, a translation that results in Precious configuring Mary as a confounding factor in her circumstances: "A long time I don't say nuffin,' jus' look at Mama" (85). The rhetorical question—"This what I come out of?"—precipitates a telescopic reflection that results in Precious symbolically articulating the effects of perinatal transmission of HIV to the impact of childhood sexual abuse and exposure to Mary's language use on Precious's sense of self, from birth through adolescence: "Like Abdul and Little Mongo come out of me. If she ever said a kind word to me I don't remember it. Sixteen years I live in her house without knowing how to read. Since I was little her husband fuck me beat me. My daddy" (85). Sherry Ziesenheim and Matthew Darling argue that reflections along these lines mark the onset of Precious using language to "speak through her wounds," rather than dissociating to cope with the stress, pain, and trauma of violent maternal interactions.[48] But the syntax, phraseologies, and tone of Precious's speech sustain Mary as a significant shaping presence even after her HIV-positive status is confirmed. Precious's struggle with language is thus revealed, here, to extend not only from the mechanics of its use in writing but also from how its use interacts with maternal influence and Precious's evolving sense of self and health in relation to HIV/AIDS.

In *The Coldest Winter Ever,* the psychophysiological risks of adolescent childbearing and HIV/AIDS are first given relief in 1984, the year that marks the nondiegetic point at which, Winter tells us, she came into full knowledge of the rituals in accordance with which her mother performed her "full-time occupation" as a "bad bitch":

Moms got her hair done once every three days. The shop we went to, 'cause she always took me, was for the high rollers' girls. These were the few women in the neighborhood who are able to hook the big money fish. They all went

---

48. Like this chapter, Ziesenheim and Darling are interested in the effects of intergenerational behavioral practices and traits on black women's health. Their study focuses on the "epigenetic marking" of trauma in Mary's "untold story" and, in distinguishing Precious's story arc from Mary's, demonstrates how dissociative disorder functions as both abusive and coping mechanism. See Ziesenheim and Darling, "Writing, Mothering, and Traumatic Subjectivity," 172–73.

to this shop to get their hair done, nails did, and, more importantly, to show off and update on shit going on. Earline's was where we could get our hair done while we collected information on the side. By the time I was seven I understood the rules perfectly. (3)

Stylized, idiomatic, and accessible, Winter's manner of speaking invokes the rules of black urban syntax, phraseology, and tone and situates the reader in the beauty shop, a space that has long been recognized as an essential cultural, social, and political site of knowledge production around black women's health.[49] As noted by sociocultural developmental psychologist Marva Lewis, the beauty shop provides a space for black mothers to foster "verbal, physical, emotional, and gender identity" for their daughters through routine interactions that center around hair.[50] The norms around hair that Winter incorporates into her "social prototype"[51] by the time she is seven derive from observing how Mrs. Santiaga monetizes her physicality and transacts it, in part, through unprotected, adolescent sex. "She was fourteen when she had me," Winter explains. "Folks said she looked great during pregnancy and would switch her ass around the neighborhood flowing easy, like water. She would wear her fine Italian leather stiletto heels even in her seventh month" (2). The materialism that Patricia Hill Collins claims Winter "bluntly embraces"[52] coalesces with the practice of transactional sex, the benefits of which Winter learns from Mrs. Santiaga, and, subsequently, uses to snag Sterling, her "first sugar daddy," as Winter describes him, by age thirteen.[53] "He got paid every two weeks and so did I," she tells us. "He worked at the store and I worked on him" (8). Winter extrapolates the material motives underlying Mrs. Santiaga's experiences with sexual intercourse during adolescence not only from listening to Mrs. Santiaga repeatedly claim that she is a "bad bitch" but also from watching her mother repeatedly model the presumptive behavior of a "bad bitch":

---

49. See, for example, Y. Lewis et al., "Building Community Trust"; Linnan and Ferguson, "Beauty Salons"; and Johnson et al., "Beauty Salon Health Intervention."

50. M. Lewis, "Black Mother-Daughter Interactions."

51. Lei et al., "How Race and Gender Shape," 1956.

52. Collins, *From Black Power*, 2.

53. Winter's age at the time she meets and initiates sex with Sterling is inferred from her reported amazement at "how in one year, from age twelve to thirteen," her "titties sprouted" and she "had the ass to match," close in time to describing Sterling's eyes "sliding in between [her] breasts," (5, 8) upon their first encounter. Winter reports having lost her virginity at age twelve, when she and Natalie "got [their] cherries busted together and lied to each other about how good the first time felt" (10).

Now a bad bitch is a woman who handles her business without making it seem like business. Only dumb girls let love get them delirious to the point where they let things that really count go undone. For example, you see a good-looking nigga walking down the avenue, you get excited. You get wet just thinking about him. You step to him, size him up, and you think, *Looks good.* You slide your eyes down to his zipper, check for the print. Inside you scream, *Yes, it's all there!* But then you realize he's not wearing a watch, ain't carrying no car keys, no jewels, and he's sporting last month's sneakers. He's broke as hell. A bad bitch realizes that she has two options: (1) She can take him home and get her groove on just to enjoy the sex and don't get emotionally involved because he can't afford her; or (2) She can walk away and leave his broke ass standing right there. Having a relationship is out. Getting emotionally involved is out. Taking him seriously is out. [. . .] Now Moms must have been a bad bitch because she had it both ways. She had the money man with the good looks, loyalty, and I know Pops was laying it down in the bedroom. (3)

Winter's unqualified buy-in to the mentality and lifestyle of a "bad bitch" reflects a complex positionality. On the one hand, she clearly demonstrates the capacity to be both deliberate and discriminating in her use of sex to bargain for what she desires in a relationship, whether physical, emotional, or financial. On the other hand, this positioning exposes deficits in her understanding of the reciprocally exploitative (and likely statutorily criminal) actions of Sterling, a presumptive major, engaging in sexual intercourse with a minor.[54] Rachel Wagner points out that Winter's experiences with sexual assault and other forms of sexual exploitation are "so deeply rooted in her life that none of them seem to stand out to her."[55] This knowledge gap interacts with HIV risk by exposing a power dynamic that underlies many black girls' participation in relationships where sex is exchanged for money or other things of value. In the United States, the dynamics of these relationships have not been the

---

54. We learn later that Sterling has been in a long-term relationship with another woman, Judy, and that he tells Judy that Winter is his seventeen-year-old cousin. This lie apparently covers not only for the fact that Sterling is in a sexual relationship with Winter but also for the fact that Winter is a minor, as Judy sardonically quips: "I will say, I was jealous at first, you know, when Sterling told me you were coming over for two weeks. Jealous of you getting all of his time and attention. I can see that he was right. You are just a kid. He was just helping out and everything worked out perfectly" (102–3).

55. Wagner, "Race, (In)Justice," 37. While she does not specifically focus on Winter's relationship with Sterling, Wagner's analysis of symbolic imprisonment in *The Coldest Winter Ever* deftly highlights the many ways in which Winter is subject to sexual exploitation and sexual assault and how these experiences illuminate black girls' distinct relationship to the prison industrial complex.

40 · CHAPTER 2

subject of extensive public health research specifically focused on the lived experiences of black girls.[56] Organizations such as the National Black Women's Justice Institute (NBWJI), Women with a Vision (WWAV), and the Institute of Women and Ethnic Studies (IWES) have labored to fill voids in the scholarship by addressing how transactional sex often facilitates economic security and protection from domestically abusive relationships for black women and girls, while simultaneously advocating for policies that promote black girls' and women's bodily autonomy.[57] The potential power imbalances in Winter's relationship with Sterling are rendered all the more obscure, not only because Winter's childhood and early teenage years are not defined by economically destitute conditions, given her father's kingpin status, but also because of the access that Winter claims her relationship with Sterling affords her to get the material things she wants. Black girl decision-making along this line cannot be discounted handily, as Yanga Zamba, Loraine Townsend, Anna Thorson, and Anna Mia Ekström recognize, because it aligns with what many black girls maintain is their ability to "meet subsistence and consumption needs" while "push[ing] social boundaries about what constitutes appropriate [sexual] relationships."[58] Nevertheless, Winter's processing of what it means to engage in transactional sex coextends from at least one belief-behavior-informed pathway to HIV infection when she connects the benefits she obtains from transactional sex with Sterling back to her mother as information source.

"The little piece of cash he provided meant a new outfit, an extra gold bangle to my collection, whatever," she declares. "Like mom says, you can never have too much" (9). Although Winter later intimates knowledge of the purpose of birth control when she takes "sample foam sponges" and "free condoms" from her social worker's office, "just in case" she needs them (126), her expressed sentiments toward teenage pregnancy are tonally in accord with

---

56. Recent US-based studies of the relationship between transactional sex and HIV risk among adolescents primarily center on gay, MSM, bisexual, and trans male and trans female populations. See, for example, Arrington-Sanders et al., "Social Determinants of Transactional Sex"; and Philbin et al., "Association between Incarceration." Studies that address the experiences of cisgender coming-of-age black girls mostly focus geographically on African countries with historically high HIV incidence rates among this demographic. See, for example, Ewing et al., "Three Integrated Elements"; Shangase et al., "Effect of Quality"; Gichane et al., "Individual and Relationship-Level Correlates"; and Stoner et al., "Differentiating the Incidence." At least one recent study encourages the development of culturally competent HIV prevention programs among adolescent girls that take into consideration the extent to which Western norms governing sex between adults and minors do not necessarily apply in non-Western societies. See Wamoyi et al., "Is Transactional Sex Exploitative?"

57. See Institute of Women and Ethnic Studies; Women with a Vision; and National Black Women's Justice Institute.

58. Zembe et al., "'Money Talks, Bullshit Walks.'"

her desire to emulate her mother and be a "bad bitch." "A definite advantage to having babies at a young age," Winter explains, is that "you get to chill with your moms like she's your sister or something. Fuck all those old stiff bastards complaining about teenage pregnancy, this and that. Me and my moms could party together" (25). As an extension of her commitment to modeling Mrs. Santiaga's mentality and behavior, Winter's embrace of the prospect of becoming a teenage mother necessarily involves having unprotected sexual intercourse and thus running the risk of exposure to HIV, because "intercourse without condom use" and with partners whose HIV status and HIV risk are unknown are among the sexual behaviors that facilitate HIV transmission.[59] No narrative elements suggest that Winter ever seeks to know Sterling's STI/STD status, or the status of any of the other men—Jamal, Bullet, Boom, and Tony[60]—with whom she has sexual intercourse. With each sexual encounter, her post-sex observations reinforce the HIV acquisition/transmission-risk characteristics of her sexual practices. "If I fucked Sterling that night I didn't know it," she remarks, before concluding: "It didn't matter. My mind was on vacation" (69). When Winter later learns that one of these unprotected sexual encounters results in pregnancy, her concern turns not to knowing whether she has been exposed to HIV or any other STI/STD, but to terminating the pregnancy, and only because she knows that Bullet cannot be the father: "I knew it wasn't [Bullet's] because I was too far along. It's Boom's or the other guy's. There was no way to be sure. I couldn't front it off. So I'd get it scraped out first thing tomorrow" (263).

Sapphire's and Souljah's concern to address risks of exposure to HIV for black girls is reflected in other narrative elements that frame Precious and Winter's stories. While much of the real-time action in *PUSH* and *The Coldest Winter Ever* occurs when Precious and Winter are, respectively, sixteen and seventeen years of age, the historical periods of past and present events in the novels witnessed rates of new HIV and AIDS infections among black women and girls that consistently outpaced national averages for nonblack women and girls. In 1986, approximately one year before Precious gives birth to Abdul and confirms that she is HIV-positive, black women comprised 51 percent of all AIDS cases among US women and had an overall AIDS rate that was three

---

59. Walter et al., "Prevalence and Correlates," 340.

60. Winter's description of, or allusion to, these sexual encounters can be found at pages 8–9, 10, 56, 186, 203–4, 216, and 241–42. Winter's encounter with Tony, GS's bodyguard, results from Winter having been tricked into having sex with him, and thus, like Winter's sexual relationship with Sterling, implicates important questions the novel raises around consent and black girl sexual health.

times higher than their white counterparts.[61] The novels' primary settings find Precious and Winter navigating life in Harlem and Brooklyn, Precious's and Winter's respective birthplaces. In 1990, New York City was one of two cities in the United States where AIDS-related complications was the leading cause of death for black women aged fifteen to forty-four.[62] While the number of US adolescents living with AIDS in the early 1990s was under 1,000, in New York City, HIV incidence rates within this demographic were substantially higher, and factors that put adolescents at risk of exposure to HIV were especially prevalent.[63] If it is true, as Stallings argues, that *PUSH* demands that all the "fictions of black girl subjectivity" be brought "into conversation with reality,"[64] then an undeniable introduction to reality that both Sapphire and Souljah compel readers to grapple with is reflected in the stark epidemiological facts and HIV/AIDS historical data that Precious's and Winter's narratives encompass.[65] And if it is also true, as Sapphire contends, that language is a "vehicle for social change,"[66] and, as Souljah insists, "knowledge [. . .] offers [. . .] the opportunity to explain and develop solutions,"[67] then it can be argued that *PUSH* and *The Coldest Winter Ever* sought to facilitate meaning-making around prevention-intervention directed action in response to the devastating effects of the HIV/AIDS epidemic among black women and girls near the turn of the twenty-first century. By highlighting the indispensable role that mothers play in transmitting the "values, attitudes, and knowledge"[68] that inform sexual protective and risk behaviors for black girls, Sapphire and Souljah pursue the more difficult, tedious task of "searching for solutions," as

61. Guinan and Hardy, "Epidemiology of AIDS"; and Ellerbrock et al., "Epidemiology of Women."

62. Cheater, "AIDS Zeros In."

63. Kaplan and Schonberg, "HIV in Adolescents"; Brunswick, "Health and Substance Use Behavior."

64. Stallings, "Erotic Literacy," 119.

65. While I agree with Elizabeth McNeil that *PUSH* leaves open the possibility that Precious's HIV-positive diagnosis is not a per se death sentence, McNeil's analysis builds on an inaccurate characterization of the 1980s as the historical period during which HIV/AIDS existed as "the most taboo and deadly of communicable diseases." See McNeil, "Un'Freak'ing Black Female Selfhood," 14. As noted, the 1980s was characterized by heightened awareness of HIV/AIDS, but within the mainstream, there was relatively little registry of the impact of the epidemic among black people generally and black women and girls specifically. Royles, "Why Black AIDS History Matters." Moreover, "skyrocketing" incidence and prevalence rates of HIV/AIDS among black women did not come into mainstream focus until 1988, prompting the CDC, in 1992, to "change the definition of AIDS" to encompass "the list of opportunistic infections that affect HIV-positive individuals, particularly women, drug users, and people of color." See Gavett, "Timeline," citing Castro et al., "1993 Revised Classification System."

66. Sapphire, "'PUSH out of Chaos,'" 35.

67. Sister Souljah, "Ask the Author," 293.

68. Crooks et al., "Protecting Young Black Female Sexuality."

Ladner puts it,[69] to the problems confronting black women and girls in the age of hip hop and HIV/AIDS. Rather than focus exclusively, or even primarily, at the macro-level, Sapphire and Souljah center the family, specifically the dynamics of black mother-daughter relationships, to enact a problem-solving approach[70] to countervailing large-scale structures that have historically adversely affected black women's health and to get down/back to the basics of coming-of-age black girl needs.

Tricia Rose has said that it is impossible to understand the needs of black girls coming of age without "having a sense of the larger contexts shaping" their experiences, "such as family dynamics, expectations surrounding gender and sexuality, economic and educational circumstances, religion, race, color, and weight."[71] Maya Corneille, Amie Ashcroft, and Faye Belgrave similarly contend that viewing the world through the lens of black adolescent girls entails appreciating their "backgrounds and experiences" and how these factors impact how black girls "interact with their environment and make decisions about how to behave."[72] When Precious asks, "What it take for my muver to see me?" (32) and Winter pretends that she is "alone, with no connection to the bald-headed weirdo" (89) seated next to her on the train, they betray longings to relate to their mothers on terms that are primal, intimate, and protective. Early revelations that many of the traumas that Precious and Winter experience throughout their adolescence are caused by their mothers' actions and inactions expose a paradox in these black girls' longings that cuts to the substance of Sapphire's and Souljah's contributions to elaborating and grappling with the complexities of the black mother-daughter dyad. By adhering to the logic that "the mother-daughter bond" is the "most important relationship" to black girls,[73] Sapphire and Souljah affirm the primacy, not the negation, of the mother,[74] and demonstrate the substantial role that black

69. Ladner, "Black Women," 14.

70. See Rehak, "Way We Live Now." In this interview with Rehak, Souljah celebrates the platform that she has been given to "propose some solutions" through writing novels, such as *The Coldest Winter Ever*. See also Dancy, *"Focus on Solutions."*

71. Rose, *Longing to Tell*, 6.

72. Corneille et al., "What's Culture?"

73. Donenberg et al., "Sexual Risk," 154. Donenberg et al. draw heavily from the findings of an earlier study of an HIV intervention program focused on black mother-daughter relationships and conducted by Mary McKernan McKay, Donna Batiste, Doris Coleman, Sybil Madison, Roberta Patkoff, and Richard Scott. See McKay et al., "Preventing HIV Risk."

74. Stallings, "Erotic Literacy," 123. Here, I also disagree with Kokkola's argument that Precious was not mothered. Kokkola, "Learning to Read Politically." Much of the physical and emotional trauma that Precious endures directly results from Mary's mothering of her. As such, the novel constructs Mary's mothering of Precious as a variable that informs the sociocultural and ecological contexts of Precious's vulnerability to exposure to HIV/AIDS.

mothers play in mediating and modulating HIV/AIDS protective and risk factors for their coming-of-age black daughters. This chapter thus proceeds by tracing a philosophy of black women's health in *PUSH* and *The Coldest Winter Ever* that posits language acquisition and use as a cornerstone of black girl identity formation and black girl sexual health. It complicates a trend in more recent hip hop feminist scholarship that, in rightfully taking respectability politics to task for its deference to middle-class white normative standards of conduct and appearance, neglects to consider the uncontested relationship among attitudes, beliefs, behaviors, and HIV/AIDS risk for black women and girls.[75] By broadening the analytic framework for understanding determinants of HIV/AIDS risk and protection for black girls to encompass the effects of language acquisition and use on black girl identity formation and black girl sexual health, this chapter demonstrates Sapphire's and Souljah's interest in looking beyond the politics of representation in order to (re)focus on how the mother-daughter relationship functions as an indispensable correlate of black women's health.

Frequent overlaps between Precious's and Winter's language and the nonverbal cues and verbal utterances of Mary Johnston and Mrs. Santiaga reveal language uses that are highly localized and derivative of Precious's and Winter's relationships and interactions with their mothers. After Mrs. Lichenstein rings the bell to Mary and Precious's apartment, Mary directs Precious to "Press LISTEN stupid!" Repeating and internalizing her mother's words, Precious interiorly responds: "I wanna say I ain' stupid but I know I am so I don't say nothin'" (14). Upon hearing Mrs. Santiaga tell Mr. Santiaga, "When a woman wants to get fucked, she gets fucked," Winter extrapolates and declares that her love for her father is countervailed only by her hatred of the "way he cock-blocked" (6). Over the course of the novels, Precious's and Winter's emergent senses of self-awareness take shape and evolve in the context of these and similar mother-daughter verbal and nonverbal exchanges. As their stories progress, a series of traumatic events displaces Precious and Winter from their homes and mothers' primary caretaking and thrusts them into survival mode. Attuned to the structural conditions of their environments and connections between these conditions and their filial relationships, Precious and Winter navigate the social terrains that interact with risk of (re)exposure to HIV/AIDS and other sexually transmitted diseases and infections. In these contexts, both Precious and Winter encounter people and situations that build their capacities for self-reflection and creative expression in response to their tenuous circumstances. At times inspired, at times demanded, these

---

75. Sikkema et al., "HIV Risk Behavior."

expressions manifest both Precious's and Winter's wills to be self-possessed through language that deploys, modifies, and deflects the language of their mothers.[76] The process of claiming evolving self-awarenesses shaped by and through their mothers' language brings the clinical mandates of HIV/AIDS risk and prevention to the fore for both Precious and Winter and underscores how mothering and language acquisition and use interact to inform black girl identity and black girl sexual health.

"Mothers Hold the Crucial Key"

TRE STYLES: (Banging on the door outside) Sheryl! Come on!
(Door opens)
TRE STYLES: Keep your baby off the street! She gonna get hit one day.
SHERYL: You got some blow? You got some rock? I'll suck your dick!
TRE: Just keep your baby off the streets! And change her diapers! They
almost smell as bad as you!

—Boyz n the Hood

Numerous scientific studies have endeavored to explain what Morrison, Kelley, Juvenile, and others immersed in black culture have long understood about the relationship between language acquisition and use and black child development and the specific roles that black mothers play in cultivating black children's linguistic and cognitive skills and physical, emotional, and social functioning.[77] A handful of studies have examined parenting practices among HIV-positive mothers in relation to children's cognitive and social developments;[78] some have analyzed the specific impact of mothering and language acquisition and use on black girls' sexual health outcomes and risk

---

76. My readings do not ignore the importance of the claims on identity that Winter and Precious make through conscious acts that defy their mothers' influence. For example, Stephanie Dunn observes, correctly, that once Mrs. Santiaga is shot in the face, Winter's image of her mother shatters and a corresponding emotional distancing from her mother sets in. Dunn, "New Black Cultural Studies." Beyond the act of Mrs. Santiaga being shot, her impact on Winter is sustained through Winter's language use and the normative beliefs about sexual practices and sexual risk that this language shapes.

77. This body of research is too voluminous to cite. For a sample, see J. Smith et al., "Association between Maternal Behavior"; Vernon-Feagans et al., "How Early Maternal Input Varies"; L. Chang et al., "Contingencies between Infants' Gaze"; Ensor and Hughes, "Content or Connectedness?"; Rasmussen et al., "Mother-Child Language Style"; and Fannin et al., "Communicative Function Use."

78. See Mebrahtu et al., "Impact of Common Mental Disorders"; and Mebrahtu et al., "Postpartum Maternal Mental Health."

46 • CHAPTER 2

for exposure to HIV/AIDS. Among the earliest studies is the collection *African American Women and HIV/AIDS: Critical Responses*. In the introduction to the section on black girls, Dorie Gilbert and Ednita Wright observe that, throughout adolescence, "mothers hold the crucial key to promoting positive self-image and gender identity among their daughters" and "make a remarkable difference in the way [their] daughters define their sexuality."[79] Echoing Gilbert and Wright in their more recent study of black girls' sexual health and risks for exposure to adverse health outcomes, Reina Evans, McKenzie Stokes, Elan Hope, Laura Widman, and Qiana Cryer-Coupet emphasize the vital role that family-level communication plays in the sexual practices, and other decision-making around sexual health and wellness, of black girls.[80] Similarly, in their study of externalizing and internalizing behaviors and related patterns of "aggressive and passive communication styles" among a group of black female adolescents and their primary female caretakers participating in the STI intervention program IMARA (Informed, Motivated, Aware and Responsible about AIDS), Ashley Kendall, Christina Young, Bethany Bray, Erin Emerson, Sally Freels, and Geri Donenberg found that black girls' overall capacities to understand, distinguish, and moderate sexual risk increased in proportion with knowledge built interactively with their mothers around the differences between "aggressive and passive communication" and "assertive communication."[81] *PUSH* and *The Coldest Winter Ever* operationalize these findings by engaging the array of issues that Venus Evans-Winters argues black girls frequently worry about—"how to survive family drama and how to get to school without beating somebody's ass and getting suspended, becoming pregnant by some boy, earning enough credits to graduate on time."[82] They also wrestle with the "troubling questions" raised by the alarming number of black girls accounting for new HIV and AIDS cases reported among youth in the United States at the dawn of the twenty-first century.[83]

At different times, Sapphire and Souljah invoked these numbers while expounding on the relationship between family dynamics and black girl identity formation. "A lot of times," Souljah noted in a 1991 speech, "how [black girls] are raised plays into how responsible or accountable [they] become as adults [. . .]. A lot of the problems that we have come out of the systems and

---

79. Gilbert and Wright, *African American Women*, 160–61.

80. Evans et al., "Parental Influence on Sexual Intentions."

81. Kendall et al., "Changes in Externalizing." Primary female caretakers, the majority of whom reported being single, self-identified as biological mothers, aunts, grandmothers, adoptive mothers, and others. Kendall et al., "Changes in Externalizing," 499.

82. Evans-Winter, *Black Feminism in Qualitative Inquiry*, 73.

83. Kelly, "African American Adolescent Girls."

the structures of the way we were raised."[84] For Souljah, understanding the specific impact of mothering as a central part of the family structure that informs black girl development requires asking a network of self-reflective questions: "How did you get here? Who was your mother? Who was your grandmother? Who was your great-grandmother? How did they live? Why did it work for them? Why didn't it work for them?"[85] Channeling Morrison, Souljah identifies mothers as sources of "emotional, mental, spiritual, and intellectual" knowledge and concludes that "the absence of a mother whose presence" provides this grounding for her daughter results in "the mother's shortcomings becom[ing] the daughter's shortcomings."[86] Sapphire drew similar conclusions while discussing the role of the family in *PUSH* in a 1996 interview during which she analogized the obligations of parents to those of pet owners:

> This morning when I woke up to feed my cat, it was me that fed my cat. I had a choice of whether I was going to pet him or kick him. [. . .] Even within slavery, in our most deprived state, we had choices. Yeah, [in the novel *PUSH*] we're looking at some people who are horribly, horribly oppressed. We can say that Precious' mother [. . .] and many of the people in the culture, find themselves in a steel box, that's how bad the oppression is. You can sit there in that steel box, you can kill yourself in that box, or you can turn on your young and kill yourself that way. Even when the choices are limited, you still have choices.[87]

Underscoring the protective role of mothers, even in oppressed conditions, Sapphire goes on to lament what she sees as the results of the breakdown in black family structures. "Large masses of black children [are] metaphorically being raised by the state. In foster homes and in jails and in poor schools," she observes, before pointing out that the novel *PUSH* "is examining Precious," and it "is also examining the family."[88] In a later discussion of the novel's film adaptation, Sapphire doubled down on her novelistic intent to "break the stranglehold of black female victimhood" by exposing the stark reality that black mothers can perpetrate abuse and victimize their children. When asked whether she was concerned that the complexities of black mothering that the novel unravels might be "co-opted by folks—including black folks," Sapphire

---

84. Sister Souljah, "State of War."
85. Sister Souljah, "State of War."
86. Sister Souljah, *Coldest Winter Ever,* 322–23.
87. Sapphire, "Sapphire."
88. Sapphire, "Sapphire."

48 • CHAPTER 2

prognostically responded: "If you are going to be actively engaged in your own health and your own recovery, then you just have to put it out there."[89] When asked again about analogies drawn disparagingly between Precious's and Mary's characterizations and "stereotypes that have historically been used to demonize and objectify black women,"[90] Sapphire rhetorically queried:

> Would *Crime and Punishment* have been written if Dostoevsky had felt he had to confine himself to "positive images" of Russian youth? Would we have Kafka's *Metamorphosis* if he had felt he could only present "positive images" of the Jewish family? To say that an artist's job is to produce "positive images" is to assign them the role of propagandist. [. . .] The artist does not necessarily seek to make people feel good (or bad). We are going after something else.[91]

In response to similar questions about whether she was concerned that *The Coldest Winter Ever* might perpetuate negative stereotypes of urban black family life, Souljah replied, "No," and remarked matter-of-factly that when she gets "a chance to write a novel about the suburbs, it'll include a lot of the same components that a novel about the ghetto includes, but it will have trees and flowers and pretty parks. I'm not under the illusion that people in the suburbs are clean and people in the projects are dirty." She concluded, "Clearly some people are, though."[92]

The dialectical relationship that Sapphire and Souljah establish between larger systemic and micro-level factors influencing black girl identity formation has an analog in the classic scene cited above, from the late John Singleton's critically acclaimed, Oscar-nominated film *Boyz n the Hood* (1991). In this scene, the audience views Tre Styles (Cuba Gooding Jr.) walking home from Doughboy's (Ice Cube's) Welcome Home Party and encountering an unattended, dirty-diaper-clad toddler in the middle of the street. In her

---

89. Sapphire, "For Colored Girls: The Sapphire Interview."

90. Claudia Müller, for example, argues that a limiting feature of the novel is its paradoxical necessary reliance on images of "the welfare queen," "the welfare mother," and "the fat poor" to advance Precious's "success narrative." See Müeller, "Welfare Mother." Heather Hillsburg argues that the novel's use of the angry black woman trope reframes anger as "a legitimate response to oppression" and builds empathy for Precious's plight among readers. Hillsburg, "Compassionate Readership."

91. McNeil et al., "'Going After Something Else,'" 353. McNeil et al. invoke Patricia Hill Collins's notion of "controlling images" of black womanhood, as originally set forth in "Learning from the Outside Within." Collins's concept builds on Michelle Wallace's germinal formulation and critique of the strong black woman archetype in *Black Macho and the Myth of the Superwoman*.

92. Rehak, "Way We Live Now."

examination of the film, veteran author and cultural critic Michele Wallace points to the ways in which the scene plays on stereotypes of black mothering. "What made me most uneasy about the portrayal of these single black mothers," Wallace observes, is "how little we're told about them, how we, as viewers, are encouraged, on the basis of crucial visual cues, to come to stereotypical conclusions about these women. We never find out what Tre's mother does for a living, whether or not Doughboy's mother works, is on welfare, or has ever been married, or anything whatsoever about the single black mother whose babies run in the street."[93] Wallace extends her analysis by locating America's confirmation of "hegemonic family values" in the success of movies like *Boyz n the Hood* because of their stereotypical representations of black mothering.[94] That Wallace provides an important critical lens for reading this scene cannot be overstated because of the historical underrepresentation of rounded depictions of black women in film, especially in the latter half of the twentieth century.[95] However, if, as Gwendolyn Pough argues, black women's roles "carry a multitude of meanings"[96] in this and similar scenes that illuminate some of the dynamics of 1980s and 1990s urban America,[97] then the nameless mother and child in the scene can be read as reference points for who sociologist Tanya Sharpe, in her poignant historiography of the epidemiology of the crack cocaine epidemic among black women, *Behind the Eight Ball: Sex for Crack Cocaine Exchange and Poor Black Women* (2005), refers to as the "nameless, faceless" black women and children affected by the HIV/AIDS epidemic during the same historical period.[98] The uneven rounding of Mary's

---

93. Wallace, "Boyz N the Hood and Jungle Fever," 123.

94. Wallace, "Boyz N the Hood and Jungle Fever," 123. For an equally provocative study of film representations of black mothers and black mothering across a larger band of films, see Rousseau, "Social Rhetoric."

95. Wallace's critique follows some of hooks's germinal observations about black women's representation in popular culture in *Ain't I a Woman: Black Women and Feminism*, which laid the groundwork for hooks's formal conceptualization of the "oppositional gaze" in *Black Looks: Race and Representation*.

96. *Check It While I Wreck It*, 130.

97. *Boyz n the Hood, New Jack City, Juice, Menace to Society, Straight Outta Brooklyn*, and *Sugar Hill* comprise a body of movies released throughout the 1980s and early 1990s that tells coming-of-age urban black male stories. The documentary style of these films was the subject of extensive criticism at the time of their releases, primarily because of their alleged "faithfulness to a monolithic black experience." See V. Smith, "Documentary Impulse." The blockbuster success of many of these films also came under fire for overshadowing an impressive spate of independent black filmmaking during the same historical period. See, for example, Camille Billops's and James V. Hatch's *Older Women and Love* (1987) and *Finding Christa* (1991), Robert Townsend's *Hollywood Shuffle* (1987), Marlon Riggs's *Tongues Untied* (1989) and *No Regrets* (1992), and Julie Dash's *Daughters of the Dust* (1991).

98. Sharpe, *Behind the Eight Ball*, 2.

50 · CHAPTER 2

and Mrs. Santiaga's characterizations suggests a correspondence between the "nameless, faceless" black women that Sharpe writes about and Mary's and Mrs. Santiaga's story arcs.

In the reader's guide to the 1999 special collector's edition of *The Coldest Winter Ever*, Souljah hints at her intent to narrow Mrs. Santiaga's characterization when identifying her as the only character in the novel that does not have a full name because, as Souljah explains, "she is a symbol of incompletion" whose "limitations transfer to her daughters."[99] The recognition by many critics that Mary Johnston[100] bears similarly flat traits opens Mary's characterization to meanings that extend beyond her obvious symbolism as a "bad" mother because she emotionally, physically, and psychologically abuses Precious and enables and participates in Carl's sexual abuse of their daughter. Mrs. Santiaga dotes on and coddles Winter, yet Winter is subject to many of the same abuses that Precious experiences.

For instance, Precious and Winter are both raped. Tony admits to raping Winter when he describes "waiting in the dark" and having sexual intercourse with her, knowing all the while that she is intoxicated and believes she is having sex with GS. "You started knocking shit over," Tony tauntingly retorts after Winter angrily accuses him of lying about the sexual assault. "You tried to suck a sip out of my Cristal bottle but I had already drank it all. But here's the hook. You got long pretty legs, big titties like cantaloupes, a small tight waist, and you love to go horse-back riding!" (216). Like Precious, Winter is subjected to domestic abuse, as when Bullet threatens to kill her if she betrays him. "The penalty for betrayal is death," he warns her. "If I catch you lying to me about anything, no matter how small, the penalty is pain" (248). The psychological and physical toll of domestic violence is repeated and reinforced for Winter, just as it is for Precious, when Bullet later monitors Winter's coming and going, confines her to their bedroom, stations rottweilers outside their bedroom door, and deprives her of food for "two nights and three mornings" (252, 267, 269–70). The vulnerabilities that Precious and Winter share and the abuses to which they both fall victim emerge within narratives that cast the War on Drugs, the crack cocaine epidemic, and the HIV/

---

99. Sister Souljah, *Coldest Winter Ever*, 340–41.

100. Susana Morris characterizes Mary as "perhaps the most fiendish literary mother in fiction" and "an abusive tyrant" (*Close Kin*, 113). In her review of *PUSH*, Susann Cokal refers to her as "a one-dimensional monolith" (186) Ziesenheim and Darling characterize her as a "monster" ("Writing," 180), and Aneeka Ayanna Henderson refers to her as "a sexual abuser who blindly follows" the leadership of Precious's abusive father, Carl Jones (*Veil and Vow*, 128). As already noted, Ziesenheim and Darling attribute greater complexity to Mary by examining her characterization in relation to various narrative tensions that implicate issues of mental health disorder and intergenerational trauma.

AIDS epidemic as concurrent developments and gesture toward crack cocaine use constituting an HIV/AIDS risk-contributing factor. When Precious likens Carl to "crack addicts and crackers" and concludes, "it why my father ack like he do" (34), she implies that Carl's sporadic presence and sexual abuse of her can be explained (not excused), at least in part, by drug addiction, and that his death from AIDS-related complications is connected to drug use.[101] Likewise, Winter's visit to Riker's Island women's prison brings substance use as an HIV/AIDS risk factor into focus when she comments on the appearances of the HIV-positive incarcerated women she encounters: "Their faces were sunken in like many crackheads I had seen back in Brooklyn. Some of them had fresh bruises and stitches. Some of them had black eyes and blotches" (179–80).[102] The well-documented history of mass incarceration in America[103] and how America's carceral systems have operated as "structural and contextual sources of HIV/AIDS risk"[104] leaves little room to doubt that the emergence of the cheaply available crystalline rock form of cocaine, known colloquially as "crack," expanded the devastating reach of HIV/AIDS in urban American communities throughout the 1980s and 1990s.[105] However, tensions in the novels that annex the crack cocaine epidemic to further insight into Precious's and Winter's evolving senses of self-awareness and sexual health flesh out through language that consistently presents Mary and Mrs. Santiaga

---

101. To be clear, the narrative leaves the question of how Carl contracts the virus unanswered. It also does not call into question Precious's implied perception of how he may have contracted the virus.

102. Precious uses similar language when describing heroin-addicted people she encounters along 124th streets: "Turn from vaykent lot n is vaykent pepul with kraters like what u see wen you look at spots on the moon, wen you see moon on space movies is holes on it, kraters, that a dope addicts arms—kraters [. . .]. There eyes is like far away space ships" (105).

103. In her weighty tome *From the War on Poverty to the War on Crime: The Making of Mass Incarceration in America* (2016), Elizabeth Hinton marks the onset of the crack epidemic in 1984, the year that Congress passed the Comprehensive Crime Control Act of 1984, which effected radical changes in the US criminal code as well as in the allocation of federal funding to address the administration of criminal justice at state and local levels. See, especially, the sections on "punitive urban policy" and "remaking black criminality," 314–32.

104. The volume of research that treats HIV/AIDS and mass incarceration as overlapping epidemics is vast and easy to find. For early and more recent public health studies, see Wohl et al., "HIV and Incarceration"; Blankenship et al., "Black-White Disparities"; and Adams et al., "Potential Drivers." For an enduringly poignant, if unevenly supported, cultural study, see Herukhuti, *Conjuring Black Funk*.

105. Edlin et al., "Intersecting Epidemics." Some more recent scholars have questioned the pervasiveness of the crack cocaine epidemic with respect to children of young black mothers in urban communities, who were born with crack cocaine in their systems. Adrianna Finamore specifically argues that the so-called "crack baby epidemic never materialized." See Finamore, "Geeking and Freaking," 61.

"Your Physical Self and Your Speech"

My muver say Farrakhan OK but he done gone too far. Too far where I wanna ax.

—Precious in *PUSH*, 40

On the train I tried to talk to Momma. I wanted to understand what was going on with her. She just seemed different to me.

—Winter in *The Coldest Winter Ever*, 89

Winter's and Precious's beliefs about crack cocaine use are unmitigated and unforgiving, as evidenced by Precious's declarations, "I hate crack addicts" (14) and "Crack addicts *disgusting!* Give race a bad name" (37)[107] and Winter rhetorically questioning who is at fault when a drug dealer refuses to sell crack to a pregnant girl from her neighborhood: "She just took her dumb ass to somebody else and got crack anyway. Then, when she had the baby boy, she tried to sell him, too" (22). These thoughts extend from raciogendered[108] language that loosely associates crack cocaine use with high-risk sexual behavior. Corene Wilson, a former crack user who appeared in the documentary *Planet Rock: The Story of Hip Hop and the Crack Generation* (2010), elucidates this relationship when describing changes in her behavior as a mother once she "got hooked" on crack cocaine: "I would leave my son in the house, and I would go around the corner and cop. And then when I'd come back, my son is standing on the stoop—two and three o'clock in the morning by himself. He was like three years old." Betty Moore, another former crack user, explains how her use of the drug modified her sexual practices: "I used to mess around with guys just to get money. Prostituting myself. I didn't—oh, my God—I didn't like it. But I did it, because I had a problem."[109] The documentary describes these women's behaviors as characteristic of crack users

---

106. MacMaster et al. distinguish between ample research that describes risks and the dearth of research that addresses internalized beliefs and practices that are pertinent to understanding risks among black women. See "Perceptions of Sexual Risks."

107. At Advancement House, Precious alludes to "bitches who act so s'perior 'n shit usta be crack addicts" (116).

108. I use this term as coined by Angeletta K. M. Gourdine. See "Colored Reading."

109. Lowe, *Planet Rock*.

known in the streets of New York City as "skeezers": "girls who will do anything to hit the (crack) pipe."[110] Commonly featured in the lexicon of hip hop, the terms "skeezer," "strawberry," "ho," "chickenhead," "cunt," and "skank" are "sounds from the streets and schoolyards"[111] that black girls situated similarly to Precious and Winter navigate. They are also standard units of Precious's and Winter's speech.

We hear it, for example, in Precious's description of Mrs. Lichenstein looking at her like she had a "bad odor out [her] pussy or something" and how she wants to reach over the desk and "yank [Mrs. Lichenstein's] fat ass out [the] chair" (8). We get it when Winter distinguishes her mother's fashion from the wardrobes of every other woman in their neighborhood: "By the time hoes sported their outfits, all their shit was played out, straight out of style" (2). In both syntax and semantics, Precious's language follows her mother's, as when Mary calls Precious a "stupid," "retarded" (14, 20, 58, 59) "fat," "slut," "nasty ass tramp!" "cunt bucket slut!" "fuckin' cow!" "whore!" and blames Precious for Carl's abandonment of her: "Nigger pig bitch! He done quit me! He done left me 'cause of you" (9, 19, 32, 55–56). Similarly, the sexual connotations embedded in the language Winter casually uses to distinguish Mrs. Santiaga from "every other woman" (2) she knows parrot Mrs. Santiaga's quip, "Don't front on me little hooker," when encouraging Winter to pursue a sexual relationship with Midnight, a man five years Winter's senior who, Winter admits, likely views her as "jailbait" (26, 7). The prevalence of this language in Winter's and Precious's speech is neither "gratuitous" nor "shocking."[112] Rather, it reinforces Souljah's and Sapphire's affirmation of the most basic things that both artists insist every black girl has: "your physical self and your speech."[113]

Mary's language resounds in Precious's speech, as when Precious reflects on the image she sometimes sees when passing a store window: "Somebody fat dark skin, old looking, someone look like my muver look back at me" (32). Seeing Mary look back at her prompts Precious to "stand in the tub" and examine the markings on her body: "it stretch marks, ripples" (32). It agitates contradictory impulses toward self-abnegation and self-embrace: "I try to hide myself, then I try to show myself" (32). And it triggers memories of Carl's violation of her body and how Mary's language use compounds the violation: "Every time I ax for money she say I took her husband, her man. Her man!

---

110. Goldstein et al., "From Bag Brides to Skeezers."

111. "Drama of the Ghetto Child," 13. See also Venable, "It's Urban, It's Real"; and Fullilove, Lown, et al., "Crack 'Hos and Skeezers."

112. Ziesenheim and Darling, "Writing," 179.

113. Sapphire, "Sapphire," 43. Souljah states it slightly, though not substantively, differently, commenting: "I am in control of myself and my words." Rehak, "Way We Live Now."

Please! Thas my motherfuckin' fahver! I hear her tell someone on phone I am heifer" (32). As previously noted, in one of many scenes in which she confronts the traumas brought on by her father sexually abusing her, Precious invokes Farrakhan's racialized critique of crack cocaine addiction, a disorder that she tacitly imputes to Carl. Brittney Cooper suggests that "for all her agreement with Farrakhan, Precious seems to know the world is not merely contained in the arc between 'crack' and 'crackers.'"[114] But even the attitude adjustment toward lesbians, which Precious's love for Ms. Rain causes her to make, is insufficient to shake Precious's faith in Farrakhan's precepts. The only narrative bend in this direction occurs when Precious reflects: "My muver say Farrakhan OK but he done gone too far. Too far where I wanna ax" (40). Precious's response to, and desire to better understand, her mother's thoughts about Farrakhan is a form of receptive and expressive language processing, an essential feature of linguistic competence. The process is clearly traceable along the pathway toward learning to read and write that Precious follows with Ms. Rain's guidance. It is also mappable, as Precious's knowledge of self in relationship to sexual health evolves. Mary's imprint on this process is, to the novel's end, indelible.

We see this, for instance, as the structure of receptive-expressive language illustrates Precious's struggle to comprehend the idea that substance use disorder can exist as a correlate of her HIV-positive status and experiences with childhood sexual abuse.[115] "I not crack addict," she states resolutely, then questions, "Why I get Mama for a mama?" (87). These thoughts follow Mary telling Precious that Carl had AIDS and is dead and feature Precious attempting to reconcile the cognitive dissonance flowing from her misunderstanding of the alignment between crack cocaine use as an HIV/AIDS risk factor and her own risk for exposure to HIV/AIDS as a victim of childhood sexual abuse. We see receptive-expressive language processing again, once Precious confirms her HIV-positive status and shares this information with Ms. Rain and the other girls at Each One Teach One: "I cry for everyday of my life. I cry for Mama what kinda story Mama got to do me like she do?" (96). It occurs, again, when Rita insists that HIV/AIDS is a "disease," not a moral judgment. "You know what she mean?" Precious asks. "Well, thas good 'cause I don't," she responds adamantly. "I cannot see how I am the same as a white faggit or crack addict" (108). In this example, Precious's pejorative characterization of at-risk groups recalls and repeats the stigmatizing language Mary uses to downplay her own

---

114. B. Cooper, "'Maybe I'll Be a Poet,'" 65.

115. The body of research that treats comorbidities of childhood sexual abuse is expansive and easy to locate. See, for example, West et al., "Adult Sexual Revictimization"; and A. Roberts et al., "Contextual Factors."

risk of exposure to HIV/AIDS because, as she tells Precious, she and Carl did not have sexual intercourse "like faggots, in the ass and all" (86). The depth of Mary's influence on Precious's language use in this instance, and the beliefs about risk groups and behaviors that Precious's language enshrines are especially pronounced in this moment because Precious knows that Mary could have been exposed to the virus, based on what Precious says she remembers from "AIDS Awareness Day at school" (86). Here, the traditional school setting, as an HIV/AIDS information source, parallels the role that Ms. Rain and Each One Teach One play in providing Precious a different pathway to literacy. However, this alternative knowledge source is unable to counterbalance Precious's impulses toward self-awareness through sexual health, which are filtered through her relationship with Mary and the language she inherits from her mother.

We see this especially as *PUSH* comes to a close, and therapy, the acquisition of basic literacy skills, and the establishment of loving and caring kinships away from Mary have tooled Precious to think about her life expectancy, given her HIV-positive status. Despite Precious's counselor informing her that the science of HIV/AIDS strongly suggests that she can "live a long time" with the virus, because she is "young, is got no disease and stuff, not no drug addict" (110), anxiety, fear, and doubt continue to beset Precious. "Something tear inside me," she explains, "I wanna cry but I can't" (137). She continues:

> It's like something inside me keeps ripping but I can't cry. I think how *alive* I am, every part of me that is cells, proteens, nutrons, hairs, pussy, eyeballs, nervus system, brain. I got poems, a son, friends. I want to live so bad. Mama remind me I might not. I got this virus in my body like cloud over sun. (137)

In this passage, words and imagery analogize the presence of HIV in Precious's body to the visceral, haunting presence of Mary in Precious's mind. The conflation of scientific, sexual, and maternal terms to capture and communicate Precious's psychosomatic condition recalls Precious's early childhood introduction to her body as violated site, and Mary as perpetrator of Precious's affliction: "Mommy please, Mommy please, please Mommy! Mommy! Mommy! MOMMY!" Precious cries, flashing back to Mary kicking her in the side of the face and calling her "Whore! Whore!" upon learning of Precious's first pregnancy (12). The memory prompts Precious to reflect on how long she has known about the mechanics of sexual reproduction: "I been knowing about that since I was five or six, maybe I always known about pussy and dick. I can't remember me not knowing," she says (12). Here, the popular euphemisms Precious uses to refer to reproductive organs echo the language Mary uses when physically and verbally assaulting Precious. This use of language configures the mechanics of acquiring language as an extension of Precious's experiences with childhood sexual abuse and maternal maltreatment. This language use, which persists from Precious's early childhood through late adolescence, cuts against any notion that HIV is "a life circumstance that [Precious] can [easily] overcome."[116] To the contrary, just as the effects of mothering and language acquisition and use contribute to Precious's health status as an HIV-positive adolescent, so, too, does the confluence of these two factors shape Precious's health prospects as she contemplates a future living with HIV.

As an indicator of how maternal influence and language acquisition and use inform black girl identity and sexual health, receptive-expressive language processing features centrally in Winter's story, just as it does in Precious's story, as evidenced primarily by shifts in Winter's thoughts, which take place once Mrs. Santiaga becomes addicted to crack cocaine. "I tried to talk to Momma," she tells us. "I wanted to understand what was going on with her. She just seemed different to me" (89). Until this narrative juncture, allusions to the crack cocaine epidemic work exclusively to demonstrate Winter's buy-in to the "bad bitch" mentality she learns from Mrs. Santiaga. We see this, for example, when Winter thanks God that she "listened to [her] Mamma's advice about always hav[ing] nice clean sexy underwear" (36). This advice recalls Winter's earlier skeptical attitude toward crack use, risky sexual behavior, and black girl identity. In this instance, Winter draws a hard distinction between her hygiene practices, an aspect of sexual health, and those of other black girls in her neighborhood. "If I was a tackhead," she tells us, invoking a colloquial term used disparagingly to refer to a financially strapped girl from the 'hood, "I could of got caught out here with some beat-up drawers on my ass, with a shit stain and a big old hole in 'em. Just the thought cracked me up" (36). The phonemic pairing intimated by Winter's direct use of the term "tackhead," and signification on the word "crackhead," again invokes Winter's earlier indictment of around-the-way girls who use crack cocaine while pregnant.

Winter's language play and attendant attitude toward crack cocaine use echo Mrs. Santiaga's early reproof of any hint of an association between her and women from the 'hood whose use of crack cocaine makes them targets of both the state and the community's contempt: "I'm not a drug addict, crackhead, or criminal," she insists (75). The salience of Mrs. Santiaga's words in shaping Winter's thoughts about crack cocaine use reveals a paradox in the operations of language. On the one hand, Winter cultivates an aversion to

---

116. Alisha Menzies and Emily Ryalls suggest that the film version of the novel constructs Precious's HIV status in this way. See Menzies and Ryalls, "Depicting Black Women," 489.

crack cocaine, which manifests as a conscious avoidance of a drug whose use is associated with several HIV/AIDS risk behaviors within the specific developmental period of black girlhood. Drs. Robert Fullilove and Mindy Fullilove outline these risks in one of their earliest studies of HIV/AIDS among black adolescents, which found that one in four black girls who reported using crack cocaine also reported participating in exchange of sex for drugs and/or money and that among black girls who used crack cocaine, 51 percent reported being pregnant at some point during adolescence, in comparison with 20 percent among nonusers who reported being pregnant.[117] On the other hand, Winter's attitude toward crack cocaine use betrays a lack of understanding of how the use of other perception-, mood-, and behavior-altering substances can interact with risk of exposure to HIV/AIDS. Ironically, Winter's use of these substances occurs in scenes that reveal her vulnerability to some of the same sexual health risks that she believes are unique to around-the-way girls who use crack cocaine.

One scene that puts this vulnerability on display occurs when Winter describes turning to marijuana as a means of relieving "tension" (24). The source of Winter's stress is Midnight and his repeated rejection of her sexual advances. The scene opens with Winter relating that she "copped a nickel bag" while in Brooklyn, and upon returning to her home in Long Island, goes into her bedroom, rolls a blunt, and opens a window to "let the breeze in to whisk the smoke out" (24). When Mrs. Santiaga abruptly enters the room, Winter covers the blunt with a towel (24), an act that implies not only that Mrs. Santiaga is unaware of her daughter's recreational drug use but also that, if known, this behavior would be met with Mrs. Santiaga's disapproval. A conversation between Winter and Mrs. Santiaga follows, wherein Winter confesses that she knows Midnight has no romantic interest in her. Mrs. Santiaga rebuffs this idea, telling Winter that the only barrier to Midnight reciprocating Winter's overtures is his fear of Winter's father: "Midnight just likes life," she quips reassuringly. "Santiaga would squeeze the life out of him" (26). The scene closes with Mrs. Santiaga preparing to leave the room. However, before she departs, Winter observes that Mrs. Santiaga "leaned her head back in and smiled," and says: "And, don't light that joint in the house" (26). Whereas Mrs. Santiaga's language regarding crack cocaine use fosters risk-averse behavior for Winter, both verbal and nonverbal cues in this scene lend approval to Winter's recreational use of marijuana. In their examination of factors contributing to the onset of adolescent substance use, Kristine Marceau, Nayantara Nair, Michelle Rogers, and Kristina Jackson identify strong correlations

---

117. Fullilove, Golden, et al., "Crack Cocaine Use," 298.

between parental knowledge "related to the tracking and monitoring" of a child's whereabouts and activities and high-risk adolescent behavior, including alcohol and substance use.[118] Similarly, Samuel Meisel, Craig Colder, and Christopher Hopwood found that "parental substance-specific communication has been positively associated with adolescent substance use."[119] Mrs. Santiaga's and Winter's interactions in this scene demonstrate that even if Winter's use of marijuana does not commence with her mother's knowledge, it continues with her mother's consent. As an indicator of risk, this affirmation circles back to, and operates co-constitutively with, Mrs. Santiaga's approval of Winter's active pursuit of a sexual relationship with Midnight, in light of Winter's description of the immediate effect that smoking marijuana has on her mental perambulations. "After the feeling of 'no worries'" takes over, Winter says she "leaned back, closed [her] eyes, and drifted into the night" (26). In this headspace, Winter imagines Midnight declaring his love for her and seeking permission from her father to marry her:

> "Winter is young," observes Santiaga.
> "Young and beautiful," responds Midnight. "Like your wife was when you two married." (27)

This scene within a scene reflects Winter's drug-induced daydream; its fantastical content and tone flow from the earlier scene wherein Mrs. Santiaga encourages Winter to pursue a romantic relationship with Midnight. At first glance, the scene seems to represent the innocent desires of an adolescent girl who wants to experience requited love and emulate the relationship conventions of her mother and father. However, following this scene, Winter attempts to seduce Midnight. This action establishes a continuum that commences with Mrs. Santiaga's words of encouragement and extends to Winter's substance-induced fantasy and risky sexual behavior.

The behavior begins with Winter positioning herself in a chair opposite the one Midnight sits in, with only a towel wrapped around her hair and a towel wrapped around her body: "I picked up my legs and placed them on the arm of my chair," she says of her actions. "I started playing games with my legs, repositioning them, opening them slowly, closing them slowly. I was making it possible for him to see the hairs on my pussy, if he only wanted to. When I got excited enough, my juices would start to flow, releasing the scent of a willing pussy, definitely something he wouldn't be able to fight" (37).

---

118. Marceau et al., "Lability."

119. Meisel et al., "Assessing Parent-Adolescent Substance Use Discussions."

When Midnight flatly rejects these advances, Winter tries to coerce Midnight by questioning his sexuality: "Are you a homosexual?" she queries. When Midnight responds again by dismissing Winter—"Go to bed little girl," he tells her—Winter drops the towels to the floor. "I wanted him to see my whole body," she explains. "I mean I was butt naked, standing in the middle of a hotel suite which was designed for fucking" (37). The insecurities and frustrations Winter earlier admits to feeling when acknowledging to Mrs. Santiaga that Midnight "straight up don't like" her and has no interest in her "as a woman" (26) results in Winter stripping down, literally, to her child's body. Midnight's recognition of Winter as a child and refusal to respond to her advances, despite her persistence, strips the scene of any hint of reciprocated romantic or sexual tension by reinforcing the age difference between Winter and Midnight, which Midnight also refuses to exploit. This action functions as a potential HIV/AIDS protective factor for Winter and contrasts the dynamics of her relationship with Sterling, which show Sterling, a major, readily engaging in the HIV/AIDS risk behavior of having condomless sex with Winter, a minor. Winter's interactions with Midnight present similar risks, not because they have unprotected sex, but because of the impact of Midnight's constant rejection on Winter's self-esteem. Studies of the relationship between self-esteem and HIV/AIDS risk determinants count early onset of sex, multiple sexual partners, condomless sex, and substance-influenced sex among the risks for exposure to heterosexual transmission of HIV for adolescent girls, and over the course of the novel, Winter engages in all of these high-risk behaviors.[120] Winter's unrequited attraction to Midnight, coupled with the encouragement she receives from Mrs. Santiaga both to use substances and to pursue a man who has no interest in her, are factors that inform Winter's participation in these high-risk behaviors.[121]

We see this again when Winter describes feeling "relaxed" after drinking the glass of "Alizé mixed with Absolut" (56) that Bullet hands her prior to

---

120. Danielson et al., "HIV-Related Sexual Risk Behavior"; and Long-Middleton et al., "Predictors of HIV Risk Reduction."

121. We see this in the dejection Winter expresses and in the subsequent risk behavior Winter engages in upon learning that Sterling not only has a girlfriend, Judy, but also that he has lied to Judy about the nature of his relationship with Winter. "So is your mother or your father Sterling's mother's sister, or brother?" Judy asks, referring to Sterling's excuse for housing Winter for two weeks. "I can see that he was right," she continues. "You *are* just a kid. He was just helping out and everything worked out perfectly" (102–3). Discovery of the "game" Sterling has run on her drives Winter to seek comfort from her girlfriends in Brooklyn, who arrive "with Hennessey and passion Alizé in hand" (104). The suppressive function of substance use for Winter is underscored by the conclusion she draws upon lighting up a "second joint" while drinking: "This is what made life worth living, good friends, free weed, and lots of laughs" (104).

60 · CHAPTER 2

their first sexual encounter. The interchange between risk of exposure to HIV/AIDS and substance use, both before and during sex,[122] manifests in Winter's suppressed sensitivity to the radio announcement that sounds as she travels to Brooklyn to have sex with Bullet: "The number one group of people dying from AIDS is young black women" (54). Daring in its articulation of sexual intercourse as a "satisfying and pleasurable" experience,[123] Winter's subsequent description of her encounter with Bullet includes no language that suggests that either of them even attempts to utilize any form of protection prior to penetration:

> I slid out of my shorts. They dropped to the floor. I began to undo his buckle and went for his zipper. When his pants fell to the floor his big penis stuck out of his boxers. I jumped on him, wrapped my legs around his waist and removed his shorts with my feet. Everything was physical the way I liked it. Watching his leg muscles go up and down, watching his ass move got me excited. I rode that dick like a professional jockey. (56)

In his provocative call for scholarship that recognizes "black radical gender and sexual praxis" as a mechanism for advancing HIV/AIDS prevention paradigms that foster sexual health among gay black men, Marlon Bailey posits that "avoiding HIV infection" is not, nor should necessarily be, the primary "logic that underpins all HIV prevention and sexual health models."[124] As a reflection of raw embrace of her own sense of sexual desire and agency, Winter's language in this scene compares to her use of language in the seduction scene with Midnight. But just as self-esteem and substance use emerge as correlates of risky sexual behavior for Winter in the seduction scene, so, too, do these factors interact with risk during her sexual encounter with Bullet. This is evidenced most notably when Winter unwittingly becomes the subject of a sex tape, which, she later learns, Bullet uses to solidify Santiaga's upending as Brooklyn's top drug lord.

---

122. In one of their many studies of the relationship between drug and alcohol use and sexual practices within a cohort of black women, veteran HIV/AIDS researchers Drs. Gina Wingood and Ralph DiClemente found that alcohol use, like crack cocaine use, among black women was substantially associated with the high-risk sexual practice of failing to negotiate condom use. Wingood and DiClemente, "Influence of Psychosocial Factors." Similarly, a 1995 study found higher rates of sexual risk-taking behaviors, including having sex without condoms, among girls with histories of alcohol and marijuana use. Koniak-Griffin and Brecht, "Linkages between Sexual Risk Taking."

123. Bailey, "Whose Body Is It?," 167.

124. Bailey, "Whose Body Is It?," 168.

"Next thing I knew," Winter says, highlighting the unexpectedness of the recording session, "Slick Kid was in the bathroom where we were with his Sharp VL video camera rolling. He was cracking up and filming me and Bullet's cool-out session in the tub." With "liquor talking," Winter begins sending shout-outs to her girlfriends, while Bullet cheers on the camera man and "add[s] in his shout outs" (57). The insult Winter later feels upon discovering that Bullet and Slick Kid circulate the sex tape at a local bar in Brooklyn is compounded by the fact that Midnight bears the news of Bullet's betrayal to Winter. "I saw your naked ass on that videotape sipping champagne with Bullet," he announces, beratingly. "Who'da ever known that Santiaga's daughter was sipping bubbly with a nigga who's a worker for the other side. While your daddy was being raided by the feds you were having drinks butt naked with the enemy" (80). The revelation leaves Winter "tongue-tied" and enraged to learn that she "had been part of a setup" (80), which, in addition to leading to Santiaga's takedown, threatens Midnight's safety and freedom. "I gotta sit in the pen for two nights for beating the shit out of a little broke-ass nigga 'cause you a *stupid bitch*," Midnight declares, referring to his assault of Slick Kid for circulating the tape and nearly "blowing [his] cover" as one of Santiaga's middle men (80). As an analog to Tony's sexual assault of her, the involuntary circulation of Winter's sexual encounter with Bullet reveals a pattern of compromised sexual positions to which Winter is subjected over the course of the novel. Mrs. Santiaga's specter looms large in this scene, as in the seduction scene, as reflected by Midnight calling Winter a "stupid bitch," a pejorative remix of the "bad bitch" nomenclature by which Mrs. Santiaga goes and Winter invoking her mother's "bad bitch" mentality to reconceptualize Midnight's verbal and physical assaults as tacit forms of affection directed toward her. "My moms was definitely right," Winter concludes. "There had to be some love in Midnight's heart for me. He fought Slick Kid for me! What other reason would he have had to beat Slick's ass? He went to jail for me, defending my name" (82). Here, again, fantasy supplants reality in Winter's mind through language that models Mrs. Santiaga's discursive tendencies. This praxis again proves perilous to Winter's sense of self and sexual health, as her discovery of Bullet's betrayal of her with the sex tape is followed closely by the revelation that Mrs. Santiaga is using crack cocaine and that Bullet is Mrs. Santiaga's dealer.

The narrative turn to Mrs. Santiaga's use of crack cocaine gives relief to the multiple traumas that Mrs. Santiaga herself endures over the course of the novel, including being shot in the face, losing custody of her children to the state, discovering her husband's infidelity, and losing the financial security she enjoys as the wife of a drug lord once Santiaga goes to jail and the government seizes his property. It also exposes the fragility of the "bad bitch" image that Mrs. Santiaga subscribes to, once her face is disfigured and she cannot maintain the physical appearance of a "bad bitch." Mrs. Santiaga's use of crack cocaine to cope with these mental and physical stressors challenges the very foundation upon which Winter's sense of self builds because of the effects that drug use has on her mother's behavior. Mrs. Santiaga's efforts to downplay her drug use and cast it as one of several actions she takes to cope with sudden changes in her life also bring receptive-expressive language as a mediator of maternal influence back into use for Winter. This process results in Winter's expressed feelings toward her mother's use of crack cocaine manifesting as a struggle that compares to the one Precious experiences when she grapples over her HIV-positive status as a victim of childhood sexual abuse and with crack cocaine use as an HIV/AIDS risk factor, because Winter's attitude toward crack cocaine use and determination to be a "bad bitch" remain unchanged, despite her mother's mental and physical conditions. These subject positions effectuate continuing threats to Winter's health that coextend with HIV/AIDS risk, beginning with her descent into denial about the impact of her mother's addiction on her own mental health and culminating with Winter going to prison. The scene that features Winter and Mrs. Santiaga in conversation on a train ride to visit Porsche in her foster placement sets these culminating events in motion.

In this scene, Winter attempts to confront her mother's use of crack cocaine head-on by directly questioning why Mrs. Santiaga suddenly decides to shave her head bald: "Seriously Momma. Why did you cut off your hair?" Winter asks. When Mrs. Santiaga deflects Winter's question, Winter grabs her mother's arm and demandingly asks, again: "Why did you cut off your hair?" (89). When Mrs. Santiaga answers elliptically—"I saw that live hoe Grace Jones. It clicked in my mind. It's a sign. I ran in the bathroom and just cut it all off"—Winter says that "for the rest of the ride" she and her mother "sat in silence." In this moment, silence both disrupts and disorients by arresting the open communication that Winter is accustomed to having with Mrs. Santiaga and positioning Winter to see Mrs. Santiaga's dissembling. This vantage point exposes and initiates Winter to dissembling as a form of communication that Mrs. Santiaga deploys to avoid confronting her drug use. Dissembling, or the mental process of concealing true motives, feelings, or beliefs, is analogous to denial, the mental process of refusing to acknowledge or accept objective facts. Both are cognitive defense mechanisms that facilitate coping. As coping tools, both also affect perception and thus can lead to high-risk behavior, especially when accompanied by other emotion-driven responses, such as withdrawal, crying, and dissociation.[125] Winter's initial refusal to engage in these coping practices, specifically when confronting her mother's drug use,[126] is consistent with the unforgiving attitude toward crack cocaine use that Mrs. Santiaga teaches Winter. We see this in Winter's disdainful characterization of how the use of crack cocaine modifies Mrs. Santiaga's behavior. "My moms had sunk to an all-time low, had been seen wearing a full-body catsuit, you know the tight two-dollar legging with the bodysuit attached with no panties underneath," Winter says, recalling her description of "tackheads." She continues, "Her head was still bald, face still twisted, and body still on crack" (132). As displacement from her family persists and uncertainty about her future deepens, however, introspection prompts Winter to confront her mother's drug addiction a second time. This action results in a search for language and a battle with words, which intensify Winter's disorientation as she labors to communicate her thoughts and feelings about Mrs. Santiaga's addiction. "What could I say about Mama?" she begins. "Well, it was unusual, but I didn't have an answer," she concedes. "Up until the time I arrived at Riker's [to visit Santiaga], went through checks and searches and the whole process. I still had no answer. Up until the time for me to sign in the book I sat nervously biting my lip about Momma" (134). The sudden loss of words to express how she feels about her mother's addiction precipitates Winter's turn to dissembling and denial to cope with her mother's addiction. The effects of this mental change figure legibly in the lies Winter subsequently tells about Mrs. Santiaga's health status[127] and insistence that no one has to worry about her mother because she "has a doctor and a specialist" (172). It flows from Winter's dissociative response to situations that conjure memories of Mrs. Santiaga, as demonstrated most notably in her refusal to cry when interacting with the HIV-positive women at Riker's Island, who, Winter admits, make her think about her mother (181). And it features in Winter's stoic decision to distribute crack cocaine to Mrs. Santiaga to prove her "loyalty" to Bullet. This transaction marks an ironic inflection point in the novel by showing Winter living in accordance with the "bad bitch" values that Mrs. Santiaga teaches and binding Winter's fate as a "bad bitch" to her mother's tragic outcome.

---

125. Aziz and Smith, "Challenges and Successes"; and Rao et al., "'You Don't Want."

126. I say as related specifically to her mother's drug use because Winter lies at other times in the narrative, sometimes for no reason at all, and at other times strategically. In these instances, lying does not function as a coping mechanism for Winter.

127. She tells Doc and Sister Souljah that Mrs. Santiaga has cancer (172). Those familiar with *The Coldest Winter Ever* know that Sister Souljah writes herself into the novel as a character.

64 • CHAPTER 2

We see this, first, in the language Winter uses to outline modifications that Bullet makes to the entrance of his residence to facilitate transferring drugs to customers. "Like Santiaga, Bullet had a double security door, with a crack slot in the outside door about two inches wide and four inches long" (250). The interchangeability Winter observes in the structures of Santiaga's and Bullet's drug operations symbolically equates the lifestyle Santiaga provides Mrs. Santiaga before his downfall and the lifestyle Winter actively pursues by moving in with Bullet, despite the "disrespect" she claims he subjects her to with the sex tape (197). We see it again in how language works to (re)introduce Mrs. Santiaga as a shaping influence on Winter's lifestyle choice in the same scene. This occurs when Winter hears a "knock at the door," which, she says, "soon turned into a scratch. The scratch," she continues, "turned into a screech" (250–51). The sound prompts Winter to place her "ear on the cold metal door" and listen "for a voice. I heard what sounded like moaning," she says.

> "Come on, come on, I'm sorry. Where you been. I need something now." The words were coming out like a whining child. The screeching was louder now, too. I slid the heavy metal slot back an inch to see where the screeching was coming from. (251)

A shift in focus from the eerie sound of a child's voice to the physical features of the woman on the other side of the door brings Mrs. Santiaga's disfigured face into Winter's eyeline and enables her to identify the "ninety-pound crackhead at the door" as her mother (251). The recognition, followed by Mrs. Santiaga's attempt to slide a "fake gold chain" into the door slot, force Winter into a fetus-like position: "With my back now against the door," she says, "I slid down to my knees, then doubled over" (251). The cyclical structure of the narrative is again reinforced by Winter's instinctive response to her mother's attempt to solicit crack cocaine. Consistent with the protective actions of a child, Winter's return to a fetal position recalls her earlier protective efforts to stage an intervention with Mrs. Santiaga about her crack use while on the train ride to visit Porsche. These protective sentiments and actions are, however, short-lived, as Bullet's arrival on the scene reorients Winter's appearance and actions to the expectations of the "bad bitch" subject position she elects to occupy. "I erased all traces from my facial expression of what I had seen," she says, and when Bullet hands her a vial of crack cocaine, she distributes it to her mother (251). The transaction carries meaning beyond the obvious harm it demonstrates Winter being willing to cause to her mother in order to maintain a relationship with Bullet. The exchange reflects the consistency with which Winter's attitudes, beliefs, and behaviors align with the "bad bitch" image she learns from Mrs. Santiaga and her dogged commitment to embodying this image. We get this, finally, as the nondiegetic narrative action of *The Coldest Winter* comes to an end, and we discover that Winter has been recounting the details of her lived experience as a "bad bitch" from prison, where she has served seven of "a mandatory fifteen-year sentence" (278). That the "bad bitch" mentality she learns from Mrs. Santiaga is the root cause of her circumstance is demonstrated by Winter's unadorned admission that she "is doing fifteen years for having a bad attitude" (281). It is signified by the reflection of Mrs. Santiaga's image in the "hideous" scar that marks Winter's face and has kept her from "bothering with the mirror for about five years" (282). And it is symbolized by the novel's ominous closing on Winter standing at the site of Mrs. Santiaga's grave. "Since mothers are so important," she explains, "I was about to enjoy the only legitimate method of leaving [prison] before a prisoner's time is served" (278). While HIV/AIDS is not explicitly identified as a complicating factor in Mrs. Santiaga's death, Winter's sentiment that her mother "was dying all along" (278) leaves the complete circumstances of Mrs. Santiaga's passing unknown. This uncertainty runs parallel to the lack of assurance Precious is left with at the close of *PUSH* and reflects another point of convergence in Souljah's and Sapphire's approaches to acknowledging and countervailing the reality of black women's health at the turn of the twenty-first century. As pioneering HIV/AIDS activist Evelynn Hammonds reminds us:

> As late as 1990, many Black women still did not perceive themselves to be at risk from the disease [of HIV/AIDS]. There were few media representations of them in public health prevention materials, and those that were shown almost universally couched Black women as being incapable of controlling their own lives in the face of AIDS. We knew that many of the African American women with AIDS were adolescents who knew little about contraception nor how to use it with male partners who were often in an older age cohort. [. . .] All of the AIDS reduction advice to Black women in the early 1990s asked women to change their behavior as if their behavior did not have a social context.[128]

Sapphire and Souljah provide frameworks for understanding some of the particularities of HIV/AIDS risk and protective factors for coming-of-age black girls by elaborating how the interplay between mothering and language acquisition and use shapes black girl identity and black girl sexual health. They

---

128. Hammonds, "AIDS," 273.

demonstrate the capacity of narrative to build knowledge about HIV/AIDS prevention in service of the health and well-being of black girls coming of age at the turn of the twenty-first century. The next chapter turns to the dramatic techniques that Nikkole Salter and Danai Gurira utilized to expand knowledge about black women's health in the age of hip hop and HIV/AIDS to a global context.

CHAPTER 3

Transnational Flow(s)

Staging Silence, Stigma, and Shame in *In the Continuum*

The co-creators of this piece (one African and one African American) felt the need to have a story told from the black woman's perspective; for her to be more than a statistic on a news report.

—Danai Gurira and Nikkole Salter, "In the Continuum," 322

Feel the finger-snapping, handclapping, thigh-pattin', chest-thumping, and footstomping and grasp the friction of their embodied cross-rhythms.

—Kyra Gaunt, *The Games Black Girls Play*, 1

The cognitive shifts that are critical for women's transformative projects take place through their interpretation of turning-point events and their assessment that they must fundamentally shift how they are conceptualizing, strategizing around, and tactically addressing their struggles.

—Celeste Watkins-Hayes, *Remaking a Life*, 144

Near the middle of the critically acclaimed 2008 documentary *I Am Because We Are,* Callista Chapola-Chimombo, Malawi's deputy minister of local government and rural affairs, calls for a break in silence around HIV and AIDS. Shortly thereafter, Flora, a Malawian woman dying from AIDS-related complications, comes into view. "My future is gone," she says. "I have failed to do what I wanted to do."[1] As the camera rolls, Flora's eyes drift to her eight-year-old son, Mavuto, sitting by her side, and her attention shifts to his future, in a less despondent tone: "I wish he could grow up. Finish his school and be well educated." An overlay of still and moving images follows, with a series of Dutch angle, medium, and extreme close-up shots of Flora's severely

---

1. Rissman, *I Am Because We Are.*

68 • CHAPTER 3

emaciated body and a group of nameless black women who embrace, caress, bathe, and ultimately bury Flora, coming into sharp focus. The women's collective movements sound a chorus over the scene that tells Flora's story. In juxtaposition with Chapola-Chimombo's call, Flora's story enacts a pattern of call-and-response that shows black women confronting the effects of HIV and AIDS in their personal lives, on their children, and in their communities, while moving mostly in silence. Paradoxically, movement infuses voice and visibility into the complex social conditions that shape these women's interrelated health contexts. Given her musical roots, it seems logical that pop icon Madonna, as writer and producer of *I Am Because We Are,* would use the power of call-and-response to break silence around—and through—telling stories about black women and HIV/AIDS.[2] This artistic choice suggests Madonna's attunement with what black creators have long understood about the capacity of call-and-response and other core elements of what Geneva Smitherman and Paul Gilroy refer to as the "communicative practices" and "distinctive kinesis" of black musical culture, to facilitate understanding, expression, navigation, and critique.[3] Four years before *I Am Because We Are's* premier, Nikkole Salter and Danai Gurira set the power of call-and-response in motion to break (through) the effects of silence and its co-constitutive indicators of mental distress, shame and stigma, on black women living with HIV and AIDS in the United States and on the continent of Africa, in the critically acclaimed play *In the Continuum.*

While not the focus of substantial literary scholarship to date, *In the Continuum* received numerous awards[4] and rave reviews from its inception, as a collaborative project, during Salter and Gurira's tenures in the graduate acting program of New York University's Tisch School of the Arts,[5] to

---

2. Rissman, *I Am Because We Are.*

3. Smitherman, "'Chain Remain the Same'"; and Gilroy, "Sounds Authentic," 113.

4. *In the Continuum* received the Global Tolerance Award from Friends of the United Nations in November 2004, an OBIE Award and Outer Critics Circle Award in 2006, and the Helen Hayes Award in 2007.

5. For general history of the play's origins, see Lunden, "Two Women, One Story," and listen to Salter and Gurira's interview with Susan Haskins and Michael Reidel (Gurira, Salter, and Jones, "'In the Continuum'"). In addition to coauthoring *In the Continuum* with Gurira, Salter is the author of the plays *Carnaval* (2013), *Lines in the Dust* (2014), *Repairing a Nation* (2015), *Freedom Rider* (2015), *Indian Head* (2017), and *Torn Asunder* (2018). Author of *The Convert* (2012), *Familiar* (2015), and the Tony Award–nominated play *Eclipsed* (2009), Gurira is perhaps as widely celebrated for her acting as she is for writing plays. On the small screen, she played Michonne on *The Walking Dead,* and on the big screen, she played the late Afeni Shakur, mother of Tupac Shakur, in *All Eyez on Me* and Okoye, the general of the Dora Milage and head of Wakandan armed forces and intel in *Black Panther* and related Marvel Cinematic Universe films.

its thirteen-week run Off-Broadway,[6] and over the course of its international tour, which began in the United States and ended in South Africa.[7] Of the play, theater critic Linda Armstrong observes that it fulfills "one of the paramount functions of a dramatic production" by giving voice to African and African American women whose "views, struggles, and tragedies are not often heard."[8] Charles Isherwood of the *New York Times* similarly lauds the play's "flesh and blood" realness. "The disturbing points the play gently makes about the status of black women both in America and in Africa," he remarks, "are humanized with such emotional vibrancy that the play leaves little aftertaste of sorrow."[9] Set in Harare, Zimbabwe, and South Central, Los Angeles, *In the Continuum* chronicles the lives of two women of African descent situated within the African Diaspora, as signified by the play's transnational settings. Abigail, a thirty-something African woman, and Nia, a black American teenager, learn they are HIV-positive in "(Scene) Three: The Diagnosis": Abigail during a prenatal visit, and Nia while being treated for shrapnel injuries sustained during a random local hip hop club shooting. Up to that point, the flow of the play builds somewhat discordantly, as the audience is introduced to seemingly sharp differences in the two characters' ages, economic backgrounds, accomplishments, and aspirations: Abigail is a news announcer for Zimbabwe's Broadcasting Corporate Studios; has her sights set on moving from the public to the private sector of the broadcast entertainment industry, where she can make "real money, shamwari!" (325); is married to Stamford Murambe, an accountant; and, with Stamford, has a soon-to-be seven-year-old son, Simbi. Nia, in contrast, is a nineteen-year-old freestyling, club-hopping, p-popping, weed-smoking, booze-drinking, intermittent ward of the state. Like Simone in *The Coldest Winter Ever,* Nia specializes in "five finger discount" (327) shopping, and, as a result of boosting one too many items from her employer, is without a job and stable housing at the start of the play. Nia's sights are set almost exclusively on NBA-bound Darnell Smith—"He practically my husband," she declares—with whom she has been in a sexual relationship for "ten months and three weeks" (326). Upon discovering that they are HIV-positive, however, Abigail's and Nia's lives are brought into synchronized relief. Monologues work in tandem with mis-en-scène, soundscape,

---

6. *In the Continuum* was originally scheduled to run Off-Broadway from September 11, 2005, through October 30, 2005; high demand and favorable reviews led to an extension of its run through February 18, 2006. See Hernandez, "*In the Continuum* World Premier"; Hernandez, "*In the Continuum* Extends"; and Sheryl Flatow, "Tales of Two Women."

7. "*In the Continuum* to Return"; and Graham, "So Far, Yet So Close."

8. Armstrong, "Theatre," 23.

9. Isherwood, "Continents Apart," E1.

and blocking to symbolically collapse the geographic space that separates the two protagonists. Salter and Gurira describe the drama that subsequently unfolds as "moments in which the worlds [of Abigail and Nia] are shuffled in such a way that both the performers and worlds flow, overlap, juxtapose, and cohabitate the stage."[10] In this framework, the audience witnesses interplay between Abigail's and Nia's social and health contexts and negotiations of silence, shame, and stigma as the characters receive their diagnoses, contemplate their futures as HIV-positive mothers, and prepare to confront their intimate partners about their positive statuses. In multiple interviews, Salter and Gurira elaborated why the antiphonic technique of cross-referencing and intersecting characters' speech and movement informs both the structure and central themes of *In the Continuum*.[11]

"On the continent [of Africa]," Gurira began, storytelling "melds into everything that needs to be done for the story to get out there. And sometimes that is breaking into song [. . .]. It's really like, movement," she continued. "The African storytelling traditions are alive" and "you launch into different characters, you launch into song, you launch into dance."[12] Salter expressed similar sentiments when reflecting on the power of storytelling. "I know that [storytelling] can move people," she said, "not merely down the path of diversion, but to the heights of . . . enlightenment, education, advancement, growth, healing, understanding, inquiry, and reflection. [. . .] The stories I tell," Salter concluded, "will entertain and, mostly importantly, spiritually and emotionally move people to act in ways that promote self, societal, and cosmic understanding."[13] "Back in the Day," the first line of the prologue, makes the congruence between Salter and Gurira's storytelling chords and black musical expression clear by establishing the play's setting through a double play on Ahmad's classic hit "Back in the Day" (1994), a hip hop tribute to childhood innocence, and the sounds and rhythms of "children playing together—Child #1 in South Central, Los Angeles, California; Child #2 in Harare, Zimbabwe." In the fifteen scenes that follow, Salter and Gurira embody "the humanity behind the statistics" and "unheard stories" of black women fighting against HIV/AIDS[14] by lyrically disrupting mainstream scientific discourses, which,

---

10. Gurira and Salter, "In the Continuum," 322. Gurira and Salter's play is reproduced in the collection *African Women Playwrights*, edited by Kathy Perkins, along with prefatory material including "How This Piece Is Performed," by Gurira and Salter, and interviews by Perkins with the writers, all gathered as one chapter titled "In the Continuum" in the volume.

11. For analysis of this technique in other dramatic works, see Yan, "Staging Modern Vagrancy."

12. Gurira, "Black Panther Star." See also Williams, "Danai Gurira."

13. Gurira and Salter, "In the Continuum," 319.

14. Gurira and Salter, "In the Continuum," 316.

at the turn of the twenty-first century, were just beginning, in earnest, to address the spread of HIV/AIDS among women of African descent in the United States and Africa.

While official reports from this historical period largely characterize changes in new incidence, prevalence, and AIDS-related death rates among black women as rapid, information about black women's risks put forth by public health officials overwhelmingly failed to consider what veteran medical and economic anthropologist and African studies scholar Brooke Grundfest Schoepf identifies as the interdependent gendered effects of knowledge and power transmission in the context of transnational HIV/AIDS prevention and intervention efforts. "Knowledge," Schoepf maintains, "is about power: the power to name and define; the power to know; the power to attract funds; the power to reduce risks of becoming infected with HIV."[15] These power dynamics were clearly not lost on Salter and Gurira, as indicated by their condemnation of the lack of honest dialogue about black women and HIV/AIDS in a 2005 interview: "HIV/AIDS require a candid conversation about sex, drugs, gender roles and empowerments," Salter maintained. "Gender issues and behavioral changes are absolutely necessary," Gurira insisted. "African women have to start talking."[16] To move black women's health in the age of hip hop and HIV/AIDS to the discursive fore, Salter and Gurira acknowledged turning, first, to science. "I started at the CDC," Salter explained, "to get the hardcore statistics for African American women, young people, and African American people in general."[17] Discovering that black women represented the "highest rate of new infections—both in the U.S. and Africa"[18] was particularly "frustrating," "upsetting," and "inflaming" to Salter and Gurira, because, as Gurira notes, "I saw the numbers, but there were no voices attached to them."[19] "Who were these women," Salter remembers asking incredulously, and "where were [their] stories?"[20] Review of scientific studies of black women's health and HIV/AIDS, from the early years of the epidemic through the year of *In the Continuum*'s Off-Broadway debut, points to the source—and validity—of Salter and Gurira's wonder and discontent.

According to 2007 HIV/AIDS Surveillance Data, between 1985 and 2005, the percentage of HIV/AIDS patients in the United States that were women increased from 8 to 27 percent, and women accounted for roughly 50 percent

---

15. Schoepf, "Women at Risk."
16. Armstrong, "Black Actresses Create," 21, 23.
17. Armstrong, "Black Actresses Create," 21, 23.
18. Gurira and Salter, "In the Continuum," 316.
19. Farley, "Show Must Go On," 138; Gurira, Salter, and Jones, "'In the Continuum.'"
20. Lee, "Putting Women's Faces," B9.

of the 33 million people living with HIV or AIDS worldwide.[21] In 2004, the same year Salter and Gurira began writing *In the Continuum,* the Global Coalition on Women and AIDS, a UNAIDS-organized initiative, was established expressly to address the HIV/AIDS crisis among women. The following year, the coalition reported that women comprised 60 percent of adults and 75 percent of people aged fifteen to twenty-four living with HIV in the sub-Saharan region of Africa.[22] In 2004, AIDS-related complications was the leading cause of death for black women aged twenty-five to forty-four in the United States and the leading cause of death for black women aged fifteen to forty-four in Africa.[23]

Despite new HIV incidence and prevalence rates among black women, and substantial numbers of black women dying from AIDS-related complications between 1985 and 2005, a keyword search of PubMed.gov[24] for scientific studies addressing the epidemic among black women between 1986 and 2006 yielded only 538 results, in comparison to 2,194 results from a keyword search of studies examining the epidemic among gay men during the same historical period. Of the 538 studies, only eighteen used stigma, shame, and silence as primary analytic points of entry.[25] Further, while the abstracts to these studies have been publicly available at no cost since 1997, an institutional affiliation

---

21. The UNAIDS reports in which these data were originally published are no longer working. The original reports are cited by Claire Pomeroy in "Virtual Mentor." The data are also reported and can be found through the US Census Bureau's HIV/AIDS Surveillance Data Base.

22. Pomeroy, "Virtual Mentor."

23. CDC, "Notice to Readers"; World Health Organization, "Global Burden of Disease."

24. PubMed.gov is maintained by the US National Library of Medicine, which is located at the National Institute of Health. The database contains over 34 million citations for biomedical literature. It does not index every article published within the biomedical and life science fields. It is, however, the largest information retrieval database that is accessible to the public online and at no cost. For this chapter, multiple PubMed.gov searches were conducted, running varying combinations of the terms "African American," "black," "female," "women," "HIV," "AIDS," "stigma," and "silence," for the period 1986 to 2006.

25. See the appendix, table 1. These studies focus especially, exclusively, or primarily on black women and disaggregate datasets according to gender and race. They also give more than cursory attention to stigma, shame, and silence. See Ford and Norris, "Urban African American and Hispanic Adolescents"; Pizzi, "Women, HIV Infection, and AIDS"; McCree et al., "Religiosity and Risky Sexual Behavior"; Murphy et al., "Correlates of HIV-Related Stigma"; Miller et al., "Sexual Diversity among Black Men"; Elford et al., "HIV in East London"; Lichtenstein et al., "Chronic Sorrow"; Jimenez, "Triple Jeopardy"; Harawa et al., "Perceptions towards Condom Use"; and Rosenthal et al., "Assessing." Again, notice should be taken that PubMed.gov does not index every article published about black women and HIV/AIDS for the historical period under review in this study. Over the course of researching extant literature, I happened upon relevant articles that were not indexed and that were not readily locatable. See, for example, Phillips et al., "Psychosocial and Physiologic Correlates."

has historically been required to access the full text of most of these studies.[26] Keyword searches of PsychArticles, the database of full-text, peer-reviewed, journal articles published by the American Psychological Association, were no more fruitful. Searching the terms "black women," "HIV," and "stigma," or their equivalents, for the period 1986 to 2006 generated zero results. Searching the terms "black women" and "HIV," or their equivalents, for the period 1986 to 2006, yielded twenty-three results, six of which did not focus especially, primarily, or exclusively on black women (appendix, table 2). This chapter proceeds on the premise that Salter and Gurira's decision to write about black women and HIV/AIDS grew out of conscious efforts not only to represent black women as "more than a statistic on a news report"[27] but also to take science to task for the paucity of knowledge and information about the particularities of black women's lived experiences and struggles with HIV/AIDS at the turn of the twenty-first century.

In this, Salter and Gurira focused their joint creative process on the "hard-hitting issues [. . .] the social-changing issues" that often go "unspoken," yet directly impact black women's health. In this way, Salter and Gurira, like Sister Souljah and Sapphire, were concerned specifically to address how language relates to risk for black women. Whereas in chapter 2 I argued that Souljah and Sapphire addressed the role of language acquisition and use in shaping sexual health risk and identity for black girls, this chapter contends that the creative impulse for Salter and Gurira to embody the truth about black women's lived experiences with HIV/AIDS was rooted in modes of communication that simultaneously invoke and defy conventional speech acts. Call-and-response, as a central technique of the black vernacular derived historically from African musical traditions and manifested in hip hop, is the mode Salter and Gurira used to build knowledge about black women's health in the age of hip hop and HIV/AIDS. Imani Perry has observed that call-and-response is not limited to

---

26. Bipartisan efforts to codify the Federal Research Public Access Act (FRPAA), which would mandate archiving and free public access to journal articles (not just abstracts) based on federally sponsored research, have repeatedly failed in Congress. For insight into debates surrounding the FRPAA, see Stebbins et al., "Public Access Failure at PubMed," 43. As previously noted, Byllye Avery's motive for founding the National Black Women's Health Project in 1984 stemmed, in part, from issues with extant research on black women's health, which she found lacking and, when existing, not readily digestible for the masses. These phenomena did not change even after the establishment of the heavily funded Women's Interagency HIV Study in 1993, because the published findings of the study remained largely inaccessible to the masses. An important, related subject, whose analysis exceeds the scope of this project, is the financial barrier that accessing research on black women's health often presents for people who are not affiliated with academic institutions yet are prevention-intervention stakeholders. See, for example, Goehl, "Editorial."

27. Gurira and Salter, "In the Continuum," 322.

"verbal response but might also manifest itself in body movements."[28] In *In the Continuum,* speech and movement work lyrically and symbolically to connect HIV-infected black women in the United States and Africa. Within this transnational framework, the mechanisms of call-and-response enable audiences to witness experiences with shame, silence, and stigma that are common to women of African descent in both geographic locations and that arise out of related social and cultural histories. We hear and see how the fear and fact of being marked as undesirable and unworthy because of an HIV-positive diagnosis agitate and evoke concomitant feelings of embarrassment, humiliation, self-blame, and distress. We hear and see how the fear and fact of social isolation, marginalization, and displacement resulting from an HIV-positive diagnosis induce denial, trauma, vulnerability, and suffering. Salter and Gurira's creative staging and negotiation of black women's struggles with and through shame, silence, and stigma, or what I call their transnational flow(s), can thus be said to have advanced a gendered discursive intervention, filling voids in predominant biomedical and public health HIV/AIDS discourses and giving voice and visibility to "unspoken" aspects of black women's lives that informed their experiences with HIV/AIDS at the start of the twenty-first century.

"More Than a Statistic"

As evidence of social forces not conventionally seen or spoken, which, nevertheless, modulate people's thoughts, feelings, and actions, silence, shame, and stigma are concepts that have historically shaped black women's sexual health and histories and, thus, influenced their risk for exposure to HIV/AIDS. Salter and Gurira's determination to wrestle with the effects of silence, shame, and stigma on black women's health was clarified when they alluded to "the issues of our cultures that [were] really inflaming" them during a 2006 interview with Susan Haskins and Michael Riedel of *Theater Talk.*[29] Gurira specifically called out "women tolerating promiscuous men who expose them to HIV" as one of the issues that "we never speak of in our culture."[30] Numerous studies[31] have documented how silence, shame, and stigma have operated coextensively with stock images of black womanhood to shape discourses of black female sexuality and subjectivity, including the "internal politics" of

---

28. Perry, *Prophets of the Hood,* 72.
29. Gurira, Salter, and Jones, "'In the Continuum.'"
30. Gurira and Salter, "In the Continuum," 319.
31. For some of the classics, see hooks, *Black Looks,* and D. Roberts, *Killing the Black Body.*

TRANSNATIONAL FLOW(S) · 75

black female identity formation,[32] the "proper" social roles for black women and the moral codes by which they should live,[33] and the underrepresentation of diverse notions of black womanhood and concomitant hypersexualizing and objectifying of black women's bodies in popular culture.[34] In one of her many discussions of the effects of silence, shame, and stigma on black women's psycho-emotional well-being and the cultural contexts of black women's risks for exposure to HIV/AIDS, veteran psychologist, sex therapist, and professor Gail Wyatt reasons that the average black woman "lives with highly personal consequences, because throughout her childhood, adolescence, and young adulthood, her sexual development takes place either in sometimes deafening silence about her sexuality or in the midst of negative messages and expectations about her ability to control it."[35] The pervasiveness and influence of these negative messages cannot be overstated because, as professor and legal scholar Dorothy Roberts points out, they are part of a system of beliefs that "represent and attempt to explain what we perceive to be the truth" about black womanhood and black female sexuality, "even in the face of airtight statistics and rational argument to the contrary."[36] Wyatt concludes that the "hazards" of these messages are evidenced not so much by society's trafficking in them as by the extent to which black women internalize and live by them. "To the degree that we allow our sexual self-image to be defined by others," she contends, "we will remain [. . .] captives [. . .] of our own experiences."[37] Gwendolyn Pough posits further that the "politics of silence" in particular "becomes a self-defeating process" when black women "do not talk about sexuality," especially, she insists, when we are aware of "the dangers that are out there."[38] The relevance of this argument to efforts to identify and address predictors of HIV/AIDS risk among black women cannot be overstated, precisely because

---

32. Melissa Harris-Perry's *Sister Citizen: Shame, Stereotypes, and Black Women in America* turns our attention to the "internal, psychological, emotional, and personal experiences" of black women, claiming that these workings are political sites that "shape the social world that black women must accommodate or resist in an effort to preserve their authentic selves and to secure recognition as citizens" (5).

33. L. Thompson, *Beyond the Black Lady,* 8. Thompson's study is part of a larger body of research inspired by Evelyn Brooks Higginbotham's germinal study of black women's political activism and the black Baptist church in which she coins the phrase "politics of respectability" to describe the practice among black women activists at the turn of the twentieth century of advocating Victorian ideals of sexuality and social decorum as part of a larger effort to promote black racial uplift and reform. Higginbotham, *Righteous Discontent,* 185.

34. hooks, *Black Looks.*

35. Wyatt, *Stolen Women,* 3–4.

36. D. Roberts, *Killing the Black Body,* 8.

37. Wyatt, *Stolen Women,* 4.

38. Carpenter, "Interview," 809.

of the role that perception of risk has historically played in informing other adverse conditions that frequently intersect with HIV/AIDS risk and impact black women's health.

For example, in a germinal study of domestic violence, Kimberle Crenshaw observes that the problem of domestic violence among black women is frequently suppressed because within black communities, people often "weigh their interests in avoiding issues that might reinforce distorted public perceptions against the need to acknowledge and address intracommunity needs. Yet the cost of suppression is seldom recognized," Crenshaw concludes, "in part because the failure to discuss the issue shapes perceptions of how serious the problem is in the first place."[39] This outcome is similar to what Shaquita Tillman, Thema Bryant-Davis, Kimberly Smith, and Alison Marks found in their study of black women survivors of childhood sexual abuse, a trauma broadly defined as unwanted or coerced sexual body contact prior to the age of eighteen.[40] Among the barriers to disclosure of childhood sexual abuse, both at the time of the occurrence(s) and in adulthood, are "stereotypical images of [black] female sexuality" and perceived "cultural mandates to protect" black male perpetrators "from actual and perceived unfair treatment in the criminal justice system."[41] These beliefs, which are culturally rooted, often coextend with perceptions of what constitutes risk in intimate interpersonal relationships and impact what Gina Wingood and Ralph DiClemente identify as the behaviors most relevant to HIV transmission. When compared to black women who did not experience childhood sexual abuse, Wingood and DiClemente found that black women who reported a history of childhood sexual abuse "were significantly more likely to report a spectrum" of risk-inducing behavior, including early onset of sexual intercourse, unprotected sexual intercourse, and multiple sexual partners.[42] Julia Jordan-Zachery highlights related findings in her study of mental illness among black women, which she maintains is a health issue often cloaked in silence because of the

---

39. Crenshaw, "Mapping the Margins," 1256–57.

40. Wyatt, Carmona, et al., "HIV-Positive Black Women."

41. Tillman et al., "Shattering Silence." This observation relies upon data that show that the perpetrators of sexual abuse of black girls and women are disproportionately black and male. See Archer, "Sex Differences in Aggression." These data reveal facets of the effects of childhood sexual abuse that are distinguishable from the effects that Sapphire and Souljah fictionalize in *PUSH* and *The Coldest Winter Ever*. Precious discloses Carl's and Mary's sexual abuse of her to health authorities, who fail to act on the disclosure as mandatory reporters. Further, as I argue in chapter 2, Winter does not perceive Sterling's statutory rape of her as violative, in large part because Mrs. Santiaga sanctions Winter's sexual relationships with men who are majors and thus, by law, cannot have consensual sex with minors.

42. Wingood and DiClemente, "Child Sexual Abuse," 382. These findings are consistent with those of sociologist Celeste Watkins-Hayes, who, like Wingood and DiClemente, has conducted decades-long research focused on black women living with HIV.

"particularly negative views of the mentally ill" that prevail in black communities. As a result of this stigmatization, Jordan-Zachery found that many black women who struggle with mental health conditions often use high-risk sexual behavior as a "coping mechanism."[43] Likewise, Rachelle Reid and Sannisha Dale found that for black women living with HIV and self-reporting low-to-no perceived social networks or support, use of substances—legal or illegal, as stimulant, depressant, hallucinogen, or painkiller—frequently coextends with lower rates of antiretroviral therapy (ART) adherence and viral suppression.[44] In this way, silence and stigma coalesce around risk for HIV-positive black women because of what Monica Melton characterizes as the fear and reality of double marginalization, of being isolated within the networks that many HIV-positive black women rely upon for social and spiritual support. "The reigning stereotypes" of HIV-positive black women as "drug addicts, sex workers, or licentious women," Melton argues, impacts decision-making not only around knowing and disclosing one's status but also around accessing and sustaining care.[45] The sum of this knowledge, derived from black women's lived experiences, shapes the complex array of social and cultural factors that defines black women's health and informs their risk for exposure to HIV/AIDS. Salter and Gurira's reflections on their collaborative creative process offer insight into why call-and-response serves as a mechanism for conveying this knowledge in *In the Continuum*.

GURIRA: We would come to each other with what we had come up with, and we'd bounce it off each other. And we knew what the other was trying to get at, we knew the issues of our cultures—
(overlapping Gurira) SALTER: That we wanted to dramatize.
(overlapping Salter) GURIRA: That we wanted to get at dramatically. And we're like, "Well, I see that, but that's not working, and that's not there. [. . .]" We listen to each other.
SALTER: And we keep each other rooted in purpose. We remind each other what we are writing the story for, what we want to get across.[46]

---

43. Jordan-Zachery, *Shadow Bodies,* 126.

44. Reid and Sannisha Dale, "Moderating Effects of Social Support." This study acknowledges that perceived social support (PSS) runs along a spectrum and thus concludes that more testing is necessary to measure the range of impacts PSS has on ART adherence and viral load among black women living with HIV.

45. Melton, "Sex, Lies, and Stereotypes," 303, 307.

46. Gurira, Salter, and Jones, "'In the Continuum.'" In a different interview, Gurira offered a similar description of the process, which also invokes call-and-response, when she explained: "I'd just get up and improvise the words. [. . .] Nikkole would say 'This works,' or 'This doesn't.' I would say, 'You're trying to say this,' or 'This sounds contrived.'" Lee, "Putting Women's Faces," B9.

78 • CHAPTER 3

The opening of *In the Continuum* underscores the central role call-and-response plays in advancing Salter and Gurira's knowledge-building purpose.

"Grasp the Friction of Their Embodied Cross-Rhythms"

As previously noted, *In the Continuum* opens with a prologue that highlights linguistic and geographic divides between black children, whose singing and dancing situate them in distinct locations: South Central, Los Angeles, and Harare, Zimbabwe. These divides soon dissolve, however, as blocking and stage directions gender the children's play. A call-and-response pattern, propelled by the speech acts and movements of black girls on the Continent and black girls in the States, emerges, invoking what Kyra Gaunt characterizes as the "unique repertoire of chants and embodied rhythms of black girlhood play," in the epigraph that opens this chapter:

> Listen in on girls' daily broadcasts from the playground and you'll hear more than "nonsense." You'll hear a sophisticated approach to nonverbal syllables. [. . .] Watch their daily routines, which mix colloquial gestures and verbal expressions, and you'll be hooked on their fascinating rhythms, their use of call-and-response from word to body. [. . .] Feel the finger-snapping, handclapping, thigh-pattin', chest-thumping, and foot-stomping and grasp the friction of their embodied cross-rhythms and social "rhythmic sections."[47]

We witness this kinesis unfold in the refrain to the play's prologue:

> Cousin's on the corner in the welfare line
> Brother's in the slammer, he committed a crime
> Preacher's in the club on the down low creep
> And yo' mama's in the gutter screamin' HIV. (324)

Set to the specific rhythm of handclapping game songs, the first three lines of the refrain metonymically signify on structural, institutional, and cultural frameworks that shape the context of sexual relationships for many black women and girls in the United States and Africa: poverty, mass incarceration, and repressed sexual fluidity. In juxtaposition with line 4, the first three lines set up a lyrical interplay between the social systems and social conditions that have informed black women's encounters with HIV/AIDS since the onset of the crisis. The invocation of what scientists now commonly refer

---

47. Gaunt, *Games Black Girls Play*, 1.

to as the "contextual issues" that "challenge health promotion efforts" to stymie the spread of HIV and AIDS among black women[48] reminds us that the conventional purpose of a prologue is to foreshadow the rising and falling action of the play and, given the prologue's allusion to systemic and social factors underlying HIV transmission among black women, the main action of *In the Continuum* logically wrestles with the interchange between these factors and black women's health. But just as Gaunt reminds us that the games that black girls play may frequently "not even register"[49] as music, as part of the cornerstone of the black vernacular tradition, or what Henry Louis Gates Jr. classically referred to as the "signifying black difference,"[50] the figurative naming—and sourcing—of risks for exposure to HIV among black women in the prologue foreshadows how the play grapples with the veritable absence of these interrelated factors in prevailing scientific research and, by extension, "fleshes" the scientific record with the particularities of black women's lived experiences. In this way, the play cuts to what Gurira and Salter refer to as the "real nitty-gritty" and root causes of the epidemic among black women, specifically, demonstrating how the process of breaking (through) silence necessitates a more reflective and accurate approach to countering and calling out the effects of silence, shame, and stigma on black women's health.[51] The stage direction "//," signaling overlapping speech, facilitates this disruptive intervention in scene "Three: The Diagnosis," as Nia and Abigail receive the results of their HIV screenings.

In this scene, science and lived experience initially juxtapose at the overlap between the nurse's announcement and Nia's verbal response.

> NURSE: You have tested HIV positive. This means you have the virus that causes Acquired Immune Deficiency Syndrome.
>
> NIA: I'm sorry what?
>
> NURSE: There is no cure for AIDS, it is generally transmitted through unprotected penetrative sex, anal or vaginal, // with a person infected with HIV. And unprotected sex means sex without a condom, male or female to protect the sexual organs and in Africa that is generally through heterosexual contact.
>
> NIA: You trying to say I'ma hoe? Do I look like a junkie? Do it look like I'm gay? Do I look like I'm from Africa? No! Every time we come in here ya'll try to make us feel like we're dirty or stupid or something. [Pulling

---

48. Duffy, "Suffering, Shame, and Silence," 13.
49. Gaunt, *Games Black Girls Play,* 1.
50. Gates, *Black*; and Gates, *Signifying Monkey.*
51. Gurira and Salter, "In the Continuum," 319.

80 • CHAPTER 3

> out her cell phone.] You don't know what the fuck you're talkin' about—
> s'cuse you—no, s'cuse you! [She exits.]
>
> NURSE: We therefore recommend that from now on [eyes follow Nia, to
> passing orderly] Ewe what are you doing? Yes I can see that—but can't
> you see those are dripping on the floor? Take them to the back, those
> are contaminated. Yes they are! You barance wemunhu. [Eyes follow him
> out. Back to Abigail.] We therefore strongly recommend you practice
> abstinence from now on; but if you must, please can you protect others,
> there are three condoms, sorry we have run out. If you want we can show
> you how to use them on a banana in the next room. [Eyes wander.] But
> then you will only have two. Excuse me. Eh, Sisi Getty, are you going to
> the shops? Please Sisi help me sha, I am so hungry can you just buy me
> a sween bun ne a coke? Thank you Sisi. Aiwa. I have the money, mirai.
> (332)

In addition to signaling overlapping speech, stage directions in this scene match Nia's verbal response with nonverbal action in a manner that foreshadows scene "Four: Nia's Denial." Rather than attend to the nurse's recitation of the clinical facts extending from an HIV-positive diagnosis, Nia pulls out a cell phone, a visual sign of turning her attention away from what the nurse has to say and, in light of the title of scene 4, an apparent sign of Nia's unwillingness to receive an HIV-positive diagnosis as a factual circumstance of her life. Pamela Foster's findings that negative stigmas associated with historically at-risk groups contribute to low rates of testing in black communities may explain why denial immediately sets in for Nia,[52] as Nia's pejorative-ladened questions invoke the myth that HIV/AIDS risk exists only for sex workers, intravenous drug users, gay people, and Native Africans. However, the overlap in speech also establishes a dialectic between Nia's denial and the nurse's reporting that sets up the structure of the health care delivery systems in which both Nia and Abigail are situated for critique. In these systems, delivery of the clinical facts extending from an HIV-positive diagnosis is a priority, but these clinical facts do not adequately equip Nia and Abigail to process and understand their diagnoses, first, because the facts are not entirely accurate, and second, because of how the facts are related.

The nurse's unresponsiveness to Nia's questions, which make Nia's misinformation about risk apparent, recalls the early years of the epidemic, when black American women's vulnerability to HIV exposure through unprotected heterosexual sex in both monogamous and multiple-partner relationships was

---

52. Foster, "Use of Stigma, Fear, and Denial."

underappreciated. Historian Evelyn Hammonds explains: "It was already clear by 1992 that a significant number of African American women had acquired AIDS through heterosexual transmission. We also knew by 1989 that the social, political, and economic problems of the urban poor [. . .] provided the means for the virus to spread rapidly through African American communities. Yet, even as this stark background became more clear to scholars, researchers, activists, health care workers, and service providers, women were by and large excluded from most of the biomedical and psychological research on AIDS."[53] The nurse's acknowledgment of risk for exposure through heterosexual sex for African women yet silence on the risk this mode of transmission poses for African American women denotes imprecision in the science upon which Nia must rely to process her diagnosis. Nia's rebuffing of a positive diagnosis sounds, as well, in her distrust of the science, as embodied by the nurse and how the nurse, as a representative of the health care system, makes Nia, as a representative black woman, feel upon seeking medical treatment. Nia's declaration, "Ya'll try to make us feel like we're dirty and stupid," recalls former senior research associate at the Joint Center for Political and Economic Studies Wilhelmina Leigh's early observations about barriers to quality health care for black women: "Access to healthcare includes both access to health insurance coverage and access to providers and facilities that render services. Adequate access to providers and facilities," she continues, means the availability of health care providers "capable of giving sensitive and competent care."[54] Nia's use of the collective, polarizing pronouns "ya'll" and "us" invokes the idea that the health care system frequently fails to affirm black women's importance as participants in the health care environment and to create a mutually respectful atmosphere for black women to enter and receive care. This commonly known, yet rarely reckoned with, awareness of black women's warranted distrust of health care systems also brings Nia's and Abigail's initially disparate reactions to their diagnoses into alliance.

Differences in Nia's and Abigail's cultural contexts are seemingly manifested in the sharp tonal contrast in their initial responses to their HIV-positive diagnoses: whereas Nia is confrontational and dismissive, Abigail literally cries in silence.

> NURSE: [Looks over at Abigail.] Ah Miss, Miss—[looks at chart] Miss Abigail, why are you crying? No, aiwa, you must think clearly. (332)

---

53. Hammonds, "AIDS."
54. Leigh, "Health of African American Women," 120.

Abigail's lack of verbal speech paradoxically resonates with Nia's belligerent retort where the nurse's disregard for Nia's brash exit from the scene overlaps with the downplaying of Abigail's grief-stricken demeanor. The nurse's frequent turn in attention away from delivering information that is pertinent to both Nia's and Abigail's health to insignificant matters, such as the orderly's clumsiness and bargaining with "Sisi Getty"[55] to purchase lunch, symbolically reinforces the lack of regard the health care system gives both women in these crucial moments of reckoning with HIV-positive diagnoses. The theme of systemic disregard for black women's health that resounds throughout "Three: The Diagnosis" extends, as well, to the directives the nurse hastily and distractedly gives Abigail at the close of the scene, while literally searching for money in her bra to pay for her lunch:

> NURSE: I see you have a son? Bring him in we can test him also. [Finds no money in bra.] Ahh, sorry Sisi I forgot my money—Oh . . . Thank you Sisi you are a life saver—surely, every time! [Looks after Sisi Getty smiling, returns to Abigail, smile fades.] Right, so, we must see your husband in the next few days—he must be formally informed and tested. (332)

Dashes inserted throughout the remainder of the nurse's instructions to Abigail redouble Abigail's silencing by revealing the nurse cutting off Abigail's only apparent attempts at speech and insisting that Abigail's husband must come to the clinic for testing: "Miss Abigail—there are no exceptions for that—I know it can be dangerous to tell him, many women are scared he will beat them and take the children—what what, even though usually it's coming from him, but, sorry you tested first. So—you must tell him and bring him for testing. Even, with the risky business of it" (333). The nurse's acknowledgment of the "risky business" of Abigail disclosing her positive status to her husband but simultaneous demand that she reveal it nonetheless, suggests gross contradictions in the science informing, and purportedly supporting, Abigail's health context. Analogous to the social mores, which, Crenshaw reminds us, frequently result in underreporting of black women as victims of domestic violence perpetrated by black men, the nurse's counsel to Abigail ultimately downplays the threat of domestic violence to which Abigail is now vulnerable because of her HIV-positive status. Science, as embodied by the nurse, prioritizes Abigail's husband's knowledge of his status over Abigail's safety in a manner that, again, recalls the early years of the epidemic, when domestic

---

55. The nurse speaks to Sisi Getty as if she is present. From the nurse's directives, we infer that Sisi Getty works at the clinic, either as an aid or in another capacity ranked lower than the nurse.

violence as a concurrent risk was an underresearched health issue for black women living with HIV/AIDS.[56] Scene "Three: The Diagnosis," closes on yet another discordant sound reverberating from the presumptive source of medical knowledge and health care, as the nurse crudely implies that Abigail and Nia brought the virus upon themselves—"You women. You go and get this HIV then you want to have a baby"—and dismisses Abigail's request for medication to prevent perinatal HIV transmission: "We don't have them here, if you have any money you can try to find them, they are very, very, expensive. Otherwise, change your diet—eat greens, negrains, nemeat. And don't breastfeed" (333). In their recent examination of the interrelated impact of health care services, information sources, and perceptions of HIV/AIDS on pregnant women, social workers Patricia King and David Pate found that for pregnant black women, barriers to initiating prenatal care stemmed as much from their experience with "delays in access to prenatal care appointments and disrespect from providers" as from unavailable or inadequate health insurance.[57] These findings are foreshadowed by scene "Three: The Diagnosis," both when Nia walks out of the emergency room and when the nurse rebuffs Abigail's request for perinatal transmission prevention medication.

Nia's and Abigail's departures from medical clinics in the United States and Africa with none of the information and tools needed to foster their safety, health, and well-being as newly diagnosed HIV-positive black women recalls accounts of events leading Dazón Dixon Diallo to establish SisterLove, an organization that has provided HIV and reproductive justice health services and care, primarily for black women in the United States and Africa, for over thirty years. As Dixon Diallo explains, when SisterLove launched in 1989, "there was nothing. There were no services, not even within the current HIV/AIDS organizations was there education, information, or service-delivery for women who were being impacted by AIDS, but more importantly [. . .], in the reproductive rights movement at that time, in that field, HIV/AIDS, especially for women, didn't having any traction, didn't reach priority."[58] She continues:

> By 1992, when [SisterLove] incorporated, we had heard lots of women's stories of pain, fear, rejection, and immobilization. And it became clear that HIV needed to be articulated and addressed in the context of women's lives. We had been dealing with women's lives in the context of HIV, and it was

---

56. Dazón Dixon Diallo, founder of SisterLove, has argued that the history of violence and domestic violence in the context of HIV/AIDS remains "untold" for black women. See Diallo, "Dr. Dazon Dixon Diallo."

57. King and Pate, "Perinatal HIV Testing."

58. Diallo, "Dr. Dazon Dixon Diallo."

84 • CHAPTER 3

a flawed strategy. Holistically speaking, we were indirectly responding to a myriad of issues—substance abuse, violence, poverty, misogyny, internalized oppression, family neglect/abandonment [. . .]. We knew that HIV was the connecting point for a lot of these experiences, but getting folks [. . .] to see the direct connection was difficult.[59]

Several scenes following "Three: The Diagnosis" introduce characters with varying degrees of relation to Nia and Abigail, whose monologues chronicle details of Nia's and Abigail's domestic and cultural backstories, or what Dixon Diallo refers to as the "context" of Nia's and Abigail's lives. In "Seven: Mama," for example, we learn that Nia is one of several children that Nia's mother has had and that Nia's newest sibling is but six months old. In "Nine: Keysha (Short for Keyshawn)," we meet Nia's transsexual cousin, who recalls introducing Nia and Darnell to one another as children, before encouraging Nia to take advantage of the financial benefits that having Darnell's child will afford her, given Darnell's NBA prospects. The same scene introduces us to the witch doctor Abigail visits with the misbegotten hopes of attaining a "cure" for HIV. "Ten: Sex Worker" shows Abigail seeking advice from a high school friend-turned-sex-worker about how to cajole Stamford into staying married to her, and "Eleven: Gail" reveals Darnell's mother responding to Nia's revelation that she is HIV-positive. Interspersed throughout this supporting cast of characters' monologues are raw commentaries on sexual practices, sexuality, and sexual health, which draw Nia and Abigail into implied dialogues with members of their familial, social, and cultural networks as the reality of their pregnancies and HIV-positive statuses sets in.

"Cognitive Reappraisal" and "Transformative Projects"

Through these exchanges, we learn that Nia's mother has known for some time that Nia is sexually active: "Don't think I didn't usta hear your little narrow behind climbin' out the window to go oochie coochie with that boy," she tells Nia. "Like you the first one discovered how to sneak out the house? I invented that shit." We also come to understand that Nia's mother clearly knows about, but theretofore never briefed Nia on, the range of risks associated with having unprotected sex: "What would you rather I say, Ms. Nia? Look at me, Strap on the jimmy? Pull the balloon over the sausage? I wish somebody had told me about this shit, half-a ya'll wouldn't be here. And now days, you can catch all

---

59. Diallo, "Reflections," 125.

kinda stuff. Stuff you can't get rid of cuz it gets in your blood. Trust me: three minutes of slappin' bellies ain't worth death. And that's what it is, death" (340). The insight Nia's mother offers into the "stuff" besides pregnancy women have to think about when having unprotected sex breaks through silence, while also illustrating how the persistence of intergenerational silence around safe sexual practices stifles the kind of openness between Nia and her mother that could have built Nia's knowledge about sexual practices and risk from early childhood. The efficacy of this knowledge, which points to social conditions that can increase or lessen risk for black women, is underscored by the results of a recent study of sexual risk behavior in a group of black women representing four generational cohorts conducted by professor of nursing Gayle Robinson. This study found that intergenerational dialogue consistently provides a "safe space for reflection, listening, and exchange of ideas" across generations of black women, because in this space, communication is "multidimensional and interpersonal [. . .]. The openness and willingness to have conversations among the women," explains Robinson, "reflect[s] a considerable degree of trust between the individuals participating in the dialogue."[60] The important role that open dialogue plays in countering the adverse effects of silence and risky sexual behavior on black women's health is a theme that also extends to exchanges that direct Nia to consider the possibility that her HIV-positive status derives from indiscriminate unprotected sex acts in which Darnell engaged outside of his relationship with Nia.

Keysha/Keshawn hints at this possibility in scene "Nine: Keysha (Short for Keyshawn)" when joking about regretting having "given" Darnell to Nia: "He was right on the line, he coulda went either way, either way" (342). The juxtaposition of stark discourse about same-sex desire with the suggestion that Darnell could be a man who has sex with men and women is stripped of stigmatizing judgment, as Keysha/Keshawn's counsel ultimately leans into encouraging Nia to think rationally about the range of STDs/STIs to which having unprotected sex could expose her. "You remember my roommate Monica?" Keysha/Keyshawn asks. "She had Chlamydia. Girl, yes! Walkin' around with it, thought it was a damn yeast infection. By the time she asked me to help her to the clinic, she couldn't even walk. And when she got there they said she had waited so long it turned into P-I-D—Pussy in Distress" (345). Keysha/Keshawn's comedic engagement of the clinical facts of sexually transmitted infections and diseases recalls, by sharply contrasting, the nurse's emotionless delivery of Nia's HIV test results in scene "Three: The Diagnosis." However, far from trivializing the issue, comedy works in scene "Nine: Keysha (Short

---

60. Robinson, "Qualitative Study."

for Keyshawn)" to ease Nia's distress, which is apparent to her cousin, and to build Nia's capacity to confront the difficult reality that her relationship with Darnell may not be monogamous: "If you're givin' it up," Keysha/Keshawn states frankly, "then you best believe he givin' it up too" (345).

Keysha/Keshawn's explicit and repeated calls to sexual intercourse as a mode of HIV transmission—regardless of how sexual partners identify by gender—are met with a response that adds yet another layer of complexity to Salter and Gurira's knowledge-building about black women's health in the age of hip hop and HIV/AIDS, as we learn at the start of scene "Eleven: Gail" that Darnell's mother is fully aware of her son's HIV-positive status. "Damn it, Darnell!" she exclaims, apparently annoyed by the revelation that Nia has the virus and by Darnell's failure to follow basic precaution and protection techniques for people living with HIV/AIDS. "I said to take your medication and use a condom. Use a condom." Subsequent repeated descriptions of Darnell as "just a boy" and "a baby," and characterization of his medical condition as a "private family matter" support the inference that Darnell's exposure to the virus was perinatal, not sexual. This seeming anomaly gains credence as Gail justifies not revealing Darnell's status—"Do you think that he would be recruited if anybody knew? Do you think he would be getting a scholarship?"—and, upon shifting pronouns, reflects, with ostensibly personal insight, on the socially isolating effects of disclosing an HIV-positive diagnosis: "You consider what people will think about you if they knew. You think they gon' treat you the same? When you mention it, even the people you thought loved you will have you eatin' outta paper plates" (349). Scene "Eleven: Gail" connects Darnell's mother's health history to Nia's and Abigail's, as HIV-positive black mothers, by recalling interrelated concerns over social perception of HIV, access to quality care, and perinatal HIV transmission prevention raised in scenes "Three: The Diagnosis" and "Ten: Sex Worker." Whereas the nurse dismissively tells Abigail that the clinic cannot provide her with antiretroviral therapy medication to prevent (or lessen the risk of) perinatal transmission, the sex worker stresses the need for Abigail to "get the doughs" and "buy the drugs" (347). She tells Abigail that she must "decide what's more important to [her]" and, in this, analogizes silence to a death sentence for Abigail and her unborn child and breaking silence as a means to life for both of them: "Remain Miss Priss Abigail, or become a survivor," the sex worker remarks starkly. "You can keep quiet about it, act as if nothing is wrong and die horribly—watching your kid die, too, all because you wanted to remain the perfect little Shona, Zimbabwean wifey. Which many have done. Or you can take care of yourself and your children" (348). Repetitions with slight revisions of speech that acknowledges the social and cultural constraints of living with HIV and stresses adherence to a cascade of care that includes condom use and pre- and postnatal antiretroviral drug therapy in scenes "Ten: Sex Worker" and "Eleven: Gail" presciently raise broader questions of black maternal health, which, in more recent years, have been focal points of mainstream scientific inquiry, including disproportionate rates of black infant mortality, black maternal morbidity and mortality, and black mother-to-child transmission of HIV.[61] One recent study notes that black HIV-positive mothers remain five times more likely to give birth to an HIV-positive infant than white HIV-positive mothers, despite the number of infants born with perinatally acquired HIV infection decreasing every year since the early 1990s.[62] The same study found that inadequate-to-no prenatal care and prenatal HIV testing among at-risk mothers are the root causes of this phenomenon and concluded that opportunities to intervene and address these causes continue to be missed.[63] Interchanges among Gail's, Nia's, and Abigail's health contexts layer and complicate this science by demonstrating how stigma impacts both pre- and postnatal health care decision-making for HIV-positive black mothers, while simultaneously reinforcing the importance of seeking and adhering to care regiments.[64]

Akin to the "therapeutic collective conversations" that undergird the "self-help" model SisterLove uses to empower black women to lay claim to their bodies,[65] Nia's and Abigail's interactions with and symbolic responses to supporting characters' monologues in scenes that follow "Three: The Diagnosis" evidence Nia's and Abigail's mental and emotional processing of their HIV-positive statuses, despite Nia and Abigail speaking very few words throughout these scenes. Nia's and Abigail's progression in and through silence narratively sets in motion the clinical correlates of what professor of public policy and sociology Celeste Watkins-Hayes, in *Remaking a Life: How Women Living with HIV/AIDS Confront Inequality,* calls "cognitive reappraisal," or "*internal* mindset shift[s]" precipitated by "*external* pivotal or set of interactions." She explains:

---

61. See, for example, Howell, "Reducing Disparities"; and Wallace et al., "Separate and Unequal."

62. Nesheim et al., "Epidemiology of Perinatal HIV." The authors concede that challenges associated with eradicating perinatal HIV transmission in the United States also stem from the fact that "the number of women with HIV delivering infants in the United States has not been accurately known since completion of the CDC's Survey of Childbearing Women in 1995" (613). Since that time, the numbers have been estimates based on data from states that routinely report rates of perinatal exposure.

63. Nesheim et al., "Epidemiology of Perinatal HIV."

64. Arora and Wilkinson, "Eliminating Perinatal Transmission."

65. Royles, *To Make the Wounded Whole,* 198–99.

88 • CHAPTER 3

Turning points, external events that affect women [living with HIV/ADS] significantly, call into question the efficacy of their preexisting strategies for economic, emotional, and physical survival. Turning points stop the negative momentum, break up routines, and inspire deep reflection. In other words, the cognitive shifts that are critical for women's transformative projects take place through their interpretation of turning-point events and their assessment that they must fundamentally shift how they are conceptualizing, strategizing around, and tactically addressing their struggles.[66]

Scenes "Thirteen: The Prayer—Bills, Bills, Bills" and "Fourteen: Abigail's Prayer" set transformative possibilities in motion for Nia and Abigail, first, by recalling Nia's and Abigail's talents and accomplishments as established in scene "One: The Beginning." "It smell like booty / I wish I could fly away / Dirty ass motel," the haiku that opens "Thirteen: The Prayer—Bills, Bills, Bills," reminds us that Nia is a prize-winning poet, while Abigail's entry onto scene "Fourteen: Abigail's Prayer," reading the certificate she received in high school upon winning "the National Interschools Public Speaking Championship, 1994, Harare, Zimbabwe," recasts her rising career in broadcast journalism as fate. Stylized mis-en-scène subsequently dramatizes the onset of Nia's and Abigail's "turning points," as we witness Nia repeatedly ball up, discard, pick up, and untangle the $5,000 "hush money" check Darnell's mother gives her, and Abigail recite her award-winning speech, an adaptation of Maya Angelou's "And Still I Rise," which pays homage to the legacies of Mbuya Nehanda, Winnie Mandela, and other African women "freedom fighters." These moments interlock and coalesce around Nia and Abigail breaking (through) silence, by simultaneously calling out Darnell and Samford for knowingly exposing them to HIV:

NIA: Because he knew. He knew. He knew the whole time. (351)

ABIGAIL: He knew, he knew, that bastard. (353)

Unguarded, open, and tinged with varying degrees of anger and frustration, these moments read like indictments of Darnell's and Samford's actions that are overlaid with confessional elements, which reveal Nia and Abigail gradually coming to grips with the responsibility they must take for their personal health:

---

66. Watkins-Hayes, *Remaking a Life,* 144.

NIA: I sold myself for $5000. Nope, baby, that's how much I cost. That's how much you cost. (351)

ABIGAIL: But I knew it, I knew it all along, with the late nights and the way he was smelling. (353)

The moments crescendo into soliloquies through which Nia and Abigail interchangeably ask God/Baba to protect their lives and the lives of their unborn children and doggedly express their determination not to let Darnell and Samford off the hook for their irresponsible sexual choices and risk behaviors, which compromised their intimate partners' healths:

NIA: I'm gonna make Darnell look me in the face and tell me I'm only worth $5000. Then, I'm going to stand there in front of all those recruiters, in front of the whole world and I'ma just say it. And then all the girls he been with's gon' know. And all the girls he was thinking about doin's gon' know. And then everybody will know. [Balling the check up and throwing it down again.] I'm worth more than this money. (353)

ABIGAIL: Okay, okay, I will tell them. But this is what I ask: Don't you let them blame me. You make them stand by me. And support me. And you make Samford stay put. You make him still love me and take care of me. Because he's still mine and I am not giving up everything I worked for. And I want my baby, so don't you let it have this illness. (354)

From these prostrate positions, Nia and Abigail simultaneously rise in scene "Fifteen: The End," and, in a moment that recalls both the rhythms of black girlhood play that opens *In the Continuum* and the synergy of Salter and Gurira's collaborative creative process, the characters "face each other in a mirror, but remain in opposite worlds" (356). In this frame, Nia and Abigail directly call-and-respond to one another, laying claims to self and body, while apostrophically demanding respect from their intimate partners:

ABIGAIL: And you must look at me and see me, Abigail Moyo Murambe.
NIA: *There's no amount you can pay me to take this away.*
ABIGAIL: You must treat me like a wife you respect—
NIA: *Naw, I don't want yo' apology!*
ABIGAIL: Because I know who I am!
NIA: *I'm changing the course of history!*

90 • CHAPTER 3

> ABIGAIL: And I am moving [gestures] forward, forward, forward—not this
> way or that. Okay! (356)

The exchange purportedly readies Nia and Abigail to move from reflecting to acting upon their situations as pregnant, HIV-positive black women. That Nia and Abigail "remain in opposite worlds," even as they call-and-respond to one another, in symbolic furtherance of each other's transformative projects, proves essential to *In the Continuum* closing with neither Nia nor Abigail following through on her commitment to disclose her HIV-positive status and confront her intimate partner. This closing points to another important theme of black women's lived experiences with silence, shame, and stigma, which flows paradoxically from the cultural and social expectation that they be strong, even when exhibiting strength will literally kill them. Folklorist and literary scholar Trudier Harris classically invited consideration of whether "this thing called strength, this thing we applaud so much in black women," might not also be "a disease,"[67] and the ending of *In the Continuum* reflects the apparent care Salter and Gurira take to avoid the trappings of the strong-blackwoman motif, by neither romanticizing nor evading the difficulties of breaking (through) silence for Nia and Abigail. The play's pursuit of knowledge and truth-telling about black women's health in the age of hip hop and HIV/AIDS does not, however, foreclose the possibility of breakthrough for Nia and Abigail. As the stage fades into blackout, Nia and Abigail "laugh in synchronicity," a sound that reinforces the unresolved discord between what they want to do and what they are expected to do, as fictional embodiments of black women living with HIV/AIDS in the United States and Africa at the turn of the twenty-first century.

This chapter has demonstrated how Nikkole Salter and Danai Gurira took on the global threat of HIV/AIDS by using the techniques of call-and-response to dramatize the impact of the epidemic on black women in the United States and Africa. As an anonymous reporter for the *New York Amsterdam News* astutely noted while *In the Continuum* was running Off-Broadway, instead of "sitting back and watching [the] epidemic unfold," Salter and Gurira "decided to take action by giving voice to the stories of Black women" living with HIV/AIDS.[68] Invoking the rhythms of movement and speech and engaging dialectically with the effects of silence, shame, and stigma on the health contexts of black HIV-positive mothers, Salter and Gurira tackled aspects of black women's struggles with HIV/AIDS that mainstream science had yet to

---

67. Harris, "This Disease Called Strength."
68. "Ms. Foundation," 37.

consider with any degree of salience or consistency at the start of the twenty-first century. By giving voice to the realities and complexities of black women's lived experiences with HIV/AIDS in both the United States and Africa, Salter and Gurira encouraged audiences to see the consequences of the neglect of black women's health in the age of hip hop and HIV/AIDS. As well, they directed audiences to understand the importance of calling out this neglect by taking actions needed to change the conditions that put black women at disproportionate risk of dying from complications related to HIV/AIDS. The next chapter considers Mara Brock Akil's issuance of a similar call to action through her work as television creator, writer, and producer.

CHAPTER 4

"Prioritized"

The Hip Hop (Re)Construction of Black Womanhood in *Girlfriends* and *The Game*

I'm doing a show about women—African-American women [. . .] and I feel that a lot of times our issues don't get national attention. Prioritized.

> —Mara Brock Akil, quoted in Chael Needle, "Girlfriends for Life"

I've been having a conversation with black women.

> —Mara Brock Akil, quoted in Sonaiya Kelley, "OWN's 'Love Is . . .'"

Accountability for sex is not just about who or who else a person may have slept with. It is also about the frequency, sincerity, variety, competence, and safety of sex. In addition to intimate partners, we are also, secondarily, accountable to our families and friends for sex.

> —Anita L. Allen, *Why Privacy Isn't Everything*, 141

When asked why four episodes of the third season of *Girlfriends* (2000–2008), the situation comedy Mara Brock Akil created and coproduced for United Paramount Network (UPN)[1] in 2000, addressed the HIV/AIDS crisis among black women in America, Brock Akil responded that she had things she wanted to say "about bridging television's gap between entertainment and education. I'm doing a show about women—African-American women," she explained, "and I feel that a lot of times our issues don't get national attention. Prioritized."[2] Over their eight- and three-season runs on UPN and the CW, respectively, *Girlfriends* and *The Game* (2006–9), the *Girlfriends*' spin-off that

---

1. Launched in 1995, UPN was acquired by CBS Corporation in 2006. *Girlfriends* and *The Game* moved from UPN to the CW the same year.

2. Needle, "Girlfriends for Life."

Brock Akil created and coproduced in 2006,[3] enjoyed solid reception among black audiences, especially black adults and women aged eighteen to thirty-four. According to Nielsen, both were consistently among the top ten African American TV rankings during their series runs, with *Girlfriends* averaging 4 million viewers and *The Game* averaging 2.3 million viewers.[4] The prioritization of black women's health issues in *Girlfriends* and *The Game* and the popularity of these programs with black viewing audiences invite inquiry into Brock Akil's creative vision and market capital. If it is true, as Brittney Cooper reminds us, that the "culture of dissemblance and the politics of respectability" were rhetorical and political strategies that black women had to navigate at the turn of the twentieth century so as to "minimize the threat of sexual assault and other forms of bodily harm routinely inflicted upon Black women,"[5] then Brock Akil complicated this politic at the turn of the twenty-first century by bringing black women's bodies into mainstream visibility.

Well before *Basketball Wives* and *The Real Housewives of Atlanta* provided scripted frameworks for black women to imagine and see themselves as financially independent, sexually autonomous subjects, Brock Akil used her artistry to call black women into dialogues about black female sexuality and agency that were not taking place anywhere on mainstream television with any degree of complexity or consistency.[6] She disrupted and created spaces for black women to explore who they are and what they want.[7] While reflecting on why she produced the drama *Love Is . . .* close to twenty years after the premiers of *Girlfriends* and *The Game,* Brock Akil pointed to the virtual nonexistence

---

3. *The Game* was twice reincarnated, running on Black Entertainment Television (BET) from 2011 to 2015, and on Paramount+ from May 2021 to June 2023.

4. Season 4 (2003–4) and season 5 (2004–5) of *Girlfriends* were UPN's highest-rated comedy series. With season 5, *Girlfriends* also became UPN's longest-running series on the air. See, generally, Nielsen Ratings Report, April 20–26, 2009. Internet links to these data are no longer available.

5. Cooper, *Beyond Respectability,* 3.

6. The closest black viewing audiences came to encountering sustained discourse around questions of black sexuality and HIV/AIDS during the same historical period as the series runs of *Girlfriends* and *The Game* was *Noah's Arc* (October 2005–October 2006), the comedy-drama television series that aired for two seasons on Logo TV. Like *Girlfriends* and *The Game,* *Noah's Arc* had an ensemble cast, but one made up of men. The series dealt with many of the same issues as *Girlfriends* and *The Game,* including same-sex dating, infidelity, indiscriminate unprotected sexual intercourse, homophobia, and antigay violence. *Noah's Arc* did not, however, have as large a viewing audience as either of Brock Akil's series.

7. Kelley, "OWN's 'Love Is . . . .'" *Love Is . . .* ran for one season before being canceled after Salim Akil, Brock Akil's husband, was accused of domestic violence directed toward a woman with whom he was allegedly having an extramarital affair. Akil was also accused of copyright infringement in using his alleged lover's screenplay as a basis for the series. See Giorgis, "Missed Opportunity."

of black women as protagonists in television series that centered the lives of modern women and said that the "conversation with black women" that *Love Is . . .* sought to draw black women into commenced with the creation of *Girlfriends* and *The Game*.[8] This chapter looks to the emergence of these series at the dawn of the twenty-first century as evidence of Brock Akil's determination to use the lived experiences of black women to effect creative intervention into what M. K. Asante Jr. describes as shifts in public discourse about historical, political, and social forces that mainstream hip hop "either failed or refused to prioritize" throughout the first decade of the twenty-first century.[9] During this period, HIV/AIDS became the leading cause of death among black women aged twenty-five to thirty-four and new rates of HIV/AIDS infection were second highest among black women (behind only gay black men). This same historical period gave way to the virtual disappearance of female MCs in mainstream hip hop, while the representation of black women's bodies, black female sexuality, and black womanhood as mere spectacles accelerated hip hop's global expansion and influence.[10]

To be certain, the decade preceding *Girlfriends'* 2000 debut produced several classic hip hop recordings by female MCs, including Salt-N-Pepa's *Very Necessary* (1993), Da Brat's *Funkdafied* (1994), Lil' Kim's *Hard Core* (1996), Foxxy Brown's *Ill Na Na* (1996), Missy Elliott's *Supa Dupa Fly* (1997), Lauryn Hill's *The Miseducation of Lauryn Hill* (1998), and Eve's *Let There Be Eve . . . Ruff Ryder's First Lady* (1999), all of which were certified platinum or multiplatinum. But as veteran MCs Trina, Missy Elliott, Yo-Yo, Rah Digga, MC Lyte, and Eve make clear in Ava Duvernay's critically acclaimed documentary *My Mic Sounds Nice: A Truth about Women in Hip Hop* (2010), at about the same time that female MCs were demonstrating their appeal, influence, and staying power with the masses, profit motives caused many industry producers to cut female hip hop artists, viewing them as too "high maintenance" in comparison with their male counterparts. In addition, the 2000s marked a shift in the production goals of the music industry: pushing units, rather than grooming artists and making quality music, became sacrosanct. As demonstrated in the list

---

8. Kelley, "OWN's 'Love Is . . . .'" Brock Akil also cites the drama *Being Mary Jane* (2014–19) as part of her "conversation" with black women.

9. Asante, *It's Bigger Than Hip Hop*, 7.

10. The latter part of the 2000s yielded a number of attempts by BET to foster dialogue about the representation of black women in hip hop music. See, especially, "Hip Hop v. America (The World)," a three-part "townhall meeting" that aired September 25 and 26, 2007. "Hip Hop vs. America." These efforts were largely criticized for not including black women critics and artists as panelists.

96 • CHAPTER 4

below, between 2000 and 2009, only one female MC—Missy Elliott—made
Billboard's list of R&B / Hip Hop Singles and Albums Chart-Toppers.

2000[11]

"Hot Boyz," Missy Elliott
Dr. Dre 2001, Dr. Dre
The Marshall Mathers LP, Eminem
And Then There Was X, DMX
Vol 3: Life & Times of S. Carter, Jay-Z

2001

*Tp-2.com, R. Kelly
"Fiesta," R. Kelly feat. Jay-Z
*Songs in A Minor, Alicia Keys

2002

The Eminem Show, Eminem
Word of Mouf, Ludacris
Nellyville, Nelly
Stillmatic, Nas
*Ashanti, Ashanti
"Hot in Herre," Nelly

2003

Get Rich or Die Tryin', 50 Cent
*Chocolate Factory, R. Kelley
Better Days, 2Pac
Kings of Crunk, Lil Jon & Eastside Boyz
*I Care 4 U, Aaliyah
"In Da Club," 50 Cent
"Ignition," R. Kelly
"Get Low," Lil' Jon

2004

*Confessions, Usher
*Diary of Alicia Keys, Alicia Keys
The Black Album, Jay-Z
College Dropout, Kanye West

---

11. Asterisks denote artists/albums/songs classified as R&B. Billboard, "Year-End Charts."

Speakerboxxxx: The Love Below, OutKast
"Tipsy," J-Kwon

2005
The Massacre, 50 Cent
**The Emancipation of Mimi,* Mariah Carey
**Destiny Fulfilled,* Destiny's Child
Encore, Eminem
The Documentary, The Game
"Lovers & Friends," Lil Jon feat. Usher & Ludacris
"Drop It Like It's Hot," Snoop Dogg

2006
**The Breakthrough,* Mary J. Blige
**Unpredictable,* Jamie Foxx
King, TI
**In My Own Words,* Ne-Yo
**Chris Brown,* Chris Brown
"Be Without You," Mary J. Blige
"It's Going Down," Yung Joc

2007
Kingdom Come, Jay
Konvicted, Akon
Graduation, Kanye West
The Inspiration, Young Jeezy
**The Evolution of Robin Thicke,* Robin Thicke
"Buy You a Drank (Shawty Snappin')," T-Pain feat. Yung Joc

2008
**As I Am,* Alicia Keys
Tha Carter III, Lil Wayne
Growing Pains, Mary J. Blige
**Just Like You,* Keyshia Cole
Paper Trail, TI
"Lollipop," Lil Wayne
"Low," Flo-Rida

2009
**I Am . . . Sasha F.,* Beyonce

98 • CHAPTER 4

Intuition, Jamie Foxx
A Different Me, Keyshia Cole
The Blueprint III, Jay-Z
808s & Heartbreak, Kanye West
"Blame It," Jamie Foxx
"Best I Ever Had," Drake
"Boom Boom Pow," Black Eye Peas

The disappearance of female MCs from mainstream scenes throughout the 2000s was counterbalanced by their sustained underground presence, a site where black women have historically deployed what anthropologist Marcyliena Morgan calls the "arsenal of symbols and information" that shape black women's experiences, from "the history of racism in the United States" to the "implications of social class in terms of services, rights, health, policing, education," and "knowledge about sexism and feminism."[12] As Gwendolyn Pough, Whitney Peoples, and a host of other hip hop feminists remind us, hip hop is "a cultural phenomenon that encompasses a variety of genres"; its "heterogeneity, widespread popularity, and sociocultural and economic currency," says Peoples, are the factors that have enabled black women to leave indelible imprints on hip hop as expressed in media, literature, film, dance, and art.[13] It is also fair to say that throughout the 2000s the diminishing presence of black women in mainstream hip hop music specifically is attributable, in part, to the movement of some of the most notable female hip hop artists—Missy Elliott, Eve, MC Lyte, Queen Latifah—to other high-profile, and profitable, locations within the entertainment industry. Indeed, it is precisely the movement of these women to other sites of influence within the industry that brings Brock Akil's disruptive channeling of hip hop feminism into focus. Brock Akil is among a sizeable body of black media producers—Nelson George, Larry Williams, Eunetta Boone, Keyna Barris, Saladin K. Patterson, Patrik-Ian Polk, Yvette Lee Bowser, Kriss Turner, Jay-Z, Sean Combs, Will Smith, Jada Pinkett

---

12. Morgan, *Real Hiphop,* 133–34.

13. Peoples, "'Under Construction.'" Fatima Robinson, who directed and choreographed high-profile music videos throughout the 2000s, also choreographed dance routines for the cult classic *Save the Last Dance* (2001), the critical and commercial hit musical film *Dreamgirls* (2006), and the 2007 and 2009 Oscar performances for Best Original Song. Kara Walker and Mickalene Thomas both had major exhibition tours in the 2000s. In 2007, Walker's widely praised silhouettes exhibit *Kara Walker: My Complement, My Enemy, My Oppressor, My Love* was featured at the ARC/Musee d'Art Moderne de la Ville de Paris, the Whitney Museum of American Art in New York, and the Hammer Museum in Los Angeles. In 2009, Thomas's installation *She's Come Undone* was featured at the Lehmann Maupin Gallery in New York.

Smith, Queen Latifah, Jamie Foxx, Lee Daniels, Tyler Perry, Shonda Rhimes, Issa Rae, Antoine Fuqua—who strategically use popular and hip hop culture to foster public discourse and critical thought about a number of pressing issues confronting black people. That Brock Akil mediated her inquiry through themes, tensions, and imagery that addressed the HIV/AIDS crisis among black women summoned for critique other neglected issues in black women's health, including sexual and domestic violence, mental illness, abandonment, homophobia, and substance use disorder. This chapter thus premises that Brock Akil's (re)construction of black women's stories in *Girlfriends* and *The Game* advanced—or attempted to advance—conversations about the representation of black womanhood in mainstream hip hop by breaking silences around HIV/AIDS and related health challenges that characterized black women's lived experiences at the start of the new millennium.

"Safe" Sex and Sisterly Redemption

Over their series runs on UPN and CW, *Girlfriends* and *The Game* centered the lives of four black women residing in Los Angeles, California, and one white and two black women residing in San Diego, California. These women's experiences in their professional careers, with family members, with one another, and with men catalyze the comedy and drama that drive plot developments. These developments form an array of images, issues, and themes that underscore widespread understandings of HIV/AIDS as a biomedical phenomenon in light of modes of HIV transmission: the only way a person can become infected with the human immunodeficiency virus (HIV) that causes acquired immune deficiency syndrome (AIDS) is through exchange of body fluids—semen, blood, vaginal secretions, and breast milk—with an HIV-infected person. Exchange is mediated via vaginal, anal, and oral sexual intercourse; sharing contaminated needles; breastfeeding; and blood transfusion. Both *Girlfriends* and *The Game* move beyond these clinical basics to address the complex array of social, sexual, and moral codes that construct HIV/AIDS as a cultural phenomenon. Recurring locations and character-driven humor provide for repetition and reinforcement of personal attitudes, social dynamics, and structural conditions that account for the prevalence, scope, and impact of HIV/AIDS among black women specifically.

Current trends in HIV incidence and diagnosis data indicate that black women account for nearly 60 percent of new HIV infections among women in the United States despite comprising less than 15 percent of the total US

100 · CHAPTER 4

population.[14] These alarming rates are accompanied by a laundry list of HIV/AIDS prevention challenges, which, throughout this project, I have argued black women continue to face, including high rates of exposure to STDs and STIs, concurrent partnerships, the perceived stigmatizing effects of receiving a positive status, social norms that stigmatize same-sex preference, and limited access to prevention education and quality health care.[15] The perils of economic dependency and the importance of self-reliance and economic self-sufficiency were overarching themes in both *Girlfriends* and *The Game*, but like Abigail in *In the Continuum*, none of the female leads in these series lives in abject poverty. Consistent with her vision of creating primetime television that would "accurately portray the urbane women of color she was familiar with,"[16] Brock Akil casted ensembles with access to resources and information about HIV/AIDS and, thus, set up repeated debunking of the myth that only poor black women are vulnerable to HIV/AIDS infection.[17] Storylines in *Girlfriends* and *The Game* worked in tandem with casting to compel understandings of what scientists call "the ecological pathways to disproportionate infection"[18] among black women by balancing consideration of characters' individual lifestyles and the effects of their lifestyle choices on the collective. The implications of this narrative structuring for sustaining discursive thinking about HIV/AIDS cannot be missed because sex and its consequences were indispensable conflict-creating agents in both series.

Of course, as Marlon Bailey reminds us,[19] not every reference to sex is relevant to HIV/AIDS; nor does every relevant reference fall under the index of deliberate HIV/AID discourse. To establish a measure of each series' HIV/AIDS discursive framework and a means for comparative analysis, therefore, I conducted an experiment. On average, a season is composed of twenty-six episodes, or roughly eight hours and forty minutes of viewing time. Seasons 1–8 of *Girlfriends* and seasons 1–3 of *The Game* are currently available on Netflix. To facilitate random selection and to secure representative samples, I viewed every third episode of the first three seasons of each series. Drawing on basic measures of website effectiveness and reach, I used "hits" to calculate the frequency with which each episode addressed HIV/AIDS directly

---

14. Ojikutu and Mayer, "HIV Prevention among Black Women."

15. Alonzo and Reynolds, "Stigma, HIV and AIDS"; and Brief et al., "Understanding the Interface."

16. Siegel, "*Girlfriends'* 100th Episode."

17. Quinn Gentry takes this persistent myth to task in her searching ethnography, *Black Women's Risk for HIV: Rough Living.*

18. Lane et al., "Structural Violence and Racial Disparity."

19. Bailey, "Whose Body Is It?"

and indirectly. Direct indicators included explicitly naming the virus and its modes of transmission (e.g., unprotected sex with an infected person). Indirect indicators included naming or alluding to risky and protective behaviors, attitudes, and conditions associated with modes of HIV transmission, as analyzed in chapters 2 and 3. These behaviors, attitudes, and conditions include having unprotected sex with multiple partners or without knowing a partner's status, having an STI or STD, trading sex for money, using drugs and alcohol (both recreationally and dependently) and judgment impairment caused by this use, believing that HIV/AIDS has a distinct look and impacts only certain populations, stigmatizing same-sex attraction or consensual same-sex sexual relationships, and normalizing same-sex desire and sexual activity.

Of the twenty-five randomly selected *Girlfriends* episodes, fourteen, or 56 percent, made at least one direct HIV/AIDS reference; six, or 24 percent, made two or more direct references. Of the twenty-one randomly selected episodes of *The Game,* four, or 19 percent, made at least one direct HIV/AIDS reference. Hits for indirect HIV/AIDS references in the twenty-five randomly selected episodes of *Girlfriends* averaged 10.5 per episode. Hits for indirect HIV/AIDS references in the twenty-one randomly selected episodes of *The Game* averaged 17.4. Indirect HIV/AIDS references in *The Game* steadily increased over time, with season 1 averaging eight per episode, season 2 averaging seventeen per episode, and season 3 averaging twenty-one per episode.

After calculating the number of references, I set about examining the structural frameworks that occasioned each reference. Patterns in story setup and conflict emerged immediately, creating story arcs within and across the two series that read like veritable reference guides to black women's health in the age of hip hop and HIV/AIDS. "Un-Treatable" from season 2 of *Girlfriends* and "The Iceman Cometh" from season 1 of *The Game* highlight the trappings of American materialism. The effects of distorted mass media images of black female sexuality and identity on the psychological and emotional stability of black women are painted with painstaking detail in "Hip-o-cracy" from season 1 of *Girlfriends* and "The Big Chill" from season 1 of *The Game.* The costly sacrifice of black women's silence in the face of cultural mores and taboos that promote homophobia and discourage honest dialogue between men and women about their respective sexual needs, desires, and preferences is candidly delineated in "They've Gotta Have It" from season 1 of *Girlfriends* and "Do the Wright Thing" from season 3 of *The Game.* Conflict resolution across these episodes coheres around similar themes of personal responsibility and sororal accountability. The repetition of these themes pushes the HIV/AIDS dialectic still further by underscoring what Anita L. Allen calls the public implications of private sex acts.

102 • CHAPTER 4

"Sex is private. But we are clearly accountable for sex. First," explains Allen, "we are accountable to our intimate partners for our sex lives."[20] She continues:

> Accountability for sex is not just about who or who else a person may have slept with. It is also about the frequency, sincerity, variety, competence, and safety of sex. In addition to intimate partners, we are also, secondarily, accountable to our families and friends for sex. This is obviously true for children and teenagers whom parents want to shelter from premature and unhealthy sex. But it can also be true of adults whose parents, extended families, or wider kinship groups assert a "say" over the choices they make about their sex lives.[21]

Girlfriends and *The Game* drive these axioms home through first-season story arcs that "make real and believable" what Brock Akil, referring specifically to Toni's (played by Jill Marie Jones) attempt to seduce Joan's (played Tracee Ellis Ross) boyfriend in *Girlfriends*' first-season cliffhanger, characterizes as the capacity of all human beings to allow selfish decision-making around sex acts to imperil the sanctity of their most cherished relationships.[22] Those familiar with the sequence of events that culminate with Joan returning from Jamaica and finding Toni and Sean (played by Dondré Whitfield) half-clad on her sofa recall that Toni's actions are motivated by a desire to retaliate against Joan for having inadvertently revealed to Greg (played by Chuma Gault), Toni's one and only true love, that Toni had not only been unfaithful but also that her partner in the infidelity—not Greg—infected her with chlamydia. The scene that closes season 1 of *Girlfriends* sets up at least two critical lines of narration in season 2 that reinforce the personal-collective sex accountability dyad about which Allen writes. First, Toni confronts the consequences of her infidelity to Greg when he reunites with her only to set her up to catch him in the act with an unidentified woman. The scene recalls both the emotional impact of the randomness of Toni's affair with Clay (played by Phil Morris) on Greg, as well as the physical risks to which the affair subjects both Toni and Greg as a result of Toni assuming that, because Clay is a doctor, he is a "safe" sex partner. Second, Toni confronts the consequences of her betrayal of Joan when Joan, determining to "learn to say no" and "save herself,"[23] terminates

---

20. Allen, *Why Privacy Isn't Everything,* 141.
21. Allen, *Why Privacy Isn't Everything,* 141.
22. Brock Akil, "We All Fall Down."
23. Season 2 episodes that address these developments in Joan's character are "Just Say No" and "Buh-Bye."

her friendship with Toni. Blocking in the breakup scene from the episode "Buh-Bye" works in tandem with dialogue to walk Toni and Joan through the series of manipulations, exploitations, and denigrations to which viewing audiences already know Toni has subjected Joan. Initially lying on the floor, Toni assumes a symbolic position of reckoning as she rises, looks Joan in the eye, and listens as Joan elaborates the pain that Toni's actions—first, in attempting to sleep with Sean, and second, in discussing Sean's battle with sex addiction with Joan's boss—cause Joan to feel. Importantly, Toni's shadowing of Joan's movement as Joan walks through every room in her house, collecting belongings and mementos of Toni and packing them in a box, invokes the proverbial sentiment that reconciliation between the two can occur only after Toni walks in Joan's shoes, and not only feels Joan's pain but also accepts responsibility for having caused that pain by a single, selfish sex act. It is no coincidence, therefore, that the scene from the episode "Trick or Truth" that completes the story arc by bringing closure to the conflict between Toni and Joan and providing for their friendship's renewal again finds Toni in a symbolically prostrate position. The dramatic effect of Toni's rising and accepting responsibility for her betrayal of Joan is heightened by their physical location in a church and the casting of Donny McClurkin's cover of the classic gospel song "We Fall Down" (1998) as the soundtrack for the face-to-face encounter:

TONI: Joan.
JOAN: Yes, Toni?
TONI: I am sorry I hurt you. I'm sorry I blamed you for Greg. For every-
thing. I did it. I made all the mistakes. I know that.

The volume of the gospel song's refrain "for a saint is just a sinner / who fell down / and got up" is neither lowered nor muted in this moment. Toni's apology is synchronized with the choir's singing, casting her as the symbolic wayward sister, who literally finds salvation in the forgiving arms of Joan, Lynn (played by Persia White), and Maya (played by Golden Brooks), all of whom embrace Toni at the scene's end.

The whole of Toni's dilemma, which is framed, on one end, by a risky sex act and, on the other end, by sisterly redemption, extends the personal-collective sex accountability thematic to a discussion of the prominence with which infectious disease and, thus, by extension, risk of exposure to HIV/AIDS, factors into the narrative equation. An analogous theme drives the story arc in season 1 of *The Game*, which culminates with Derwin (played by Pooch Hall) sleeping with Drew Sidora (as herself) and, in the cliffhanger episode, Melanie (played by Tia Mowry) discovering the infidelity, breaking off

FIGURE 2. A scene from season 2, episode 1 of *The Game*, "Diary of a Mad Black Woman Redux." Originally aired October 1, 2007. Melanie Barnett (Tia Mowry) confronts Derwin Davis (played by Pooch Hall) about cheating. Screenshot captured online from video uploaded by ParamountPlus.com.

her engagement to Derwin, and declaring, as she walks out on him, that she hopes he didn't wear a condom with that "skank [Drew]," because he deserves "whatever [he] get[s]" ("Diary of a Mad Black Woman, Redux"; see figure 2). However, whereas the fallout from Toni's affair immediately sensitizes her to the personal risks associated with selfish sex acts, the fallout from Derwin's indiscretion cuts to the core of Melanie's emotional and mental foundations, making her more vulnerable to high-risk sexual behavior.

Initially evidenced by her one-night stand with Trey Wiggs (played by Chaz Shepherd) the night after she and Derwin break up, the psychosomatic effects of Derwin's infidelity on Melanie crest when she attempts to seduce Malik (played by Hosea Chanchez) after she thinks Derwin has betrayed her again. "Come on, Malik," she tells him. "Just do this for me, OK. I just want to feel better" ("Fool Me . . . I'm the Damn Fool"). Tasha's (played by Wendy Raquel Robinson) introduction into the scene at this moment is significant because it compels Melanie to question the logic of her actions. "You done lost yourself, Melanie," Tasha tells her. "You done lost yourself in this world. It's time you called your parents." The directive nudges Melanie out of a self-destructive state of mind and into a more self-reflective space. Although it does not solve immediate problems extending from her lack of financial resources, Tasha's advice has the effect of restoring Melanie's sense of accountability to herself and to others, besides Derwin, with whom she has intimate relationships.

What is revealed in the trajectory of images that compose Toni's and

Melanie's negotiation of the public implications of private sex acts are two women struggling to ground themselves, to come to terms with who they are, what they want, what they will tolerate from others, and what others are willing to tolerate from them. Out of Toni's and Melanie's related identity crises we can derive definitions of black womanhood that view it as a condition of becoming, rather than of already being. These definitions are indispensable to an understanding of the larger aesthetic principles underlying Brock Akil's systematic reconstruction of black womanhood for turn-of-the-twenty-first-century viewing audiences.

Of "Shades of Gray" and (Sister) Circles

> TEE-TEE: All I'm saying is, you gotta find a greater meaning. I mean, what's your rhyme about?
> MALIK: Losing the game.
> TEE-TEE: No, see, it's bigger than that. See, the game is a metaphor for a bigger loss. Think about it: it's not about losing the game; it's about losing your daddy.
> MALIK: I didn't lose him. I just don't know where he is.
> TEE-TEE: Then explore that.
> —"The Iceman Cometh," season 1, *The Game*

Malik Wright, a.k.a. "40 million," is the son of Tasha Mack, the "elder" among *The Game*'s three female leads. A running theme in the growth of Tasha's character during season 1 is the balance she must strike between mothering Malik and managing his career as the Sabers' (the fictional San Diego–based professional football team at the center of *The Game*) superstar starting quarterback. Among the events that make up Tasha's backstory and complicate this balancing act are Malik's father's abandonment of Tasha when he learns that she is pregnant at sixteen, Tasha giving birth to Malik and becoming a teenage mother, Tasha cultivating Malik's athletic talents, and Tasha negotiating Malik's $40 million contract once he is drafted to the pros. While the last two of these developments make clear Tasha's seriousness and skill as a businesswoman, the first two impute vulnerable dimensions to her character that are introduced in season 1 and fleshed with detailed specificity in seasons 2 and 3.[24] Exploration of Tasha's character flaws is mediated through a range of hip

---

24. Two episodes from season 3 are worth mentioning here: "Punk Ass Chauncey," in which Malik meets his biological father, and "The Third Legacy," in which Tasha vocalizes and comes to terms with the anger she's harbored toward Malik's father for not staying with and supporting her during her pregnancy.

hop significations, as exhibited in the dialogue above between Malik and Tee-Tee.[25] The dialogue is excerpted from a scene where Malik is putting together rhymes for Tee-Tee to critique. The deeper meaning that Tee-Tee drives Malik to discover compels reflection on his upbringing without a father, but it also mandates audience consideration of the economic and emotional tolls of single parenting on Tasha. While Malik's method of rhyming invokes mainstream hip hop, his lyrical content pushes the discursive practice to a level that contemplates the multiple capacities and dimensions of subjectivity that shape Tasha's experiences as a black woman. The effect works doubly to model and advance a hip hop feminist aesthetics, the larger value system underlying the construction of black womanhood in both *Girlfriends* and *The Game*.

As noted in chapter 1, Joan Morgan outlines fundamental elements of hip hop feminism in her germinal memoir, *When Chickenheads Come Home to Roost* (1999), through reflections on how she came to understand the kind of discordant harmony that exists between the social conditions and power dynamics that shaped the lives of her mother's generation of black women and cultural forces molding the experiences of her generation of black women. "As a child of the post-Civil Rights, post-feminist, post-soul hip-hop generation," she begins, "my struggle songs consisted of the same notes [as my mother's] but they were infused with distinctly different rhythms" (22). Whereas the process of self-definition for her mother's generation involved shedding "the restrictive costumes of domestic, mother, and wife" (20), for Morgan's generation, the process involved being "willing to take an honest look at ourselves—and then tell the truth about it. Much of what we'll see will be fly as hell," she quips; "a lot," she admits bluntly, "will be painful and trifling" (23).

This process of introspection and acknowledgment is nevertheless indispensable for black women living in the age of hip hop to go through, Morgan maintains, because "only when we've told the truth about ourselves—when we've faced the fact that we are often complicit in our oppression—will we be able to take full responsibility for our lives" (23). And taking responsibility means, on the one hand, coming to terms with the fact that the problems that plagued past generations of black women—"racism, sexism, poverty, inadequate education, escalating rates of incarceration, piss-poor health conditions, drugs, and violence" (22)—persist and, on the other hand, determining "to push [our] foremothers' voices far enough away to discover [our] own" (26). For black women living in the age of hip hop, she deduces, "love no longer

---

25. Although Tee-Tee's origins are never fully explained, more than one episode implies that he is a relative (possibly a nephew or cousin) taken in by Tasha, who becomes Malik's personal assistant in the tradition of Farnsworth Bentley, best known for his work as Sean "Diddy" Combs's valet and personal assistant.

presents itself wrapped in the romance of basement blue lights, lifetime commitments, or the sweet harmonies of The Stylistics and The Chi-Lites. Love for us, is raw like sushi, served up on sex platters" (61–62). Thus, "more than any other generation before us," Morgan reasons, black women need "a feminism committed to 'keeping it real.' We need a voice like our music—one that samples and layers many voices, injects its sensibilities into the old and flips it into something new, provocative, and powerful. And one whose occasional hypocrisy, contradictions, and trifleness guarantee us at least a few trips to the terror-dome, forcing us to finally confront what we'd all rather hide from. We need a feminism that possesses the same fundamental understanding held by any true student of hip hop," and that is, "truth can't be found in the voice of any one rapper but in the juxtaposition of many. The keys that unlock the riches of contemporary black female identity," Morgan concludes, "lie at the magical intersection where those contrary voices meet—the juncture where 'truth' is no longer black and white, but subtle, intriguing shades of gray" (62). In a 2004 interview with *The Hollywood Reporter*'s Tatiana Siegel, Brock Akil echoed Morgan's sentiments in describing precisely what about black women's lives she sought to introduce to television as a creator-writer-producer. "I thought that what I could add," she explained, "were all of our shades of gray and our complexities. I didn't see a lot of vulnerabilities in [the depictions of black women on television]. A lot of times, I think we are represented as very fearless, tough women. The word 'sassy' gets used a lot." To appeal to audiences in a "more real and tangible way," therefore, Brock Akil set about combating the stereotype that "black women are either the sister-girl or the asexual judge with no life. I can be fearless at work, but I can also be stupid over a guy. I can be all those things at once. I wanted to show how fashionable we are. The fashion and the femininity, I really wanted to talk about that," she says.[26] In a nutshell, Brock Akil concluded, she wanted to see the multifaceted existences of black women "validated."[27] The benefits gained from this validation surface especially clearly in episodes of *Girlfriends* and *The Game* whose narrative lines center the complexities of black women's sexual lives in the age of hip hop and HIV/AIDS and the range of social, psychological, and health considerations that black women must make in their efforts to enjoy fulfilling, safe sexual relationships. "The Pact" from *Girlfriends* and "The Big Chill" and "The Side Part, Under" from *The Game* are, in this regard, representative and thus deserving of close examination.

---

26. Siegel, "*Girlfriends*' 100th Episode."
27. Givhan, "Echoes of TV's First Lady," C01.

108 • CHAPTER 4

Among all of the episodes in *Girlfriends'* eight-season run, "The Pact" offers the most visually detailed and densely narrated representation of HIV/AIDS infection among black women. In it, Kimberly Elise stars as Reesie Jackson, a mate of Joan, Lynn, and Toni, with whom Joan has a falling out in college because, according to Joan, Reesie stole and eventually married Joan's boyfriend, Brian (played by Timon Durrett). A series of flashbacks, filtered through Joan's and Reesie's points of view, recall a scene wherein Brian arrives in Joan's dormitory room with two tickets to an MC Hammer concert and discovers that Joan is unable to attend the concert because of a prescheduled study group. Joan's recollection of the scene casts Reesie as a provocatively clad predator who captures her prey—Brian—upon using Joan's ticket to accompany him to the concert. Reesie's recollection depicts Joan as a bookworm, annoyed by Brian's invitation and presence and content to cast him off on Reesie. The naming of the year of Joan and Reesie's falling out—1991—situates its terms within larger developments shaping black expressive culture at the time, including the resuscitation and mass marketing of black-power rhetoric, fueled by the commercial and critical success of hip hop artists Public Enemy. In addition to the MC Hammer concert reference in the flashbacks, Lynn, adorned in red and black coveralls and green, black, red, and yellow block T-shirts and jackets, serves as a visual reminder of Public Enemy's influence on the scene, as she vows to aid Joan in bringing Reesie down "by any means necessary" after Brian, in fact, leaves Joan for Reesie. The naming of the year also locates the consequences of the falling out within a historical period, which, I argue in chapters 2 and 3, is paradoxically distinguished, on the one hand, by increased rates of HIV/AIDS diagnoses among black women and girls and, on the other hand, by the underreporting of this phenomenon in mainstream media outlets as well as a dearth of medical and public health discourse regarding the root causes of this phenomenon. As Cathy Cohen explains in her study of black political responses to HIV/AIDS throughout the 1990s, black politicians especially were determined to depict HIV/AIDS as "a disease equally threatening to all in the general public or affecting those respectable and innocent segments of communities of color—women and children—that deserved sympathy and support. Disproportionately, black members sought to highlight the plight of 'respectable' victims—women and children—living with AIDS, minimizing the attention directed at black gay men and black men who sleep with men."[28] In 1991, "the down low" was a signifier within black popular culture for infidelity of any nature and had not yet come to stand in for the specific sexual practice whereby black men who

---

28. Cohen, *Boundaries of Blackness,* 313.

socially identify as heterosexual have sexual relationships with other men, the race-neutral equivalent of men having sex with men, or MSM, in CDC parlance.[29] Thus, both knowledge and communication gaps existed around the complex routes—male-male, male-female, and male-male-female—by which the virus could be transmitted as well as the sexual, cultural, and identity politics surrounding this basic clinical process. In Joan's and Reesie's flashbacks, Lynn again symbolically highlights this discursive void, as her general presence and expressed eagerness to attend the concert with Brian, when he announces that he has a second ticket, are conspicuously ignored. Lynn further symbolically signals the poignancy of disregard afforded the cultural circumstances of black women's vulnerability to HIV/AIDS in the early years of the epidemic when audio and visual affects twice attempt, but fail, to enact flashbacks of Lynn's memory of the larger context shaping Joan and Reesie's dispute: "O.K.: January 1991," she announces. The screen blurs and disperses with flashback sound effects once, twice, then she states flatly: "I got nothing."

Reesie's subsequent entry onto the scene initially purposes an occasion for Joan to indict Reesie in person, to hold her accountable for Joan's besieged status as a thirty-something unmarried black woman—despite Joan's considerable professional success. "If it weren't for you," Joan argues, "I would be the one that was married, I would be the one with two kids, and I would be living your happy life." Joan's begrudged socioeconomic plight is among *Girlfriends'* core themes and underscores much of the drama—and comedy—framing Joan's characterization and, thus, driving plot development both within and across individual episodes. Almost immediately after this indictment, however, we learn that the conflict between Reesie and Joan that opens "The Pact" is designed not to set the controlling narrative of Joan's characterization up for reinforcement but rather to bring Reesie's story into sharp focus. The focal

---

29. The success of E. Lynn Harris's self-published novel *Invisible Life* (1994) fueled conversations about professional black men who lead public lives as heterosexuals but privately have sex with men or both men and women. Another ten years would pass before the term "down low" would be narrowly redefined and applied to this phenomenon. The publication of J. L. King's highly controversial *On the Downlow: A Journey into the Lives of Straight Black Men Who Sleep with Men* mainstreamed conversations about black men who have sex with men after King appeared on *The Oprah Winfrey Show*. *On the Downlow* characterizes black MSMs as driven by selfish primal desires and tacitly implicates them in the spread of HIV/AIDS among black women. Keith Boykin's *Beyond the Downlow: Sex, Lies, and Denial in Black America* (2005) was among the first in a series of responses to King's book, which clarified the dangers in playing the "blame game" with HIV/AIDS as well as not accounting for the complex social, psychological, emotional, and cultural dynamics that inform questions of identity and sexuality among black men. In a 2010 appearance on *The Oprah Winfrey Show,* King recanted much of what he argued about black MSMs in *On the Downlow* and appears now to embrace his identity as a gay black man.

shift is bluntly perfected through a discordant antiphony that highlights the naivety of Joan's assumptions about marriage in general and Reesie's marriage to Brian specifically:

> REESIE: You want my happy life!
> JOAN: Yes!
> REESIE: You want Brian!
> JOAN: Yes!
> REESIE: Then you can have him. And you can have the AIDS he gave me, too!

After Reesie's announcement, a mise-en-scène reflective of Brock Akil's envisioned prioritization and validation of black women's complex identities and issues takes shape. In piecemeal fashion, Lynn, Toni, and Joan approach Reesie, bearing items intended to comfort (and humor) her—a blanket, an apple, and a heating pad—as they settle into symbolically supportive spaces that encircle Reesie, who sits on the sofa. Maya's initial location outside the circle, with arms akimbo and legs stiffly spread apart, visually represents the hesitation, and often outright rejection, with which HIV/AIDS-infected people are met with the revelation of their status. Maya's apparent dishevelment (see figure 3), when Reesie states that she has full-blown AIDS and is not "simply" HIV-positive, yet steady movement toward the sofa facilitate the audience's observation of her transition from a symbolically guarded—and perhaps even reactionary—position to a location from which she, like Joan, Toni, and Lynn, can listen, and learn, as Reesie details the plight of a black woman living with AIDS.

Plain expository dialogue among the women strips Reesie's testimony down to its clinical basics at the same time that it fosters analysis of the cultural dynamics that instance and impact her management of her status:

> LYNN: Do you know how Brian got it?
> REESIE: From another man.
> JOAN: Oh my God. He couldn't use a condom.
> REESIE: No, because if he put a condom in his pocket, then he'd be admitting to himself that he was going out to have sex with men, and that would make him gay, which, according to him, he's not.

In a moment rare for situation comedy, let alone black entertainment television in the early 2000s, the concept of MSM is explicitly voiced and explicated. Because it is integrated into Reesie's larger discourse on living with

FIGURE 3. A scene from *Girlfriends*, season 3, episode 19, "The Pact." Originally aired March 17, 2003. Reesie Jackson (played by Kimberly Elise) sits with Joan (played by Tracee Ellis Ross) and Lynn (played by Persia White) and discusses living with AIDS. Screenshot captured online from video uploaded to YouTube by Cornelius Wilson, January 21, 2017.

AIDS, it does not control her narrative. Rather, the articulations work doubly to clarify, without stigmatizing, the sexual practice and to bring the narrative arc of "The Pact" full circle, as we are invited to infer that Brian's struggles with his sexual identity preceded his relationship with Reesie and, thus, likely overlapped with his relationship with Joan. In this moment of reconciling the cultural contexts informing Reesie's, Joan's, and Brian's interrelated backstories with their respective present conditions, the imprint of Brock Akil's hip hop feminism becomes markedly clear. The moment emboldens Reesie to acknowledge to Joan—and, perhaps, for the first time to herself—that she did in fact steal Brian. "You've been right all along," she confesses. "I stole him. He was fine. Karma's a bitch, hun?" she quietly quips. "Don't say that," Joan insists, "don't even think that." The scene closes on a less somber note when Toni makes a joke about Reesie having ashy feet. Importantly, however, the chords of truth-telling, reckoning, and healing that the sister circle gives rise to reverberate beyond the scene, setting the tone for sustained, informed discourse both among black women *and* about black women and HIV/AIDS.

The Game incorporates fewer direct references to HIV/AIDS than *Girlfriends*. As a whole, however, the occasions it presents for deep reflection on the epidemic and its specific impact on black women are no less compelling. Indirect references that abounded over *The Game*'s three-season run engage what Gail Wyatt, Nell Forge, and Donald Guthrie refer to as the constellation of cultural factors, including gender role expectations, myths about black

112 • CHAPTER 4

female identity, and taboos about black female sexuality, that influence black women's "decision making skills and communication with partners in sexual relationships" and, thus, impact their risk for exposure to HIV/AIDS.[30] These considerations lead back to issues raised by Tasha's and Melanie's characterizations and the conflicts that structure their narratives.

Tasha's status as a successful single black mother extends from storylines that engage the motley of themes and images of black womanhood, which, Tricia Rose argues, has historically worked to "marginalize, pathologize, and condense" black women's experiences and, thus, reduce their representations in popular culture to single dimension.[31] "The Big Chill" sets up the proposition that Tasha's embodiment of the "angry black woman" stereotype causes her relationship with Kenny (played by Rocky Carroll), the Sabers' offensive team coach, to fail. Rather than reinforce this myth, Brock Akil appropriates it precisely to mobilize the principles of hip hop feminism in accordance with the ambiguities, ambivalences, and complexities of Tasha's and Melanie's characters that are revealed, analyzed, and embraced. This process unfolds in scenes that recall and revise key elements of the truth-telling, reckoning, and healing propelled in "The Pact" and thus brings HIV/AIDS within the purview of *The Game*'s rhetorical focus.

The pivotal conflict in "The Big Chill" initiates when Kenny informs Tasha that when she meets his friends, he wants her to "skip the drama." Prior to this exchange, which takes place outside a coffee shop, Tasha, believing that a fellow customer cut in front of her in line, creates a scene inside the coffee shop. The audience is not privileged to the exchange that ultimately leads the manager to ban Tasha and Kenny from the establishment, but the loudness and crudeness with which she initially reacts to the customer and the cashier who attempts to diffuse the situation suggests strongly that Tasha's attitude plays a key role. The coffee shop scene provides an occasion for Kenny to confront Tasha about a number of preceding incidences, all of which, he claims, escalate out of control because of Tasha's confrontational demeanor. He infers further that if she does not adjust her attitude before meeting his friends, he will break off their relationship. The warning is important for what it reveals about the differences in Kenny's and Tasha's respective understandings of the dynamics of their relationship up to the point where she is set to meet his friends and thus deserves exact quoting:

---

30. Wyatt, Forge, et al., "Family Constellation and Ethnicity."
31. Rose, *Longing to Tell,* 9.

KENNY: I want them to meet the Tasha I fell in love with. The sexy, beautiful, smart Tasha.

TASHA: Now how many other Tasha's you know.

KENNY: Well, let's see, a "I don't take no mess, Tasha," the "Aw, hell no! Tasha," and, oh yeah, everybody's favorite, the "Now what, now?" Tasha.

TASHA: Ok. Well don't forget the, "I rocked your world last night, Tasha."

KENNY: Well, I appreciate that one. But outside of the bedroom, I need peace. I need softness.

TASHA: I'm soft. I'm peaceful. And I'm sorry, Kenny. I didn't know it was an issue.

The exchange demonstrates Kenny's capacity to recognize the multiple dimensions of Tasha's subjectivity, among which is clearly a strong personality. Kenny has apparently known about this specific dimension for some time but does not criticize it until he turns to the question of the impression that he expects Tasha to make with his friends. In the midst of essentially commanding that she adjust her attitude for the benefit of these friends, Kenny embraces the aggression that Tasha displays in the bedroom, as signified by the "rock your world" metaphor she uses to characterize her sexual disposition, a disposition that Kenny maintains he "appreciates." Tasha's response to Kenny's reproof is worth noting because it drives her reflection inward, compelling her to contemplate the roles her attitude and actions play in defining and sustaining their relationship.

In this self-reflective mode, Tasha seeks advice from Kelly (played by Brittany Daniels) about how to "fix" her attitude. Their exchange occasions the explicit naming of the "angry black woman" stereotype and several other myths associated with black and white womanhood about which they initially lightly joke. "Kenny's got this big dinner party tomorrow night, and I got to be on my best behavior," Tasha begins. "And you white women know how to make your man feel more important than he is, so, teach me" she commands. Kelly retorts, "Please. I can't turn water into wine." When Tasha betrays that her desire to appease Kenny stems from her fear of becoming a statistic—"If I don't fix this, I may die alone. Forty-two percent of black women under thirty are never going to get married"—Kelly teases: "Ooooh, that's awful. Someone should organize a telethon." Eventually, however, the conversation strikes a serious chord, as Tasha explains why she believes black women are justified in being angry—"We always gotta shoulder the burden of everybody"—and Kelly advises that "it's all about picking your battles. Every little thing doesn't have to be about a power struggle. Like tomorrow night. It's his night. His friends. So, just, go with the flow, and be his woman."

114 • CHAPTER 4

Heeding Kelly's advice and determining not to become a statistic, Tasha initially enters the dinner party scene prepared to recode her behavior, adjusting it to fit the public persona Kenny expects her to perform. Almost immediately, however, Tasha is confronted with the challenges of pretending to be—or act like—someone she is not, as Kenny's friends welcome her to "the circle."

The backstory of the circle, which is composed of Kenny, two white women, and two white men, reveals that at different times, all three of the men dated, or were married to, one of the women in the circle.

KENNY: Penny and I dated first.
MIKE: Until I stole her away from him.
RICK: And he pawned her off on me.
PENNY: They love me so much they just had to keep me in the circle.

When Tasha pulls Kenny to the side to inquire about this dynamic—"Is this some sort of swingers club?" she asks—Kenny responds: "No, they're cool people. They're just messing with you." However, as the evening progresses, sexual overtones in the conversation do not diminish; at one point, Rick even attempts to engage Tasha in a discussion of the shape and size of Penny's behind. What becomes clear to Tasha—and to the audience—as the scene unfolds is that certain models of social identity that are available to Kenny and his circle of friends are not as easily accessed and displayed by Tasha. Here it is worth noting that the loudness and abrasiveness of Tasha's behavior at the coffee shop are matched by the tactlessness and lewdness the circle exhibits in assuming that Tasha is—or should be—comfortable with their conversation, what the conversation reveals about the dynamics of their sexual interrelationships, and the implications of these dynamics for her, as Kenny's current mate and sexual partner. In this respect, the scene is further revealing in that it demonstrates the apparent ease with which at least one of the white women in the circle negotiates sexual relationships with all three of the men. Tasha's access to this model of sexual practice is restricted not only for its mythic implications for her as a single black mother but also because of the risks it presents to her as a single black woman living in the age of HIV/AIDS. It is well settled that HIV/AIDS is "as much a social process as it is a biomedical one";[32] thus, risk of exposure to the virus among black women is particularly pronounced when both social and geographic boundaries among potential sex partners are so narrow as to blur the boundaries between high- and low-risk

---

32. Brijnath, "It's about TIME," 372.

populations.[33] Here, again, we cannot miss fundamental distinctions in the operations of the circle motif, which in "The Pact" functions as a safe space for black women to inform and support one another, but in "The Big Chill" symbolizes the risks of exposure to HIV/AIDS and other STDs and STIs that black women take when entering casual sex spaces.

As the scene progresses, Tasha's blackness and womanness become increasingly inextricably bound and distinguished by sexual and social codes in which she cannot traffic without the risk of compromising both her emotional and physical health. It is no coincidence, therefore, that the catalyst for removing her from "the circle" involves a play on language that invokes Jannis Androutsopoulos's theory of "cultural referencing," the process whereby the language of hip hop provides for both the conservation and borrowing of experiential domains mapped along racial, gender, and geographic lines.[34] Tasha walks away from the circle, initially to help Kenny clean up, and says that she is going to let the rest of the members "conversate." Mike seizes the opportunity to make light of Tasha's use of a colloquialism, pointing out that the "real word" is "converse." Offended by Mike's teasing and its racial implications, Tasha threatens to "bust him in his damn throat." Kenny enters the scene in a manner that recalls the cashier's earlier efforts to diffuse the tensions mounting between Tasha and the line-cutter at the coffee shop. But Kenny's efforts are met with the same resistance as Tasha dresses down individual members of the circle and dismisses the entire group as "a bunch of swingers." The repercussions of her actions and attitude are hardest felt when Kenny later arrives at Tasha's house to officially end their relationship. The breakup is signified by the return of various items of Tasha's lingerie, a telling rejection of the sexual intimacy Kenny shared with Tasha in favor—we must assume— of the preservation of the sexual relationships shared within/between/among members of "the circle." Tasha's devastation by Kenny's rejection is, however, short-lived, as the closing scene brings back into focus the various ways in which her unapologetic approach to "being" and "doing" herself has kept Tasha honest and safe, if single. Importantly, Malik enters the scene to convey these sentiments in words that underscore his truth about his mother: "The right guy is out there for you," he asserts. "I'm sure there's a man out there that'll put up with you."

---

33. Tillerson, "Explaining Racial Disparities."
34. Androutsopoulos, "Language and the Three Spheres."

116 · CHAPTER 4

Brock Akil's Hip Hop Feminism:
Predecessors and Prospects

In a 2004 article for *ESSENCE Magazine* titled "Quitting Hip-Hop," Angela Michaela Davis, founding editor of *Vibe Magazine* and former editor-in-chief of *Honey,* declared: "If there is not a shift in how the hip hop industry portrays women, then our 20 year relationship is officially O-V-E-R."[35] At the heart of Davis's contention with the culture on which she built her career as one of hip hop's foremost fashion stylists and journalists was the danger she observed in a male-dominated industry that tended to "view women as moneymakers (as in the kind you shake). Few of us," she lamented, "are in a position to be decision makers."[36] This chapter has argued that throughout the early 2000s, Mara Brock Akil provided the goods for Davis and other hip-hop-generation artists, critics, and consumers seeking diverse, salient popular cultural representations of black womanhood—representations that, at the time, mainstream hip hop music was not willing to offer. As creator-writer-producer of *Girlfriends* and *The Game,* Brock Akil challenged viewing audiences to look beyond the mere spectacle that hip hop music made of black women's bodies, black female sexuality, and black womanhood to acknowledge the complexity of black women's existences and struggles. Merging elements of situation comedy with her own brand of hip hop feminism, Brock Akil constructed narratives predicated on the specific values and assumptions of a diverse cast of forward-thinking hip-hop-generation female characters who were unafraid to let their sensibilities, sensitivities, and vulnerabilities show. Beyond providing for the development of rounded characters, these narratives produced textual space for exploring the particular health challenges confronting the masses of black women to and for whom Joan, Maya, Toni, Lynn, Tasha, Melanie, and Kelly spoke at the turn of the twenty-first century. Foremost among these challenges was HIV/AIDS.

To be sure, *Girlfriends* and *The Game* were preceded by a number of black television series[37] that addressed disease and the racial, gender, sexual, and cultural mores that contribute to black-white health disparities in America.

---

35. Davis, "Quitting Hip Hop," 155.

36. Davis, "Quitting Hip Hop," 155.

37. Consideration of the treatment of HIV/AIDS among black women in series not typically characterized as "black television" exceeds the scope of this chapter. Worth mentioning briefly is the 2004 episode of *Law and Order: Special Victims Unit* "Low Down," which guest-starred Michael Beach. Beach plays Andy, an assistant district attorney on the "down low," who murders his white male coworker/lover after being pressured to leave his black wife and children. Andy's guilt is established through a series of events that reveals that both Andy and his wife are HIV-positive and results in Andy disclosing to his wife that he is gay.

Who can forget the classic scene from *Good Times* (1976) when Mary Ann, J.J.'s ex-girlfriend, confronts him with her STD-positive status, proclaiming, "J.J., I got V.D. and you da one gave it to me." Or Stacy Dash's and Lela Rochon's small-screen debuts on *The Cosby Show* (1984–92) playing Michelle, a friend of Denise's, who is afraid to talk with her parents about "a feminine issue," and Veronica, a pregnant teenager for whom Denise hosts a baby shower. Most of us can probably remember the interruption of regularly scheduled broadcasts on November 7, 1991, the day Magic Johnson announced his retirement from the NBA because he had "attained" the HIV virus. How many remember that nearly a year to the date earlier, *A Different World* aired "Time Keeps on Slippin'" (1990) and acknowledged the growing problem of HIV/AIDS at historically black colleges and universities (HBCUs) by putting "a condom" in the 1990 Hillman time capsule?[38] A few months later, in "Monet is the Root of All Evil" (1991), the series again acknowledged the epidemic by exploring the crisis in interpretation and generational conflict created when a hip hop artist's painting of a presumptively crack-addicted mother, cast in the image of the Madonna and nursing her baby, is displayed in the Hillman Art Gallery. The very next episode marked the climax in the series' first HIV/AIDS story arc by letting Josie, a minor character, adeptly acted by Tisha Campbell, take center stage to reveal her HIV-positive status. Memorably, Whoopi Goldberg, who guest-starred as the Hillman professor who builds Josie's confidence to disclose her status, warns students who initially shun Josie in a calm, steady tenor: "AIDS is not a moral judgment." Social-contextual and structural factors heightening black women's vulnerability to HIV/AIDS exposure were signified in a second story arc in *A Different World* that addressed Kim's repressed issues with self-esteem and body image brought to the surface by an exhibition of black women featuring Mammy ("Mammy Dearest," 1991), the campus visit of Freddie's formerly incarcerated pen pal ("Prisoner of Love," 1992),[39] and Gina's involvement in an abusive relationship with her rapper boyfriend Dion ("Love Taps," 1992).

The layering and gynocentric points of view that shaped *A Different World*'s HIV/AIDS storylines are part of the larger creative revisioning that Susan Fales Hill and Debbie Allen brought to the series after its first season. In an encyclopedia entry for the Museum of Broadcast Communications, Darnell Hunt describes Allen's tenure as director-producer of *A Different World* as particularly transformative because, under Allen's leadership, the series took

---

38. In 1991, when the episode originally aired, the Federal Communications Commission would not allow the condom to be displayed. In syndication, the condom is visible.

39. Freddie's "pen pal" turns out to be an undercover reporter writing a story about black students' attitudes toward ex-convicts at historically black colleges and universities.

on "a range of social and political issues rarely addressed on television—let alone in situation comedies. Featured characters regularly confronted such controversial topics as unplanned pregnancy, date rape, racial discrimination, AIDS, and the 1992 Los Angeles uprisings." The series also lauded "the virtues of higher education for African American youth at a time when many black communities were in crisis." In closing, Hunt concluded that *A Different World* would perhaps best be remembered for "its cultural vibrancy" and "commitment to showcasing black history, music, dance, fashion and attitude"—qualities that Hunt attributes to Allen, as producer-director, and Fales Hill, as head writer.[40] On multiple levels, *A Different World* achieved what even *The Cosby Show* was unable to accomplish, by entertaining, engaging, and enlightening the masses through narratives that centered the specific social, political, and cultural plights of upwardly mobile, high-achieving hip-hop-generation black youth. It is of little surprise, therefore, that Brock Akil cites *A Different World* as one of her influences: it provided a blueprint for black situation comedy that arguably remained unmatched in primetime television until *Girlfriends'* 2000 debut.[41]

Of course, between 1993 and 2000, other black comedies enjoyed varying levels of success on network television. For example, Fox's *Living Single* (1993–98) created and executive-produced by Yvette Lee Bowser, gave Brock Akil the opportunity to see herself and her friends for the first time on network television in its ensemble cast of educated, middle-class black men and women. Costarring Queen Latifah as the founding editor of the hip hop magazine *Flava, Living Single* also broadened the parameters of hip hop feminism's media influence.[42] Yet, as Brock Akil maintains, in creating *Girlfriends,* she believed she "had something to add to the conversation that [*Living Single*] started about African-American women."[43] In a 2004 interview with *The Hol-*

---

40. Hunt, "Different World." It is now well documented that *A Different World* was responsible for increased student enrollments at HBCUs throughout the late 1980s and early 1990s.

41. Siegel, "*Girlfriends'* 100th Episode." A respectful nod must be made here to the Fox Network Television series *Roc* (1991–94), which starred the inimitable Charles S. Dutton and Ella Joyce. This underrated series merged "the stage" with "the set" by broadcasting live episodes of the entire second season. Roc is also the first black situation comedy after *A Different World* to pointedly address the HIV/AIDS crisis in the black community in the touching series finale episode, "You Shouldn't Have to Lie" (1994).

42. As Beretta Smith-Shomade points out, when Latifah landed a lead role in *Living Single,* her influence with mainstream audiences was already evidenced by her success as an MC as well as her appearances in supporting roles in several high-profile films, including *Jungle Fever* (1992). See Smith-Shomade, *Shaded Lives,* 50–51, 52–53, 55–56. In 2007, Latifah garnered an Emmy nomination for her gripping performance as Anna, an HIV-positive community activist, in the HBO movie *Life Support* (2007).

43. Siegel, "*Girlfriends'* 100th Episode."

lywood Reporter, Brock Akil hinted at what she set out to "add," in describing the legacy she hoped to leave with *Girlfriends*: "[I want to show that] black women were here, we were thriving, we were stylish, we were professional, we were vulnerable and we were human. We wanted the same things everybody else wanted. So, I feel in a way like a documentarian."[44] Likening her objectives to those of a documentarian underscores Brock Akil's intent to bring a level of truth to popular cultural representations of black womanhood that she clearly found lacking at the turn of the twenty-first century. Her ability to do this resulted, in part, from her attunement to the aesthetic sensibilities of her generation. The beneficiaries of the hard-fought social movements of the 1950s and 1960s, blacks born after the civil rights and black power movements, also bore witness to abject institutional and structural failures that beset cities across America throughout the 1970s, 1980s, and 1990s, giving rise to a host of social, political, and cultural challenges. In response to these challenges, Brock Akil set out to "tell the dirty little secrets of black women," the biggest one of which, she announced tongue-in-cheek during a 2007 interview with *Black Enterprise,* is that "we're just human beings trying to make it like everyone else."[45] When UPN merged with the WB (Warner Bros.) to form the CW Television Network in 2006, the fall lineup included both *Girlfriends* and *The Game.* Explaining why within three years both series were canceled ironically provides for a summative review of some of the very social and cultural issues that Brock Akil aimed to highlight through the creative reconstruction of black womanhood in *Girlfriends* and *The Game.*

Brock Akil has always acknowledged that a great deal of her success in the television industry today can be attributed to the opportunities that the WB Television Network and United Paramount Network created throughout the 1990s for black actors, writers, producers, and directors to "get their feet in the door,"[46] and, as Lynette Rice puts it, tell black stories to black viewing audiences.[47] Indeed, it was while working as a writer for the UPN series *Moesha* (1996–2001) that Brock Akil began pitching her ideas for *Girlfriends* to UPN network executives. At the time, both the WB and UPN were affectionately known among black viewing audiences as the "black TV stations" because of these networks' long list of situation comedies starring black actors. That these stations also seemed concerned to match entertainment with enlightenment was another source of attraction to large black viewing audiences, who regularly tuned in to follow storylines that addressed current events and develop-

---

44. Siegel, "*Girlfriends*' 100th Episode."
45. Richardson, "Top 50 Power Brokers."
46. Brock Akil, "We All Fall Down."
47. Rice, "Is the Black Situation Comedy Dying?" 9.

120 • CHAPTER 4

ments in black communities. In 2003, for example, the UPN took the bold step of teaming up with the Kaiser Family Foundation and Viacom to launch the "Know HIV/AIDS" campaign, a multimedia year-long initiative aimed at encouraging groups hardest hit by HIV/AIDS to get tested and know their status. In addition to the four episodes of season 3 of *Girlfriends* that prominently featured HIV/AIDS storylines during this campaign, "The Test" (2003) aired on the UPN series *One on One* (2001–6) and "She's Positive," a 2004 episode of *The Parkers* (1999–2004), aired on World AIDS Day. "The Test" highlighted the importance of knowing one's status and the status of potential new sexual partners. "She's Positive" starred Rozanda "Chili" Thomas of the R&B group TLC, as an HIV-positive woman tasked with the challenge of disclosing her status to a new love interest. In a network television and business climate readily responsive to the social needs and interests of black constituencies and resourced with the financial support and creative talent required to meet those needs and interests, it is of little surprise that the distinctive brand of hip hop feminism that Brock Akil introduced to network television with *Girlfriends* and *The Game* was able to take root and thrive throughout the 2000s.

Yet, as David Wyatt, a former writer for *The Cosby Show*, *Martin* (1992–97) and *Fresh Prince of Bel-Air* (1990–96) explains, once the UPN, like the WB and Fox before it, began pursuing more advertisers, their stock in programs aimed at black audiences substantially dropped. Consequently, the actors, writers, producers, and directors on the network's black television shows either lost their jobs or were forced into entry-level positions at other major networks, where they had little to no decision-making authority.[48] When the WB and UPN merged in 2006 to form the CW Television Network, the station picked up *Girlfriends, All of Us* (2003–7), *The Game*, and *Everybody Hates Chris* (2005–9) but cut *One on One* (2001–6), *Eve* (2003–6), and *Half & Half* (2002–6). The following year *All of Us* was gone. *Girlfriends* did not have a series finale when it ended in 2008, partly because of the 2007–8 Writers Guild strike, but mostly, many critics believe, because the CW concluded that a *Girlfriends* finale would be too costly to produce. The cynicism of CW critics seems warranted given the predictable fate the network subjected *The Game* to in its final season on the CW by moving the series to the 8/9c Friday night "death" slot in the network's 2008 fall lineup: at the end of the season, the CW announced the show's cancellation.[49]

The pathway that Brock Akil charted with *Girlfriends* and *The Game* parallels those charted by female MCs of the 1990s in that both point to the

---

48. McCombs, "Death of a Network."

49. *Everybody Hates Chris* (2005–9) was afforded the same fate: it was moved to the Friday night 7/8 c time slot and was subsequently canceled in 2009.

adeptness and creativity with which black women artists made their marks on the entertainment industry. The eerie echoing sounded in the rationales hip hop executives gave for declining to bankroll female MCs beyond the '90s, the rationale CW executives gave for not giving *Girlfriends* a proper closing, and the method used to bring *The Games'* series run on the CW to an end points to larger issues of racism, sexism, and capitalism in the media with which, the late bell hooks and many other black feminist theorists remind us, black women have always struggled. However, the global influence that hip hop has enjoyed for over four decades adds a distinctive layer of complexity to these struggles for black women artists who not only identify with hip hop but also draw upon hip hop for creative inspiration.

In ways both powerfully subtle and fully expressed, Mara Brock Akil channeled her hip hop sensibilities into creating, writing for, and producing two situation comedies that did for black women of the 2000s what female MCs accomplished the decade before: represented black womanhood in all its complex forms. Debuting *Girlfriends* and *The Game* at a time when HIV/AIDS constituted the prevailing health issue confronting people of African descent worldwide, Brock Akil provided for the mapping of black American women's distinctive struggles with the epidemic onto network television landscapes. In syndication and on demand through streaming, these series continue to facilitate the absorption of Brock Akil's own brand of hip hop feminism into discourses of black female identity, sexuality, and subjectivity that currently prevail in mainstream hip hop. The importance of this process of discursive integration cannot be overstated, given the substantial possibilities it creates for reformulating mainstream media constructions of black womanhood, black women's health, and HIV/AIDS in the twenty-first century. If, as W. J. T. Mitchell observes, "hypervisibility—being remarked, noticed, stared at—can only be understood if it is placed in some relation to its dialectical twin: invisibility,"[50] then situating and sustaining HIV/AIDS and other black women's health issues as focal points of rounded representations and narrations require vigilant attention to the array of forces that control black women's presence and absence in mainstream information and media outlets. Placing *Girlfriends* and *The Game* side by side, as this chapter has done, renders more easily visible how clearly each series elaborated Brock Akil's vision of black womanhood at the turn of the twenty-first century. Both shows employed similar strategies of documenting the various challenges confronting black women in the new millennium through storylines that were at once highly entertaining and critically enlightening. Among the most important issues

---

50. Mitchell, "Seeing Disability," 393.

brought to light are those related to black women's health in the age of hip hop and HIV/AIDS. *Girlfriends* and *The Game* remind us that representations of black female sexuality and subjectivity carry weight beyond the contexts of their lyrical expression in hip hop music. This weight bears substantially on current conditions of black women's health as well as the conditions we can expect future hip hop generations to inherit and endure. Will their future be one in which the risk of contracting HIV is no longer real for roughly one-third of black women and girls throughout the world? Stay tuned.

CHAPTER 5

In Memoriam—and in Life

We must go to the root and see that that is sound and healthy and vigorous and not deceive ourselves with waxen flowers and painted leaves of mock chlorophyll.

—Anna Julia Cooper, *A Voice from the South*, 62

How do I give voice to my quests so that other women can take what they need from my experiences?

—Audre Lorde, *The Cancer Journals*, 17

That's what I*'m* talking about.

—Jason Merrill Perry, May 3, 1972–April 18, 2018

My cousin Jason had a funny way of letting you know what he liked. He would say, "Now, that's what I*'m* talking about," dragging out and savoring the sound of "m," like nectar on his lips. My earliest memory of hearing this sound coincides with Jason telling me, for the first time, that he "like[d] boys." We were twelve. Lying side by side on our backs, legs propped on the headboard of a king bed in the back room of Big Mama's house, Jay read *Giovanni's Room* and I read *Tar Baby* . . .

> All of a sudden, Jay leaps up, throws his book against the wall, and shouts: "Now that's what I'm talking about!" The startling effect of his actions is immediately snuffed out by the deliciousness of that sound—m. It lingers over the hours we spend talking about how much Jay relates to the character, David, and how much he wishes he could tell the rest of the family what he is telling me. At first, I try joking my way out of his frustration—"So that's why you been walkin' 'round here dressed like Boy George: you want to be a white man!" Eventually, though, I settle (back) into the space of openness and trust that Jay and I always share. "I love you," I say to him. "Whoever you like, I like." "Now that's what I'm talking about," he smiles . . .

Over the years, that sound became synonymous with Jay's extraordinary flair for making me laugh out loud, even in my most unjoyful moments. It

124 • CHAPTER 5

embodied his knack for living without fear, sorrow, or regret, and never letting anyone feel sorry for him. It held me together on February 21, 2018, the night Jay summoned me to witness his last will and testament. It was with me the night his spirit left the room on April 18, 2018. And it comforts me now, as I write this closing chapter. In closing, as in opening, I relate memories of my cousin, Jason Merrill Perry, as testimony of his importance to me, the depth of my love for him, and how very much I miss him. I also tell these stories, in keeping with lessons learned from Anna Julia Cooper, Audre Lorde, and my other black feminist foremothers, which teach me that fostering the health and well-being of black women requires that I first "go to the root" and give voice to my own lived experiences. Jason's fierce commitment to living with HIV and AIDS provided my point of entry into understanding the HIV/AIDS epidemic. It directed my pursuit of competency in HIV/AIDS education and prevention through my work as a certified testing counselor with the NO/AIDS Task Force in New Orleans, Louisiana.[1] It inspired me to establish the Black Women's Health Conference Task Force, a cohort of practitioners, researchers, and community activists, who, since 2012, have biennially organized and convened the Black Women's Health Conference at Tulane University, to address the range of health disparity issues that black women and girls face.[2] And it influenced the broad thinking about black women's health that has shaped this study's findings and contributions.

As I have noted throughout this study, the habitual underfunding and neglect of black women's health within mainstream scientific, political, and popular cultural spheres has left the responsibility—and privilege—of building knowledge about black women's health mostly to black women. As guide and model, throughout this study, I have used both the practical and theoretical tenets of hip hop feminism to fill voids in empirical research on the status of black women's health at the turn of the twenty-first century and to offer an alternative disciplinary perspective on the work that remains to be done if the threat that HIV/AIDS continues to present to the health and well-being of black women and girls is to be eradicated. I want to close, therefore, by briefly highlighting some of the more recent issues that I see in discourses around HIV/AIDS and black women's health, which implicate many of the dynamics of language use, silencing, and visibility that I have explored in this book. While this study does not afford space to address each of these issues in depth, their relevance to the question of how hip hop feminism should continue to

---

1. I was certified in 2009 and worked as a counselor for one year. The NO/AIDS Task Force opened in the early 1980s and in 2014 restructured and reorganized under the name CrescentCare.

2. Black Women's Health Conference.

equip the masses to understand and act in service of black women's health points to the kind of future scholarly research that this study hopes to inspire. Because Jason has been a constant guiding force in my completion of this book, it seems only fitting that Dave Chappelle, Jay's favorite comedian, provided the occasion for me to reflect on and synthesize my closing observations, as I viewed his 2021 Netflix standup comedy special, *The Closer*.[3]

This seventy-minute performance features Chappelle using humor to engage the customary themes of his comedy, that is, the pervasiveness of white supremacy and its pernicious influence on American systems and values. Those familiar with Chappelle's style of comedy know that he holds no punches; in this regard, *The Closer* is noteworthy for repeated blunt references to HIV/AIDS that Chappelle makes to draw in his audience and thread the string of critical reflections that compose his performance.

The opening, for example, tethers the clinical uncertainties of the early years of the HIV/AIDS epidemic to unknowns associated with the recent COVID-19 pandemic through wordplay, which highlights clinically confirmed commonalities in the latency stage of HIV and asymptomatic COVID-19.[4] "I didn't get sick at all," Chappelle quips, describing his health condition upon receiving a positive COVID-19 screening. "I am the Magic Johnson of Coronavirus."[5] In another, explicit invocation of HIV/AIDS, Chappelle alludes to the following remarks hip hop artist DaBaby made during a Rolling Loud concert, approximately two months before *The Closer*'s premier:

> If you didn't show up today with HIV, AIDS, any of them deadly sexually transmitted diseases that'll make you die in two, three weeks, then put your cellphone light up. Ladies, if your pussy smell like water, put a cellphone light them up. Fellas, if you ain't sucking dick in the parking lot put your cellphone light up. Keep it real.[6]

The callout was widely, and rightfully, criticized for misinformation about the clinical progression of HIV/AIDS that DaBaby peddled to his massive audience. But, as Chappelle's reflections on the controversy bring to light, little to no consideration was given to how reactions to DaBaby's comments, and efforts to "cancel" him, reinforced the historical tendency of mainstream media and music industries to selectively police and license presumptively

---

3. *The Closer* is the last of five specials that Chappelle recorded as part of a multimillion-dollar deal inked with Netflix in 2016.

4. Bogart et al., "Covid-19-Related Medical Mistrust."

5. Chappelle, *The Closer*.

6. DaBaby, Rolling Loud Concert. See also DaBaby, "DaBaby's Message"; and "DaBaby Goes On Homophobic Rant."

offensive speech by artists. To these observations, I would add that the fall-out from DaBaby's speech reinforced the tendency of mainstream media and music outlets to coopt and obscure HIV/AIDS and present it as a health condition that exclusively affects LGBTQ people and communities.

The Elton John AIDS Foundation, for example, condemned DaBaby for spreading "HIV misinformation and homophobia," declaring that both "have no place in the music industry."[7] Dua Lipa, who collaborated with DaBaby on the critical and commercial hit "Levitating,"[8] put out a statement saying that she was "surprised and horrified" by his comments, did not see how they could be associated with the artist she worked with, and stood "100% with the LGBTQ community. [. . .] We need to come together to fight the stigma and ignorance around HIV/AIDS," she concluded.[9] Shortly after DaBaby's comments went viral, GLAAD (the Gay and Lesbian Alliance Against Defamation) released the results of a survey that measured the number and substance of media coverage of issues impacting LGBTQ people and condemned the disproportionate attention given to DaBaby's misinformation in comparison to "the efforts and victories of people fighting for LGBTQ populations and those with HIV."[10] Public maintenance of HIV/AIDS as (primarily or exclusively) LGBTQ-related, even when advocating for education that combats the adverse effects of discriminatory attitudes on people living with HIV or AIDS, atomizes the disease and enacts an erasure of the range and complexities of black women's lived experiences in relation to the long history of HIV/AIDS.[11] This is one reason why both the likes of DaBaby's comments and critical responses to such comments warrant further scrutiny.

This is also why I believe that the commendable efforts by pharmaceutical companies to mainstream the visibility of LGBTQ people living with HIV/AIDS in PrEP and ART advertisements warrant further inquiry. A few years ago, when I began this study, there were virtually no advertisements for Cabenuva, Dovato, Apretude, or Biktarvy[12] running on cable networks or

---

7. Elton John AIDS Foundation, "HIV Misinformation."

8. Lipa, "Levitating."

9. Lipa, "Instagram Stories."

10. Gibbons et al., "South Lags in LGBTQ Coverage," 3a.

11. This project's consideration of the correlates of HIV/AIDS risk for black women countervails the spurious perspective on vaginal health also voiced by DaBaby. A cursory review of statements issued in the aftermath of his comments reveals no criticism of his exclusionary call to women whose pussies "smell like water."

12. Apretude is an HIV-1 pre-exposure prophylaxis approved for use by the FDA in December 2021; Biktarvy, Cabenuva, and Dovato are prescription medications for treating HIV and AIDS, respectively approved for use by the FDA in February 2018, January 2021, and April 2019. The timing of FDA approval may explain why advertisements for these medications were rare a few years ago, but it does not explain the lack of representation of black women.

streaming services. Since December 2022, when I began tracking them, commercials for these products have featured during prime and nonpeak viewing hours on ABC, CBS, NBC, CNN, USA, TNT, and FOX, as well as on HULU, Peacock, and Starz.[13] This is obvious progress. While black women are visible in some of these commercials, they appear more frequently as support to HIV-positive black, white, and Hispanic men than as people living with HIV or AIDS. Moreover, whereas narration that accompanies these commercials regularly gives voice to the experiences of HIV-positive men, black women rarely speak to their stories with HIV/AIDS.[14] This study has consistently clarified the necessity of seeing and hearing the range of black women's experiences with HIV/AIDS.

In keeping with this objective, I want to return briefly to *The Closer,* and the part of the performance where Chappelle acknowledges his investment in "gender constructs" and maintains that he is "not indifferent to the suffering" of others. Sarah Balkin suggests that these concessions, coupled with Chappelle's seeming conciliation to the LGBTQ community at the start of the special, ultimately reveal him leaning into "the persona of a homophobic, transphobic comedian" and making "a platform out of [. . .] accusations leveled at him following the release of *Sticks and Stones,*"[15] the 2019 Netflix comedy special that brought Chappelle under fire for using the experiences of gay and transgender people as punchlines. As I see it, Chappelle's "lean into" current debates at the crosscurrents of identity politics, sexual politics, and naming[16] underscores the overarching, affirmative perspective that *The*

---

13. I first noticed these advertisements running on December 9, 2022, and began documenting the dates and times that I encountered them on December 29, 2022. Noteworthy examples include a Biktarvy ad that ran on TNT on May 2, 2023, during the first game of the Lakers-Warriors Western Conference Semi-Finals and an ad for Cabenuva that ran on FOX while I sat in a nail salon at 9:45 a.m. on May 23, 2023.

14. See, for example, Cabenuva, "Orlando." A notable exception is a recent commercial for Biktarvy that opens with a compilation of voices and images, which includes a black female, before transitioning to a voiceover. Biktarvy, "Testimonial."

15. Balkin, "On Quitting."

16. As briefly noted in the introduction, debates over gender definitions and the sexuality spectrum date back at least to the turn of the twentieth century. Chappelle rejects the notion that people not assigned "female" at birth can claim the signifier "woman" at the same time that he decries the enactment of laws that purport to diminish or otherwise impinge on the constitutional rights and entitlements of people who identify as nonbinary and/or trans. Federal jurisprudence continues largely to develop in support of this legal position. See, for example, *Bostock v. Clayton County, Georgia,* 140 S.Ct. 1731 (June 15, 2020); *Gloucester County School Board v. G.G., by His Next Friend and Mother, Deirdre Grimm,* 137 S. Ct. 1239 (March 6, 2017); *A.M. By Her Mother and Next Friend, E.M. v. Indianapolis Public Schools and Superintendent,* 617 F.Supp.3d 950 (July 26, 2022); and *Brandt v. Rutledge,* 2023 WL 4073727 (June 20, 2023). Exceptions to this trend include the 6th Circuit Federal Court of Appeals' and 11th

Closer takes on the right that people of diverse backgrounds and experiences have to hold different opinions and the obligation that people of diverse backgrounds and experiences have to acknowledge and respect each other's shared humanities. This insight is essential for thinking about black women's health in the current age of hip hop and HIV/AIDS, particularly in light of evidence showing that cisgender and transgender black women face equally alarming rates of risk of exposure to HIV/AIDS, common barriers to HIV/AIDS-related care, and similar impediments to accessing resources that impact their overall health statuses.

A recent study of adverse childhood events (ACEs), gender-based violence, intimate partner violence, and housing insecurity as correlates to risk of exposure to HIV and other sexually transmitted diseases and infections among a group of 230 black women, for example, found that one-third of study participants "experienced 3 to 9 ACEs" and 40 percent had been exposed to some form of adult sexual violence. Forty-one percent of the study group reported having multiple comorbidities that included exposure to an STI/STD.[17] A similar study measuring depression among a group of black women living with HIV/AIDS and the effects of "mindfulness-based therapy" on addressing mental health within this demographic found shared experiences with adverse childhood events, family stressors, and pressure to conform to the strong-blackwoman schema among women in the group identifying as cisgender and women identifying as transgender.[18] These findings are consistent with reports from a 2021 study that comparatively measured HIV-testing behaviors among cisgender and transgender black women.[19] Similarly to the studies of HIV/AIDS risk among cisgender black women and girls cited throughout this book, the 2021 study counted exposure to intimate partner violence, substance use, and high-risk sexual behavior among the confounding health factors for transgender black women living with HIV. The results of the study showed negligible differences in "reported lifetime HIV testing" for cisgender

---

Circuit Federal Court of Appeals' recent decisions to deny injunctive relief to plaintiffs seeking to enjoin state laws denying youth access to gender-affirming care to go into effect. See *L.W., by and through her parents and next friends, Samantha Williams and Brian Williams, et al. v. Jonathan Thomas Skrmetti, in his official capacity as the Tennessee Attorney General and Reporter, et al.* (6th Cir. Ct. of Appeals, 3:23-cv-00376) and *Paul A. Eknes-Tucker, et al. v. Governor of the State of Alabama, et al.* (11th Cir. Ct. of Appeals, 22-11707).

 17. Tsuyuki et al., "Characterising a Syndemic," 9.

 18. Hunter-Jones et al., "Process and Outcome Evaluation," 592.

 19. Rutledge et al., "HIV Testing."

and transgender black women.[20] As I see it, debates over who can and should claim use of pronouns and gender signifiers are immaterial to the question of whether alliances across the spectrum of gender and sexual identities should build to address the range of issues impacting quality of life for black people living with HIV and AIDS, or at risk of infection. The obvious answer to this question is "yes." This book has proffered hip hop feminism as an indispensable mechanism for building these alliances so as to sustainably cultivate and act on knowledge that fosters the health and well-being of all people affected by HIV/AIDS.

---

20. Other studies have found more substantial differences in measures of the experiences of black cisgender and black transgender women living with HIV/AIDS. Pamela Klein, Demetrios Psihopaidas, Jessica Xavier, and Stacey Cohen, for example, found that black cisgender women living with HIV were more likely than black transgender women living with HIV to be retained in care and to achieve viral suppression status. See Klein et al., "HIV-Related Outcome Disparities." Klein and colleagues acknowledge the limitations of their findings due to a "lack of robust transgender data collection and research." Jaleah Rutledge, Kaston Anderson-Carpenter, and Jae Puckett also highlight the need for more research that addresses the "distinct and independent" experiences of trans people and that utilizes analytic methods that do not take "the typical, dichotomous understanding of gender" as a given. Rutledge et al., "HIV Testing and Associated Characteristics," 150.

APPENDIX

Empirical Studies of Black Women, Silence, Shame, Stigma, and HIV/AIDS, 1986–2006

TABLE 1. Studies from PubMed.gov, 1986–2006

SHORT TITLE	AUTHOR(S)	PUBLICATION	YEAR/ VOLUME	SYNOPSIS
"Prevention Implications of AIDS Discourses among South African Women"	Anna Strebel	*AIDS Education and Prevention*	1996 8(4)	Study based on focus-group discussions with 95 South African women; examines effects of stigma on denial of risk
"Resources, Stigma, and Patterns of Disclosure"	Richard Sowell et al.	*Public Health Nursing*	1997 14(1)	Interview-based study of 56 black and 26 white HIV-positive women residing in Georgia; examines needs and access to care based on geography
"Patterns of Resistance: African American Mothers and Adult Children with HIV Illness"	Joyceen Boyle et al.	*Scholarly Inquiry for Nursing Practice*	1999 13(2)	Interview-based study of 14 rural-based black mothers of HIV-infected children; examines factors influencing caregiving and support

(continued)

132 • APPENDIX

SHORT TITLE	AUTHOR(S)	PUBLICATION	YEAR/ VOLUME	SYNOPSIS
"Hope and Coping in HIV-Infected African American Women"	Kenneth Phillips et al.	*Journal of National Black Nurses Association*	2000 11(2)	Examines the relationship between hope and coping strategies used by HIV-positive black women
"Levels of Hope in HIV-Infected African American Women"	Kenneth Phillips et al.	*Clinical Excellence for Nurse Practitioners*	2000 4(2)	Interview-based study of 49 HIV-positive African American women; examines hope and quality of relationship with primary care physician
"Physical and Mental Health in African American Mothers with HIV"	Margaret Miles et al.	*Journal of Association of Nurses in AIDS Care*	2001 12(4)	Questionnaire-based study of 34 black women participants over period of 2 years to assess physical and mental health
"Calculating the Risks and Benefits of Disclosure"	Beth Black et al.	*Journal of Obstetric, Gynecologic, and Neonatal Nursing*	2002 31(6)	Survey-based study of 48 HIV-positive black women; analyzes threat of stigma and feelings of shame influencing willingness to disclose status
"Stigma, Disclosure, and Psychological Functioning"	Heather Clark et al.	*Women's Health*	2003 38(4)	Qualitative study of perception of stigma on psychological functioning and disclosure for 98 HIV-infected and 146 noninfected black women
"HIV Testing Attitudes, AIDS Stigma, and Voluntary HIV Counselling"	Seth Kalichman et al.	*Sexually Transmitted Infections*	2003 79(6)	Survey-based study of 224 black men and 276 black women residing in Cape Town township; assesses attitudes toward testing and testing history

(continued)

SHORT TITLE	AUTHOR(S)	PUBLICATION	YEAR/VOLUME	SYNOPSIS
"HIV Self-Care Symptom Management Intervention"	Margaret Miles et al.	*Nursing Research*	2003 52(6)	Clinical trial in which 109 black women enrolled; study designed to measure efficacy of an HIV self-care symptom management intervention in reducing emotional distress and improving health
"Traditional Beliefs about the Causes of AIDS and AIDS-Related Stigma in South Africa"	Seth Kalichman et al.	*AIDS Care*	2004 16(5)	Survey-based study of 487 black South African men and women; examines knowledge base related to cause(s) of HIV transmission/infection
"Women from Africa Living with HIV in London"	Jane Anderson et al.	*AIDS Care*	2004 16(1)	Interview- and questionnaire-based study of 62 women from 11 African countries residing in the UK; examines impact of stigma and religion on access to care and resiliency
"Experience of African American Women Living with HIV"	Anne Norris et al.	*Journal of the Association of Nurses in AIDS Care*	2005 16(2)	Focus-group-based study of four black women living with HIV; examines impact of storytelling through film as intervention
"The Politics of Invisibility"	Elizabeth Arend	*Journal of Homosexuality*	2005 49(1)	Interview- and survey-based study of 14 black and 2 Latina women of color who have sex with women; examines coping and perceptions of access to care
"Constrained but Not Determined"	Aaron Buseh et al.	*Women's Health*	2006 44(3)	Interview-based study of 29 HIV-positive black women; explores experiences with and responses to stigma

(continued)

SHORT TITLE	AUTHOR(S)	PUBLICATION	YEAR/ VOLUME	SYNOPSIS
"Social Construction of Gender Roles, Gender-Based Violence, and HIV/AIDS"	Anna Strebel et al.	*Journal of Social Aspects of HIV/ AIDS*	2006 3(3)	Interview-based study of 78 African men and women; examines perceptions of gender roles and risk for gender-based violence and exposure to HIV
"Perceived Social Support and HIV/AIDS Medication"	Lorece Edwards	*Qualitative Health Research*	2006 16(5)	Semi-structured interview study of 33 HIV-positive black women; examines perceptions of social support for accessing and sustaining treatment
"In Our Grandmother's Footsteps"	Donna Shambley-Ebron et al.	*Advances in Nursing Science*	2006 29(3)	Interview-based study of 10 HIV-positive black women with one or more HIV-infected children; examines "strong black woman" buy-in as source of resiliency

APPENDIX · 135

TABLE 2. Studies from PsychArticles, 1986–2006

SHORT TITLE	AUTHOR(S)	PUBLICATION	YEAR/ VOLUME	SYNOPSIS
"Culturally-Tailored HIV/ AIDS Risk Reduction Messages Targeted to African American Urban Women"	Seth Kalichman et al.	*Journal of Consulting and Clinical Psychology*	1993 61(2)	PSAs with culturally relevant and relatable deliveries used to test impact on motivation to know status/get tested among 106 low-income black women
"Medical Adherence among Prenatal, HIV-Seropositive, African American Women"	Darlene Shelton et al.	*Family Systems Medicine*	1993 11(4)	Interview-based study of 4 HIV-positive black women and their families to determine relationship between kinship networks and access to and use of care
"Context Framing to Enhance HIV-Antibody-Testing Messages Targeted to African American Women"	Seth Kalichman et al.	*Health Psychology*	1995 14(3)	Video messaging with culturally relevant and relatable deliveries used to test impact on motivation to know status/get tested among 100 black women
"Women's Self-Disclosure of HIV Infection"	Jane Simoni et al.	*Journal of Consulting and Clinical Psychology*	1995 63(3)	Survey-based study of 65 women of diverse ethnicities to assess factors contributing to disclosure/ nondisclosure to family members and within sexual networks
"Experimental Component Analysis of a Behavioral HIV Prevention-Intervention for Inner-City Women"	Seth Kalichman et al.	*Journal of Consulting and Clinical Psychology*	1996 64(4)	Sexual communication and self-management skills assessed in randomly allotted group of 87 inner-city women to determine impact on knowledge and risk behavior
"Distress and Coping among Women with HIV Infection"	Mark S. Kaplan et al.	*American Journal of Orthopsychiatry*	1997 67(1)	Stress coping mechanism analyzed among multiethnic group of 53 women living with HIV/AIDS

(continued)

136 • APPENDIX

SHORT TITLE	AUTHOR(S)	PUBLICATION	YEAR/ VOLUME	SYNOPSIS
"The Impact of Maternal HIV Infection on Parenting in Inner-City African American Families"	Beth Kotchick et al.	*Journal of Family Psychology*	1997 11(4)	Parenting behavior and impact on children's psychosocial development assessed in study groups of 86 HIV-positive women and 148 HIV-negative women
"Family Constellation and Ethnicity"	Gail Wyatt et al.	*Journal of Family Psychology*	1998 12(1)	Analyzes relationship among sexual risk-taking, family formation, and economic stability in randomly collected sample of 835 women of various ethnicities
"Children Whose Mothers Are HIV Infected"	Shannon Dorsey et al.	*Journal of Family Psychology*	1999 13(1)	Examines impact of HIV-positive status on mothering and child psychosocial development in study group of 249 inner-city HIV-positive black women
"The Gynecological, Reproductive, and Sexual Health of HIV-Positive Women"	Gail Wyatt et al.	*Cultural Diversity and Ethnic Minority Psychology*	1999 5(3)	Comparatively analyzes intersecting health issues in group of 290 HIV-positive women of diverse ethnicities
"Motherhood in the Context of HIV Infection"	Tanya Tompkins et al.	*Cultural Diversity and Ethnic Minority Psychology*	1999 5(3)	Comparatively analyzes family structure and parenting challenges in group of 199 HIV-positive women of diverse ethnicities
"Psychiatric Disorders in African American Men and Women Living with HIV"	Hector Myers et al.	*Cultural Diversity and Ethnic Minority Psychology*	1999 5(3)	Comparatively examines prevalence of major psychiatric disorder, dependency, stressors, and coping in 234 black men and 135 black women
"Impact of Relationship Violence, HIV, and Ethnicity on Adjustment in Women"	Julie Axelrod et al.	*Cultural Diversity and Ethnic Minority Psychology*	1999 5(3)	Comparatively analyzes impact of domestic violence, HIV, and ethnicity on psychological distress in study group of 415 women of diverse ethnicities

(continued)

APPENDIX • 137

SHORT TITLE	AUTHOR(S)	PUBLICATION	YEAR/ VOLUME	SYNOPSIS
"Infant Birth Weight among Women with or at High Risk of HIV Infection"	Jeannette Ickovics et al.	*Health Psychology*	2000 19(6)	Examines correlates between child birth weight and HIV status for pregnant women
"HIV Prevention for Intimate Couples"	Nabila El-Bassel et al.	*Families, Systems, and Health*	2001 19(4)	Examines impact of participation in relationship-based HIV-intervention program on sex practices of 217 black and Latino heterosexual couples
"Spirituality and Psychological Adaptation among Women with HIV/ AIDS"	Jane Simoni et al.	*Journal of Counseling Psychology*	2002 49(2)	Interview-based study of 230 HIV-positive black and Puerto Rican women; examines spirituality as coping mechanism
"Structural Ecosystems Therapy for HIV-Seropositive African American Women"	Jose Szapocznik et al.	*Journal of Consulting and Clinical Psychology*	2004 72(2)	Examines impact of structural ecosystems therapy on reducing psychological distress among HIV-positive black women

BIBLIOGRAPHY

Adams, Joëlla, Mark Lurie, Maximilian King, Kathleen Brady, Sandro Galea, Samuel Friedman, Maria Khan, and Brandon Marshall. "Potential Drivers of HIV Acquisition in African-American Women Related to Mass Incarceration: An Agent-Based Modelling Study." *BMC Public Health* 18 (2018): 1387. https://doi.org/10.1186/s12889-018-6304-x.

Aguayo-Romero, Rodrigo. "(Re)centering Black Feminism into Intersectionality Research." *American Journal of Public Health* 111 (January 2021): 101–3.

Akintobi, Tabia, Jennie Trotter, Donoria Evans, Tarita Johnson, Nastassia Laster, DeBran Jacobs, and Tandeca King. "Applications in Bridging the Gap: A Community-Based Partnership to Address Sexual Health Disparities among African American Youth in the South." *Journal of Community Health* 36, no. 3 (2011): 486–94.

Allen, Anita L. *Why Privacy Isn't Everything: Feminist Reflections on Personal Accountability.* New York: Rowman & Littlefield, 2003.

Alonzo, Angelo, and Nancy Reynolds. "Stigma, HIV and AIDS: An Exploration and Elaboration of a Stigma Trajectory." *Social Science and Medicine* 41, no. 3 (1995): 303–15.

Anderson, Martin, and Robert Morris. "HIV and Adolescents." *Pediatric Annals* 22, no. 7 (July 1993): 436–46.

Androutsopoulos, Jannis. "Language and the Three Spheres of Hip Hop." In *Global Linguistic Flows: Hip Hop Cultures, Youth Identities, and the Politics of Language,* edited by H. Samy Alim, Awad Ibrahim, and Alastair Pennycook, 43–62. New York: Routledge, 2009.

Archer, John. "Sex Differences in Aggression between Heterosexual Partners: A Meta-Analytic Review." *Psychological Bulletin* 126 (2000): 651–80.

Arledge, Elizabeth. *Out of Control: AIDS in Black America.* New York: The Documentary Group, 2006.

Armstrong, Linda. "Black Actresses Create Candid Drama about HIV/AIDS." *New York Amsterdam News,* September 15–21, 2005, 21, 23.

140 • BIBLIOGRAPHY

———. "Theatre: Women with AIDS Infected by Callous Husbands." *New York Amsterdam News,* December 22–28, 2005, 23.

Arora, Kavita, and Barbara Wilkinson. "Eliminating Perinatal Transmission in the United States: The Impact of Stigma." *Maternal Child Health Journal* 21 (2017): 393–97.

Arrington-Sanders, Renata, Aubrey Alvarenga, Noya Galai, Joyell Arscott, Andrea Wirtz, Rashida Carr, Alexander Lopez, Chris Beyrer, Rebecca Nessen, and David Celentano. "Social Determinants of Transactional Sex in a Sample of Young Black and Latinx Sexual Minority Cisgender Men and Transgender Women." *Journal of Adolescent Health* 70, no. 2 (February 2022): 275–81.

Asante, M. K. *It's Bigger Than Hip Hop: The Rise of the Post-Hip Hop Generation.* New York: St. Martin's Press, 2009.

Avery, Byllye. "Breathing Life into Ourselves: The Evolution of the National Black Women's Health Project." In *Feminism and Community,* edited by Penny Wise and Marilyn Friedman, 147–53. Philadelphia: Temple University Press, 1995.

———. Interview by Loretta Ross. Voices of Feminism Oral History Project, Provincetown, MA, July 21–22, 2005.

Aziz, Mariam, and Kimberly Smith. "Challenges and Successes in Linking HIV-Infected Women to Care in the United States." *Clinical Infectious Diseases* 52, no. 2 (January 15, 2011): S231–S237.

Aziz, Sulayman, and David Sweat. "Subsequent HIV Diagnosis Risk after Syphilis in a Southern Black Population." *Sexually Transmitted Diseases* 45, no. 10 (October 2018): 643–47.

Bailey, Marlon. "Whose Body Is It: On the Cultural Possibilities of a Radical Black Sexual Praxis." *American Quarterly* 71, no 1 (March 2019): 161–69.

Balkin, Sarah. "On Quitting: Dave Chappelle's The Closer and Hannah Gadsby's Nanette." *TDR* 67, no 1 (2023): 149–66.

Ballom, Te Cora. "Prevention of Overweight and Obesity among African American Girls." In *Black Girls and Adolescence: Facing the Challenges,* edited by Catherine Fisher Collins, 75–95. Santa Barbara, CA: Praeger, 2015.

Bambara, Toni Cade. Preface to *The Black Woman: An Anthology.* New York: Signet, 1970.

Banks, Nina. "Black Women in the United States and Unpaid Collective Work: Theorizing the Community as a Site of Production." *Review of Black Political Economy* 47, no. 4 (2020): 343–62.

Barch, Deanna, Michael Harms, Rebecca Tillman, Elizabeth Hawkey, and Joan Luby. "Early Childhood Depression, Emotion Regulation, Episodic Memory, and Hippocampal Development." *Journal of Abnormal Psychology* 128, no. 1 (2019): 81–95.

Bedimo, Ariane, Marsha Bennett, Patricia Kissinger, and Rebecca Clark. "Understanding Barriers to Condom Usage among HIV Infected African American Women." *Journal of the Association of Nurses in AIDS Care* 9 (1998): 48–58.

Biktarvy. "Testimonial." Commercial Archivist, May 2, 2023. YouTube video, 1:00. https://www.youtube.com/watch?v=p7QPHrqaaYA.

Billboard. "Year-End Charts." https://www.billboard.com/charts/year-end/.

Black Women's Health Conference. https://bwhconference.com/.

Blankenship, Kim, Amy Smoyer, Sarah Bray, and Kristin Mattocks. "Black-White Disparities in HIV/AIDS: The Role of Drug Policy and Corrections Systems." *Journal of Health Care for the Poor and Underserved* 16, no. 4B (2005): 140–56.

BIBLIOGRAPHY • 141

Bodell, Lindsay, Thomas Joiner, and Nicholas Ialongo. "Longitudinal Association between Childhood Impulsivity and Bulimic Symptoms in African American Adolescent Girls." *Journal of Consulting and Clinical Psychology* 80, no. 2 (2012): 313–16.

Bogart, Laura, Bisola Ojikutu, Keshav Tyagi, David Klein, Matt Mutchler, Lu Dong, Sean Lawrence, Damone Thomas, and Sarah Kellman. "Covid-19-Related Medical Mistrust, Health Impacts, and Potential Vaccine Hesitancy among Black Americans Living with HIV." *Journal of Acquired Immune Deficiency Syndrome* 86, no. 2 (February 2021): 200–207.

Borrego, Silvia Pilar Castro. "Re(Claiming) Subjectivity and Transforming the Politics of Silence through the Search for Wholeness in *PUSH* by Sapphire." *ATLANTIS: Journal of the Spanish Association of Anglo-American Studies* 36, no. 2 (December 2014): 147–59.

Brawner, Bridgette, Loretta Sweet Jemmott, Gina Wingood, Alicia Lozano, and Alexandra Hanlon. "Project GOLD: A Pilot Randomized Controlled Trial of a Novel Psychoeducational HIV/STI Prevention Intervention for Heterosexually Active Black Youth." *Research in Nursing and Health* 42, no. 1 (February 2019): 8–28.

Brief, Deborah J., A. R. Bolinger, M. J. Vielhauer, J. A. Berger-Greenstein, E. E. Morgan, S. M. Brady, L. M. Buondonno, and T. M. Keane for the HIV/AIDS Treatment Adherence, Health Outcomes and Costs Study Group. "Understanding the Interface of HIV, Trauma, Post-Traumatic Stress Disorder, and Substance Use and Its Implications for Health Outcomes." *AIDS Care* 16, no. 1 (2004): 97–120. https://www.tandfonline.com/doi/full/10.1080/09540120412301315259.

Brijnath, Biana. "It's about TIME: Engendering AIDS in Africa." *Culture, Health, and Sexuality* (July–August 2007): 371–86.

Brock Akil, Mara. "Mara Brock Akil on Bringing *Girlfriends* to Netflix, Conversations with Culture, History + More." Interview by Angela Yee, Charlamagne Tha God, and DJ Envy. *The Breakfast Club,* September 11, 2020. YouTube video, 51:58. https://www.youtube.com/watch?v=vBejxZLJgio.

———. "We All Fall Down: A Closer Look at Trick or Truth." *Girlfriends: The Second Season.* Hollywood: CBS DVD, Paramount Home Entertainment, 2007.

Brown, Ruth Nicole. *Black Girlhood Celebration: Toward a Hip-Hop Feminist Pedagogy.* New York: Peter Lang, 2009.

Brunswick, A. F. "Health and Substance Use Behavior: The Longitudinal Harlem Health Study." *Journal of Addiction Disorder* 11, no. 1 (1991): 119–37.

Buehler, James, Debra Hanson, and Susan Chu. "The Reporting of HIV/AIDS Deaths in Women." *American Journal of Public Health* 82, no. 11 (November 1992): 1500–1505.

Cabenuva. "Orlando: Living with HIV." Commercial Archivist, April 21, 2023. YouTube video, 1:00. https://www.youtube.com/watch?v=xo-93UipPfI.

Carpenter, Faedra. "An Interview with Gwendolyn D. Pough." *Callaloo* 29, no. 3 (2006): 808–14.

Castro, Kenneth G., John W. Ward, Laurence Slutsker, James W. Buehler, Harold W. Jaffe, and Ruth L. Berkelman. "1993 Revised Classification System for HIV Infection and Expanded Surveillance Case Definition for AIDS among Adolescents and Adults." *MMWR* 41 (December 18, 1992). https://www.cdc.gov/mmwr/preview/mmwrhtml/00018871.htm.

Centers for Disease Control and Prevention. "Cases of HIV Infection and AIDS in the United States." *HIV Surveillance Report* 14 (2002). https://www.cdc.gov/hiv/pdf/library/reports/surveillance/cdc-hiv-surveillance-report-2002-vol-14.pdf.

———. "Current Trends Mortality Attributable to HIV Infection/AIDS—United States, 1981–1990." *Morbidity and Mortality Weekly Report* 40, no. 3 (January 25, 1991): 41–44.

142 • BIBLIOGRAPHY

———. "Diagnoses of HIV Infection in the United States and Dependent Areas." *HIV Surveillance Report* 31 (2018). Updated May 2020. https://www.cdc.gov/hiv/library/reports/hiv-surveillance/vol-31/index.html.

———. "Diagnosis of HIV Infection in the United States and Dependent Areas, 2020." *HIV Surveillance Report* 33 (2021). https://www.cdc.gov/hiv/library/reports/hiv-surveillance/vol-33/index.html.

———. "Epidemiologic Notes and Reports Persistent, Generalized Lymphadenopathy among Homosexual Males." *Morbidity and Mortality Weekly Report* 31, no. 19 (1982): 249–51.

———. "Estimated HIV Incidence and Prevalence in the United States, 2015–2019." *HIV Surveillance Supplemental Report* 26, no. 1 (2021). http://www.cdc.gov/hiv/library/reports/hiv-surveillance.html.

———. *Morbidity and Mortality Weekly Reports* 30, no. 21 (June 5, 1981): 1–3. https://www.cdc.gov/mmwr/preview/mmwrhtml/june_5.htm.

———. "Mortality Attributable to HIV Infection among Persons Aged 25–44 Years—United States, 1994." *Morbidity and Mortality Weekly Report* 45, no. 6 (February 16, 1996): 121–25.

———. "Notice to Readers: National Black HIV/AIDS Awareness Day, February 7, 2004." *Mortality and Morbidity Weekly Report* 53, no. 4 (February 6, 2004): 86. https://www.cdc.gov/mmwr/preview/mmwrhtml/mm5304a5.htm.

Chang, Jeff. *Can't Stop, Won't Stop: A History of the Hip-Hop Generation*. New York: Picador, 2005.

Chang, Lucas, Kaya de Barbaro, and Gedeon Deák. "Contingencies between Infants' Gaze, Vocal, and Manual Actions and Mothers' Object-Naming: Longitudinal Changes from 4 to 9 Months." *Developmental Neuropsychology* 41, no. 5–8 (July–December 2016): 342–61.

Chappelle, Dave. *The Closer*. Netflix, October 5, 2021.

Cheater, M. "AIDS Zeros In on Women and Children." *World Watch* 3, no. 6 (November–December 1990): 34–35.

Chinn, Juanita, Iman Martin, and Nicole Redmond. "Health Equity among Black Women in the United States." *Journal of Women's Health* 30, no. 2 (2021): 212–19.

Christian, Barbara. "The Race for Theory." *Cultural Critique* 6 (Spring 1987): 51–63.

Clair, Brittany. *Carrying On: Another School of Thought on Pregnancy and Health*. New Brunswick, NJ: Rutgers University Press, 2022.

Cohen, Cathy J. *The Boundaries of Blackness: AIDS and the Breakdown of Black Politics*. Chicago: University of Chicago Press, 1999.

Cokal, Susann. "Review of *PUSH*." *Review of Contemporary Fiction* 17, no. 1 (Spring 1997): 186.

Collins, Patricia Hill. *Black Feminist Thought: Knowledge, Consciousness, and the Politics of Empowerment*. New York: Routledge, 1990.

———. *From Black Power to Hip Hop: Racism, Nationalism, and Feminism*. Philadelphia: Temple University Press, 2006.

———. "Learning from the Outside Within: The Sociological Significance of Black Feminist Thought." *Social Forces* 33, no. 6 (October–December 1986): S14–S32.

Cooper, Anna Julia. *A Voice from the South: By a Black Woman of the South*. Oxford: Oxford University Press, 1990. First published 1892.

Cooper, Brittney. *Beyond Respectability: The Intellectual Thought of Race Women*. Urbana: University of Illinois Press, 2017.

———. "'Maybe I'll Be a Poet, Rapper': Hip Hop Feminism and Literary Aesthetics in *PUSH*." *African American Review* 46, no. 1 (Spring 2013): 55–69.

Copeland, Valire, Christina Newhill, Lovie Jackson Foster, Betty Braxter, Willa Doswell, Allen Lewis, and Shaun Eack. "Major Depressive Disorder and Cardiovascular Disease in African-American Women." *Journal of Social Service Research* 43, no. 5 (2017): 624–34.

Corneille, Maya, Amie Ashcroft, and Faye Belgrave. "What's Culture Got to Do with It? Prevention Programs for African American Adolescent Girls." *Journal of Health Care for the Poor and Underserved* 16, no. 4 (November 2005): 38–47.

Crenshaw, Kimberle. "Mapping the Margins: Intersectionality, Identity Politics, and Violence against Women of Color." *Stanford Law Review* 43, no. 6 (July 1991): 1241–99.

CrescentCare. https://www.crescentcare.org/.

Crooks, Natasha, Barbara King, and Audrey Tluczek. "Protecting Young Black Female Sexuality." *Cultural Health Sex* 22, no. 8 (August 2020): 871–86.

Curran, James, Harold Jaffe, Ann Hardy, W. Meade Morgan, Richard Selik, and Timothy Dondero. "Epidemiology of HIV Infection and AIDS in the United States." *Science* 239 (February 5, 1988): 610–16.

DaBaby. "DaBaby's Message to His Gay/Homo Fans at Rolling Loud: Rant and Response Full Video." Chris Song, July 31, 2021. YouTube video, 4:40. https://www.youtube.com/watch?v=S6RJ393ahPA.

———. Rolling Loud Concert. Hard Rock Stadium, Miami Gardens, FL, July 25, 2021.

"DaBaby Goes on Homophobic Rant during Rolling Loud Set." *TMZ,* July 26, 2021. https://www.tmz.com/watch/2021-07-26-072621-dababy-1211631/.

Dagbovie, Sika. "From Living to Eat to Writing to Live: Metaphors of Consumption and Production in Sapphire's *PUSH*." *African American Review* 44, no. 3 (Fall 2011): 435–52.

Dale, Sannisha, Yue Pan, Nadine Gardner, Sherence Saunders, Ian Wright, Cheri Nelson, Jingxin Liu, Arnetta Phillips, Gail Ironson, Allan Rodriguez, Maria Alcaide, Steven Safren, and Daniel Feaster. "Daily Microaggressions and Related Distress among Black Women Living with HIV during the Onset of the Covid-19 Pandemic and Black Lives Matter." *AIDS Behavior* (May 27, 2021): 1–8.

Dancy, Barbara. "*Focus on Solutions*: A Community-Based Mother/Daughter HIV Risk-Reduction Intervention." In *African American Women and HIV/AIDS: Critical Responses,* edited by Dorie Gilbert and Ednita Wright, 183–89. Westport, CT: Praeger, 2003.

Danielson, Carla, Kate Walsh, Jenna McCauley, Kenneth Ruggiero, Jennifer Brown, Jessica Sales, Eve Rose, Gina Wingood, and Ralph DiClemente. "HIV-Related Sexual Risk Behavior among African American Girls." *Journal of Women's Health* 23, no. 5 (2014): 413–19.

David, Marlo. "'I Got Self, Pencil, and Notebook': Literacy and Maternal Desire in Sapphire's *PUSH*." *Tulsa Studies in Women's Literature* 35, no. 1 (Spring 2016): 173–99.

Davis, Angela Michaela. "Quitting Hip Hop." *ESSENCE,* October 2004, 155.

Davis, Dana Ain. *Reproductive Injustice: Racism, Pregnancy, and Premature Birth.* New York: New York University Press, 2019.

Des Jarlais, Don, Samuel Friedman, and Jo Sotheran. "The First City: HIV among Intravenous Drug Users in New York City." In *AIDS: The Making of a Chronic Disease,* edited by Elizabeth Fee and Daniel Fox, 279–95. Berkeley: University of California Press, 1992.

Diallo, Dazon Dixon. "Dr. Dazon Dixon Diallo: Women and AIDS: Surviving Voices." National AIDS Memorial, December 5, 2017. YouTube video, 5:39. https://www.youtube.com/watch?v=OAdrp3fdfqM.

———. "Reflections of a Human Rights Educator." *Meridians* 4, no. 2 (2004): 124–28.

DiClemente, Ralph, and Gina Wingood. "A Randomized Controlled Trial of an HIV Sexual Risk Reduction Intervention for Young African American Women." *JAMA* 274 (1995): 1271–76.

Diesel, Jill, Amy Peterson, and Thomas Peterman. "Reported Chlamydia and Gonorrhea are Decreasing among Young Black Women: Good News or Bad News? A Narrative Review." *Sexually Transmitted Diseases* 48, no. 12 (2021): e228–e235.

Donenberg, Geri, Erin Emerson, and Mary Ellen Mackesy-Amiti. "Sexual Risk among African American Girls: Psychopathology and Mother-Daughter Relationships." *Journal of Consulting and Clinical Psychology* 79, no. 2 (2011): 153–58.

Duffy, Lynne. "Suffering, Shame, and Silence: The Stigma of HIV/AIDS." *Journal of the Association of Nurses AIDS Care* 16, no. 1 (January–February 2005): 13–20. https://doi.org/10.1016/j.jana.2004.11.002.

Dugger, Celia W. "HIV Incidence Rises among Black Mothers: Infection Rate Drops for White Women." *New York Times*, May 1, 1992, B3.

Dunn, Stephanie. "A Hip Hop Afro-Feminist Aesthetic of Love: Sister Souljah's *The Coldest Winter Ever*." *Langston Hughes Review* 21 (Fall 2007): 39–53.

———. "The New Black Cultural Studies: Hip Hop Ghetto Lit, Feminism, Afro-Womanism, and Black Love in *The Coldest Winter Ever*." *Fire!!! The Multimedia Journal of Black Studies* 1, no. 1 (2012): 83–99.

Durham, Aisha, Brittany C. Cooper, and Susana M. Morris. "The Stage Hip-Hop Feminism Built: A New Directions Essay." *Signs* 38, no. 3 (Spring 2013): 721–37.

Duvernay, Ava, dir. *My Mic Sounds Nice: A Truth about Women in Hip Hop*. Forward Movement, 2010.

Edlin, Brian, Kathleen Irwin, Sairus Faruque, Clyde McCoy, Carl Word, Yolanda Serrano, James Inciardi, Benjamin Bowser, Robert Schilling, Scott Holmberg, and the Multicenter Crack Cocaine and HIV Infection Study Team. "Intersecting Epidemics—Crack Cocaine Use and HIV Infection Among Inner-City Young Adults." *New England Journal of Medicine* 331, no. 21 (November 24, 1994): 1422–27.

Elford, Jonathan, Jane Anderson, Cecilia Bukutu, and Fowzia Ibrahim. "HIV in East London: Ethnicity, Gender, and Risk: Design and Methods." *BMC Public Health* 9, no. 6 (June 2006). https://www.ncbi.nlm.nih.gov/pmc/articles/PMC1524742/pdf/1471-2458-6-150.pdf.

Ellerbrock, Tedd, Timothy Bush, Mary Chamberland, and Margaret Oxtoby. "Epidemiology of Women with AIDS in the United States, 1981 through 1990: A Comparison with Heterosexual Men with AIDS." *JAMA* 265 (1991): 2971–75.

Elton John AIDS Foundation. "HIV Misinformation and Homophobia Have No Place in the Music Industry." Instagram, July 28, 2021. https://www.instagram.com/p/CR35rNQjyPy/.

Ensor, Rosie, and Claire Hughes. "Content or Connectedness? Mother-Child Talk and Early Social Understanding." *Child Development* 79, no. 1 (January–February 2008): 201–16.

Espinosa, Mariola. "The Question of Racial Immunity to Yellow Fever in History and Historiography." *Social Science History* 38, no. 3–4 (Fall/Winter 2014): 437–53.

Evans, Reina, McKenzie Stokes, Elan Hope, Laura Widman, and Qiana Cryer-Coupet. "Parental Influence on Sexual Intentions of Black Adolescent Girls: Examining the Role of Gendered-Racial Socialization." *Journal of Family Psychology* 36, no. 2 (2022): 318–23.

Evans-Winter, Venus. *Black Feminism in Qualitative Inquiry*. New York: Routledge, 2019.

Ewing, Sarah, Angela Bryan, Tutu Alicante, P. Todd Korthius, Karen Judson, and Travis Lovejoy. "Three Integrated Elements of Empowerment: HIV Prevention with Sub-Saharan African Adolescent Females Involved in Transactional Sex." *Clinical Practice in Pediatric Psychology* 6, no 4 (2018): 355–63.

Fannin, Danai, Oscar Barbarin, and Elizabeth Crais. "Communicative Function Use of Preschoolers and Mothers from Differing Racial and Socioeconomic Groups." *Language, Speech and Hearing Services in Schools* 49 (April 2018): 306–19.

BIBLIOGRAPHY • 145

Farley, Christopher. "The Show Must Go On: Playwrights Danai Gurira and Nikkole Salter Hit the Stage to Give Voice to the AIDS Crisis Devastating Black Women." *ESSENCE* 31, no. 10 (2006): 138.

Finamore, Adrianna. "Geeking and Freaking: Black Women and the 1980s Crack Epidemic." *California History* 99, no. 2 (Summer 2022): 59–80.

Flatow, Sheryl. "Tales of Two Women." *Playbill*, July 20, 2006. https://playbill.com/article/tales-of-two-women-com-133862.

Ford, Kathleen, and Anne Norris. "Urban African American and Hispanic Adolescents and Young Adults: Who Do They Talk to About AIDS and Condoms? What Are They Learning?" *AIDS Education and Prevention* 3, no. 3 (Fall 1991): 197–206.

Foster, Pamela H. "Use of Stigma, Fear, and Denial in Development of a Framework for Prevention of HIV/AIDS in Rural African American Communities." *Family Community Health* 30, no. 4 (2007): 318–27.

Foucault, Michel. *The Care of the Self*. Vol. 3 of *The History of Sexuality*. New York: Knopf Doubleday Publishing Group, 1988.

———. *The Use of Pleasure*. Vol. 2 of *The History of Sexuality*. New York: Knopf Doubleday Publishing Group, 1986.

Freeman, Robert, Marya Gwadz, Elizabeth Silverman, Alexandra Kutnick, Noelle Leonard, Amanda Ritchie, Jennifer Reed, and Belkis Martinez. "Critical Race Theory as a Tool for Understanding Poor Engagement along the HIV Care Continuum among African American/Black and Hispanic Persons Living with HIV in the United States: A Qualitative Exploration." *International Journal for Equity in Health* 16 (2017). https://www.ncbi.nlm.nih.gov/pmc/articles/PMC5364619/pdf/12939_2017_Article_549.pdf.

Fullilove, Mindy. Foreword to *African American Women and HIV/AIDS: Critical Responses*, edited by Dorie Gilbert and Ednita M. Wright, ix–x. Westport, CT: Praeger, 2003.

Fullilove, Mindy, Robert Fullilove, Katherine Haynes, and Shirley Gross. "Black Women and AIDS Prevention: A View towards Understanding the Gender Rules." *Journal of Sex Research* 27 (1990): 47–64.

Fullilove, Mindy, Eve Golden, Robert Fullilove III, Randy Lennon, Deborah Porterfield, Sandra Schwarcz, and Gail Bolan. "Crack Cocaine Use and High-Risk Behaviors among Sexually Active Black Adolescents." *Journal of Adolescent Health* 14 (1993): 295–300.

Fullilove, Mindy, E. Ann Lown, and Robert Fullilove. "Crack 'Hos and Skeezers: Traumatic Experiences of Women Crack Users." *Journal of Sex Research* 29 (November 1992): 275–87.

Fuselier, Herman. "A Party until Sunrise, Kingfish Was the Place to Be." *Daily Advertiser*, April 12, 2018. https://www.theadvertiser.com/story/news/2018/04/12/party-until-sunrise-kingfish-place/509181002/.

Gates, Henry Louis, Jr. *Black: Words, Signs and the "Racial" Self*. New York: Oxford University Press, 1987.

———. *The Signifying Monkey*. New York: Oxford University Press, 1988.

Gaunt, Kyra D. *The Games Black Girls Play: Learning the Ropes from Double-Dutch to Hip-Hop*. New York: New York University Press, 1998.

Gavett, Gretchen. "Timeline: 30 Years of AIDS in Black America." *Frontline*, July 10, 2012. https://www.pbs.org/wgbh/frontline/article/timeline-30-years-of-aids-in-black-america/.

Gentry, Quinn. *Black Women's Risk for HIV: Rough Living*. New York: Routledge, 2007.

Gibbons, Sammy, Petruce Jean-Charles, and Claire Thornton. "South Lags in LGBTQ Coverage." *USA Today*, September 28, 2021, 3a.

146 · BIBLIOGRAPHY

Gichane, Margaret, Nora Rosenberg, Catherine Zimmer, Audrey Pettifor, Suzanne Maman, Bertha Maseko, and Kathryn Moracco. "Individual and Relationship-Level Correlates of Transactional Sex among Adolescent Girls and Young Women in Malawi: A Multilevel Analysis." *AIDS and Behavior* 26, no. 3 (March 2022): 822–32.

Gilbert, Dorie, and Ednita M. Wright, eds. *African American Women and HIV/AIDS: Critical Responses*. Westport, CT: Praeger, 2003.

Gilroy, Paul. "Sounds Authentic: Black Music, Ethnicity, and the Challenge of a Changing Same." *Black Music Research Journal* 11, no. 2 (Autumn 1991): 111–36.

Giorgis, Hannah. "The Missed Opportunity of *Love Is . . .*" *The Atlantic*, January 2, 2019. https://www.theatlantic.com/entertainment/archive/2019/01/revisiting-love-after-salim-akil-allegations/579277/.

Givhan, Robin. "Echoes of TV's First Lady: Michelle Obama's Last True Cultural Antecedent Is Cosby's Claire Huxtable." *Washington Post*, June 19, 2009, C01.

Godleski, Stephanie, Rina Eiden, Shannon Shisler, and Jennifer Livingston. "Parent Socialization of Emotion in a High-Risk Sample." *Developmental Psychology* 56, no. 3 (2020): 489–502.

Goehl, Thomas. "Editorial: Access Denied." *Environmental Health Perspectives* 115, no. 10 (October 2007): A482–A483.

Goldstein, Paul, Lawrence Ouellet, and Michael Fendrich. "From Bag Brides to Skeezers: A Historical Perspective on Sex-for-Drugs Behavior." *Journal of Psychoactive Drugs* 24, no. 4 (1992): 349–61.

Gomez, Estaban, and Katherine Strasser. "Language and Socioemotional Development in Early Childhood: The Role of Conversational Turns." *Developmental Science* 24, no. 5 (September 2021): 1–12. https://doi.org/10.1111/desc.13109.

Goodman, Elizabeth, and Alwyn Cohall. "Acquired Immunodeficiency Syndrome and Adolescents: Knowledge, Attitudes, Beliefs, and Behaviors in a New York City Adolescent Minority Population." *Pediatrics* 84, no. 1 (1989): 36–42.

Gourdine, Angeletta K. M. "Colored Reading: Or, Interpretation and the Raciogendered Body." In *Reading Sites: Social Difference and Reader Response,* edited by Patricinio P. Schweickart and Elizabeth A. Flynn, 60–82. New York: Modern Language Association of America, 2004.

Graham, Trey. "So Far, Yet So Close: An Off-Broadway Hit Strikes All the Right Notes for Audiences in Harare, Zimbabwe." *American Theatre* (July/August 2006): 50–53.

Greig, Russell, and Beverly Raphael. "AIDS Prevention and Adolescents." *Community Health Studies* 13, no. 2 (1989): 211–19.

Gueron-Sela, Noa, Michael Willoughby, Marie Camerota, Lynn Vernon-Feagans, and Martha J. Cox. "Maternal Depressive Symptoms, Mother-Child Interactions, and Children's Executive Function." *Developmental Psychology* 54, no. 1 (2018): 71–82.

Guinan, Mary, and Ann Hardy. "Epidemiology of AIDS in Women in the United States." *JAMA* 257, no. 15 (April 17, 1987): 2039.

Gurira, Danai. "Black Panther Star as a Fierce Warrior." Interview by Peter Travers. *Popcorn with Peter Travers*, February 22, 2018.

———. "HIV/AIDS in Africa: Danai Gurira Speaks at the 2016 Global Citizen Festival." Global Citizen, September 24, 2016. YouTube video, 2:03. https://www.youtube.com/watch?v=Orn4rytckqk.

Gurira, Danai, and Nikkole Salter. "In the Continuum." In *African Women Playwrights,* edited by Kathy A. Perkins, 318–60. Urbana: University of Illinois Press, 2009.

Gurira, Danai, Nikkole Salter, and Sarah Jones. "'In the Continuum' and 'Bridge and Tunnel.'" Theater Talk Archive, August 13, 2013. Original tape date January 28, 2006. YouTube video, 25:23. https://www.youtube.com/watch?v=TQKudzTMnWE.

Hammonds, Evelyn. "AIDS: The Secret, Silent Suffering Shame." In *Still Brave: The Evolution of Black Women's Studies,* edited by Stanlie M. James, Frances Smith Foster, and Beverly Guy-Sheftall, 268–80. New York: The Feminist Press, 2009.

———. "Gendering the Epidemic: Feminism and the Epidemic of HIV/AIDS in the United States, 1981–1999." In *Feminism in 20th Century Science, Technology, and Medicine,* edited by Angela Creager, Elizabeth Lunbeck, and Londa Schiebinger, 230–44. Chicago: University of Chicago Press, 2001.

Harawa, Nina, John Williams, Hema Ramamurthi, and Trista Bingham. "Perceptions towards Condom Use, Sexual Activity, and HIV Disclosure among HIV-Positive African American Men Who Have Sex with Men: Implications for Heterosexual Transmission." *Journal of Urban Health* 83, no. 4 (July 2006): 682–94.

Harris, Trudier. "This Disease Called Strength: Some Observations on the Compensating Construction of Black Female Character." *Literature and Medicine* 14, no. 1 (1995): 109–26.

Harris-Perry, Melissa. *Sister Citizen: Shame, Stereotypes, and Black Women in America.* New Haven, CT: Yale University Press, 2011.

Heckler, Margaret M. *Report of the Secretary's Task Force on Black and Minority Health.* US Department of Health and Human Services, August 1985. https://archive.org/stream/reportofsecretaroousde#page/n9.

Henderson, Aneeka Ayanna. *Veil and Vow: Marriage Matters in Contemporary African American Culture.* Chapel Hill: University of North Carolina Press, 2020.

Herman, Robin. "A Disease's Spread Provokes Anxiety." *New York Times,* August 8, 1982, 31.

Hernandez, Ernio. "*In the Continuum* Extends Final Time Off-Broadway before African and U.S. Tour." *Playbill,* January 17, 2006.

———. "*In the Continuum* World Premier Opens Oct. 2 at Off-Broadway's Primary Stages at the 59E59 Theater." *Playbill,* October 2, 2005.

Herukhuti. *Conjuring Black Funk: Notes on Culture, Sexuality, and Spirituality.* New York: Vintage Entity Press, 2007.

Higginbotham, Evelyn Brooks. *Righteous Discontent: The Women's Movement in the Black Baptist Church, 1880–1920.* Cambridge, MA: Harvard University Press, 1993.

Highberg, Nels. "The (Missing) Faces of African American Girls with AIDS." *Feminist Formations* 22, no. 1 (Spring 2010): 1–20.

Hill, Bianca, Viraj Patel, Lorlette Haughton, and Oni Blackstone. "Leveraging Social Media to Explore Black Women's Perspectives on HIV-Pre-Exposure Prophylaxis." *Journal of Association of Nurses in AIDS Care* 29, no. 1 (2018): 107–14.

Hill, Marc Lamont, Biany Peréz, and Decoteau J. Irby. "Street Fiction: What Is It and What Does It Mean for English Teachers?" *English Journal* 97, no. 3 (January 2008): 76–81.

Hillsburg, Heather. "Compassionate Readership: Anger and Suffering in Sapphire's *PUSH.*" *Canadian Review of American Studies* 44, no. 1 (2014): 122–47.

Hinton, Elizabeth. *From the War on Poverty to the War on Crime: The Making of Mass Incarceration in America.* Cambridge, MA: Harvard University Press, 2016.

"Hip Hop vs. America Pt 1: 'Oprah . . . Wasn't Fair to Hip Hop.'" BlackTree TV, January 3, 2008. YouTube video, 4:18. http://www.youtube.com/watch?v=Rk3U1iR3vfU.

148 • BIBLIOGRAPHY

"HIV/AIDS Education: First National Women and Girls HIV/AIDS Awareness Day." *Science Letter* (March 28, 2006): 789.

HIV.gov. "Global Statistics: The Global HIV and AIDS Epidemic." Updated November 15, 2023. https://www.hiv.gov/hiv-basics/overview/data-and-trends/global-statistics.

Hogan, Katie. "Gendered Visibilities in Black Women's AIDS Narratives." In *Gendered Epidemic: Representations of Women in the Age of AIDS*, 165–90. New York: Routledge, 1998.

———. *Women Take Care: Gender, Race, and the Culture of AIDS.* Ithaca, NY: Cornell University Press, 2001.

Holloway, Karla. *Private Bodies, Public Texts: Race, Gender, and a Cultural Bioethics.* Durham, NC: Duke University Press, 2011.

hooks, bell. *Ain't I a Woman: Black Women and Feminism.* Boston: South End Press, 1981.

———. *Black Looks: Race and Representation.* Boston: South End Press, 1992.

———. *Reel to Real: Race, Sex, and Class at the Movies.* New York: Routledge, 1996.

Howell, Elizabeth. "Reducing Disparities in Severe Maternal Morbidity and Mortality." *Clinical Obstetrics and Gynecology* 61, no. 2 (June 2018): 387–99.

Hunt, Darnell. "A Different World." Museum of Broadcast Communications Encyclopedia of Television. https://interviews.televisionacademy.com/shows/different-world-a.

Hunter-Jones, J., S. Gilliam, C. Davis, D. Brown, D. Green, C. Hunter, A. Carswell, and N. Hansen. "Process and Outcome Evaluation of a Mindfulness-Based Cognitive Therapy Intervention for Cisgender and Transgender Women Living with HIV/AIDS." *AIDS and Behavior* 25 (2021): 592–603.

Hurston, Zora Neale. "My Most Humiliating Jim Crow Experience." In *I Love Myself When I Am Laughing and Then Again When I Am Looking Mean and Impressive,* edited by Alice Walker, 163–68. New York: Feminist Press, 1979.

Institute of Women and Ethnic Studies. https://www.iwesnola.org/.

"*In the Continuum* to Return to South Africa in July." *BBW News Desk,* July 2, 2007.

Isherwood, Charles. "Continents Apart, Two Odysseys on Parallel Tracks." *New York Times,* October 10, 2005, E1.

Jeffries, Michael P. "Hip Hop Feminism and Failure: A Commentary." *Palimpsest* 1, no. 2 (2012): 277–84.

———. *Thug Life: Race, Gender, and the Meaning of Hip Hop.* Chicago: University of Chicago Press, 2011.

Jemmott, Loretta S., and John B. Jemmott. "Increasing Condom-Use Intentions among Sexually Active Black Adolescent Women." *Nursing Research* 41, no. 5 (1992): 273–79.

Jimenez, Antonio. "Triple Jeopardy: Targeting Older Men of Color Who Have Sex with Men." *Journal of Acquired Immune Deficiency Syndrome* 33 (June 1, 2003): S222–S225.

Johnson, Latasha, Penny Ralston, and Ethel Jones. "Beauty Salon Health Intervention Increases Fruit and Vegetable Consumption in African American Women." *Journal of the American Dietetic Association* 110, no. 6 (2010): 941–45.

Jordan-Zachery, Julia. *Shadow Bodies: Black Women, Ideology, Representation and Politics.* New Brunswick, NJ: Rutgers University Press, 2017.

Juvenile. "Mamma Got Ass." *Project English.* Santa Monica, CA: Universal, 2001.

Kadivar, Hajer, Patricia Garvie, Christine Sinnock, Jerry Heston, and Patricia Flynn. "Psychosocial Profile of HIV-Infected Adolescents in a Southern US Urban Cohort." *AIDS Care* 18, no. 6 (2006): 544–49.

BIBLIOGRAPHY • 149

Kaplan, Marjorie, and Kenneth Schonberg. "HIV in Adolescents." *Clinics in Perinatology* 21, no. 1 (March 1994): 75–84.

Kelly, Ella Mizzell. "African American Adolescent Girls: Neglected and Disrespected." In *African American Women and HIV/AIDS: Critical Responses*, edited by Dorie Gilbert and Ednita Wright, 163–81. Westport, CT: Praeger, 2003.

Kelley, Robin D. G. *Yo' Mama's Disfunktional: Fighting the Culture Wars in Urban America*. Boston: Beacon Press, 1997.

Kelley, Sonaiya. "OWN's 'Love Is . . .': The Love Story of a Powerful Hollywood Couple Hits Prime Time." *Los Angeles Times,* June 19, 2018. https://www.latimes.com/entertainment/tv/la-et-st-love-is-feature-20180619-story.html.

Kendall, Ashley, Christina Young, Bethany Bray, Erin Emerson, Sally Freels, and Geri Donenberg. "Changes in Externalizing and Internalizing Symptoms among African American Female Adolescents over 1 Year Following a Mother-Daughter Sexual Health Intervention." *Journal of Consulting and Clinical Psychology* 88, no. 6 (2020): 495–503.

King, Patricia Lee, and David Pate. "Perinatal HIV Testing among African American, Caucasian, Hmong, and Latina Women: Exploring the Role of Healthcare Services, Information Sources, and Perceptions of HIV/AIDS." *Health Education Research* 29, no. 1 (2014): 109–21.

Kitwana, Bakari. *The Hip Hop Generation: Young Blacks and the Crisis in African American Culture*. New York: Basic Books, 2003.

Klein, Pamela, Demetrios Psihopaidas, Jessica Xavier, and Stacey Cohen. "HIV-Related Outcome Disparities between Transgender Women Living with HIV and Cisgender People Living with HIV Served by the Health Resources and Services Administration's Ryan White HIV/AIDS Program: A Retrospective Study." *PLOS Medicine* (May 28, 2020). https://doi.org/10.1371/journal.pmed.1003125.

Klonoff, Elizabeth, Hope Landrine, and Delia Lang. "Introduction: The State of Research on Black Women in Health Psychology and Behavioral Medicine." *Women's Health: Research on Gender, Behavior, and Policy* 3 (1997): 165–81.

Kokkola, Lydia. "Learning to Read Politically: Narratives of Hope and Narratives of Despair in *PUSH* by Sapphire." *Cambridge Journal of Education* 43, no. 3 (2013): 391–405.

Koniak-Griffin, Deborah, and Mary-Lynn Brecht. "Linkages between Sexual Risk Taking, Substance Use, and AIDS Knowledge among Pregnant Adolescents and Young Mothers." *Nursing Research* 44, no. 6 (November–December 1995): 340–46.

Kramer, Larry. *The Normal Heart*. New York: Samuel French, 1985.

Kukura, Elizabeth. "Better Birth." *Temple Law Review* 93, no. 2 (2021): 243–300. https://papers.ssrn.com/sol3/papers.cfm?abstract_id=3823504.

Kumpf, Terence. "From Queering to TransImagining: Sookee's Trans/Feminist Hip Hop." *Transgender Studies Quarterly* 3, no. 1–2 (May 1, 2016): 175–84.

Ladner, Joyce. "Black Women Face the 21st Century: Major Issues and Problems." *The Black Scholar* 17, no. 5 (September–October 1986): 12–19.

Lane, Sandra, Robert Rubinstein, Robert Keefe, Noah Webster, Donald Cibula, Alan Rosenthal, and Jesse Dowdell. "Structural Violence and Racial Disparity in HIV Transmission." *Journal of Healthcare for the Poor and Underserved,* no. 3 (August 15, 2004): 319–35.

Lee, Felicia R. "Putting Women's Faces on the Grim Statistics about AIDS." *New York Times,* October 1, 2005, B9.

Lei, Ryan, Rachel Leshin, Kelsey Moty, Emily Foster-Hanson, and Marjorie Rhodes. "How Race and Gender Shape the Development of Social Prototypes in the United States." *Journal of Experimental Psychology* 151, no. 8 (2021): 1956–71.

150 · BIBLIOGRAPHY

Leigh, Wilhelmina A. "The Health of African American Women." In *Health Issues for Women of Color: A Cultural Diversity Perspective,* edited by Diane Adams, 295–314. Thousand Oaks, CA: Sage, 1995.

Lewis, Marva. "Black Mother-Daughter Interactions in Hair-Combing Rituals." In *Afrikan American Women: Living at the Crossroads of Race, Gender, and Culture,* edited by Huberta Jackson-Lowman, 345–68. San Diego: Cognella Academic Publishing, 2014.

Lewis, Nghana. "Black Women's Health in the Age of Hip Hop and HIV/AIDS: A Model for Civic Engagement and Feminist Activism." *On Campus with Women* 38, no. 3 (Winter 2010). https://go.gale.com/ps/i.do?p=AONE&u=anon~7722950b&id=GALE|A229720143&v=2.1&it=r&sid=bookmark-AONE&asid=f25434b9.

Lewis, Yolanda, Lara Shain, Sandra Crouse Quinn, Katherine Turner, and Timothy Moore. "Building Community Trust: Lessons from an STD/HIV Peer Educator Program with African American Barbers and Beauticians." *Health Promotion Practice* 3, no. 2 (2002): 133–43.

Lewis-Thornton, Rae. "Facing AIDS." *Essence* 25, no. 8 (December 1994): 62–67.

Liang, Yue, Jiayao Li, Hongjian Cao and Nan Zhou, and Limin Zhang. "Early Home Learning Environment Predicts Early Adolescents' Adjustment through Cognitive Abilities in Middle Childhood." *Journal of Family Psychology* 34, no. 8 (2020): 905–17.

Lichtenstein, Bronwen, Mary Laska, and Jeffrey Clair. "Chronic Sorrow in the HIV-Positive Patient: Issues of Race, Gender, and Social Support." *AIDS Patient Care and STDs* 16, no. 1 (2002): 27–38.

Lindsey, Treva. "Let Me Blow Your Mind: Hip Hop Feminist Futures in Theory and Praxis." *Urban Education* 50, no. 1 (2015): 52–77.

Linnan, Laura, and Yvonne Owens Ferguson. "Beauty Salons: A Promising Health Promotion Setting for Reaching and Promoting Health among African American Women." *Health Education and Behavior* 34, no. 3 (2007): 517–30.

Lipa, Dua. "Instagram Stories." https://www.rollingstone.com/music/music-news/dua-lipa-dababy-homophobic-remarks-rolling-loud-1203152/. Orig. posted July 27, 2021.

———. "Levitating." *Future Nostalgia.* Warner, October 1, 2020.

Long-Middleton, Ellen, Pamela Burke, and Sally Rankin. "Predictors of HIV Risk Reduction in Adolescent Girls." *MCN* 44, no. 3 (May/June 2019): 150–56.

Lorde, Audre. *The Cancer Journals.* New York: Spinsters Ink Press, 1980.

Lowe, Richard, dir. *Planet Rock: The Story of Hip Hop and the Crack Generation.* VH1, 2010.

Lunden, Jeff. "Two Women, One Story, *In the Continuum.*" *NRP,* January 12, 2006.

MacMaster, Samuel, Randolph Rasch, Mark Kinzly, R. Lyle Cooper, and Susan Adams. "Perceptions of Sexual Risks and Injection for HIV among African American Women Who Use Crack Cocaine in Nashville, Tennessee." *Health and Social Work* 34, no. 4 (November 2009): 283–91.

Marceau, Kristine, Nayantara Nair, Michelle Rogers, and Kristina Jackson. "Lability in Parent and Child-Based Sources of Parental Monitoring Are Differentially Associated with Adolescent Substance Use." *Prevention Science* 21, no. 4 (2020): 568–79.

McCombs, Alexis. "The Death of a Network." *Black Enterprise,* May 1, 2006.

McCree, Donna Hubbard, Gina Wingood, Ralph DiClemente, Susan Davies, and Katherine Harrington. "Religiosity and Risky Sexual Behavior in African American Adolescent Females." *Journal of Adolescent Health* 33, no. 1 (July 2003): 2–8.

McKay, Mary McKernan, Donna Batiste, Doris Coleman, Sybil Madison, Roberta Patkoff, and Richard Scott. "Preventing HIV Risk Exposure in Urban Communities: The CHAMP Family Model." In *Working with Families in the Era of HIV/AIDS*, edited by Willo Pequegnat and José Szapocznik, 67–88. London: Sage Publications, 2000.

McNeil, Elizabeth. "Un'Freak'ing Black Female Selfhood: Grotesque-Erotic Agency and Ecofeminist Unity in Sapphire's *PUSH*." *MELUS* 37, no. 4 (2012): 11–30.

McNeil, Elizabeth, Neal Lester, DoVeanna Fulton, and Lynette Myles. "'Going After Something Else': Sapphire on the Evolution from *PUSH* to *Precious* to *The Kid*." *Callaloo* 37, no. 2 (Spring 2014): 352–57.

Mebrahtu, Helen, Lorraine Sherr, Victoria Simms, Helen Weiss, Rudo Chingono, Andrea Rehman, Patience Ndlovu, and Frances Cowen. "The Impact of Common Mental Disorders among Caregivers Living with HIV on Child Cognitive Development in Zimbabwe." *AIDS Care* 32 (2020): 198–205.

———. "Postpartum Maternal Mental Health Is Associated with Cognitive Development of HIV-Exposed Infants in Zimbabwe: A Cross-Sectional Study." *AIDS Care* 30 (2018): 74–82.

Mehra, Rena, Lisa Boyd, Urania Magriples, Trace Kershaw, Jeannette Ickovics, and Danya Keene. "Black Pregnant Women 'Get the Most Judgment': A Qualitative Study of the Experiences of Black Women at the Intersection of Race, Gender, and Pregnancy." *Women's Health Issues* 6 (November–December 2020): 484–92.

Meisel, Samuel, Craig Colder, and Christopher Hopwood. "Assessing Parent-Adolescent Substance Use Discussions Using the Continuous Assessment of Interpersonal Dynamics." *Journal of Personality Assessment* 104, no. 6 (2022): 800–812.

Melton, Monica. "Sex, Lies, and Stereotypes: HIV Positive Black Women's Perspectives on HIV Stigma and the Need for Public Policy as HIV Prevention Intervention." *Race, Gender and Class* 18, no. 1–2 (2011): 295–313.

Menzies, Alisha, and Emily Ryalls. "Depicting Black Women, the Politics of Respectability, and HIV in *Precious*." *Howard Journal of Communications* 31, no. 5 (2020): 481–92.

Miller, Maureen, Malin Serner, and Meghan Wagner. "Sexual Diversity among Black Men Who Have Sex with Men in an Inner-City Community." *Journal of Urban Health* 82, no. 1 (March 2005): 26–34.

Mitchell, W. J. T. "Seeing Disability." *Public Culture* 13, no. 3 (Fall 2001): 391–98.

Morgan, Joan. *When Chickenheads Come Home to Roost: A Hip-Hop Feminist Breaks It Down.* New York: Simon and Schuster, 1999.

Morgan, Marcyliena. *The Real Hiphop: Battling for Knowledge, Power, and Respect in the LA Underground.* Durham, NC: Duke University Press, 2009.

Morgan, Marcyliena, and Dionne Bennett. "Hip-Hop and the Global Imprint of a Cultural Form." *Daedalus* 140, no. 2 (Spring 2011): 176–96.

Morris, Susana. *Close Kin and Distant Relatives.* Charlottesville: University of Virginia Press, 2014.

Morrison, Toni. "Toni Morrison Interview on *Jazz* (1993)." *Charlie Rose*, May 7, 1993.

"Ms. Foundation and *In the Continuum* Help Women of Color Break the Silence." Review of *In the Continuum*, *New York Amsterdam News*, February 9–15, 2006, 37.

Müeller, Claudia. "The Welfare Mother and the Fat Poor: Stereotypical Images and the Success Narrative in Sapphire's *PUSH*." *Current Objectives of Postgraduate American Studies* 14, no. 1 (2013): 1–18.

Murphy, Debra, Erika Austin, and Lisa Greenwell. "Correlates of HIV-Related Stigma among HIV-positive Mothers and Their Uninfected Adolescent Children." *Women's Health* 44, no. 3 (2006): 19–42.

National Black Women's Justice Institute. https://www.nbwji.org/.

152 • BIBLIOGRAPHY

Needle, Chael. "Girlfriends for Life: Mara Brock Akil, Creator of UPN's Girlfriends, Shares with A&U's Chael Needle the Inside Scoop on the Show's HIV Story Lines and the State of Sexual Health on TV." *The Media Project,* 2003. https://web.archive.org/web/20111126024415/http://www.themediaproject.com:80/news/itn/040103.htm. Orig. printed in *A&U: America's AIDS Magazine,* no. 102 (April 2003): 26.

Nesheim, Steven, Lauren Fitzharris, Kristen Gray, and Margaret Lampe. "Epidemiology of Perinatal HIV Transmission in the United States in the Era of Its Elimination." *Pediatric Infectious Disease Journal* 38, no. 6 (June 2019): 611–16.

O'Daniel, Alyson. *Holding On: African American Women Surviving HV/AIDS.* Lincoln: University of Nebraska Press, 2016.

Ofori-Atta, Akoto. "Sister Souljah: More than a Street Lit Author." *The Root,* June 2, 2011. https://www.theroot.com/sister-souljah-more-than-a-street-lit-author-1790864199.

Ogur, Barbara. "Smothering in Stereotypes: HIV-Positive Women." In *Talking Gender: Public Images, Personal Journeys, and Political Critiques,* edited by Nancy Hewitt, Jean O'Barr, and Nancy Rosebaugh, 137–52. Chapel Hill: University of North Carolina Press, 1996.

Ojikutu, Bisola, and Kenneth Mayer. "HIV Prevention among Black Women in the US—Time for Multimodal Integrated Strategies." *JAMA* 4, no. 4 (2021). https://jamanetwork.com/journals/jamanetworkopen/fullarticle/2778348.

O'Leary, Ann, and Lorretta Jemmott, eds. *Women at Risk: Issues in Primary Prevention of AIDS.* New York: Plenum, 1995.

Oribhabor, Geraldine, Maxine Nelson, Keri-Ann Buchanan-Peart, and Ivan Cancarevic. "A Mother's Cry: A Race to Eliminate the Influence of Racial Disparities in Maternal Morbidity and Mortality Rates among Black Women in America." *Cureus* 12, no 7. (2020): e9207. https://pubmed.ncbi.nlm.nih.gov/32685330/.

Overby, Kim, and Susan Kegeles. "The Impact of AIDS on an Urban Population of High-Risk Female Minority Adolescents: Implications for Intervention." *Journal of Adolescent Health* 15 (1994): 216–27.

Pappas, Christine. "'You Hafta Push': Using Sapphire's Novel to Teach Introduction to American Government." *Journal of Political Science Education* 3, no. 1 (2007): 39–50.

Pau, Alice, and Jomy George. "Antiretroviral Therapy: Current Drugs." *Infectious Disease Clinics of North America* 28, no. 3 (September 2014): 371–402.

Pearl, Nancy. "[Review of] *The Coldest Winter Ever.*" *Library Journal* 124, no. 7 (April 15, 1999): 146–47.

Peoples, Whitney. "'Under Construction': Identifying Foundations of Hip-Hop Feminism and Exploring Bridges between Black Second-Wave and Hip-Hop Feminism." *Meridians* 8, no. 1 (2008): 19–52.

Perkins, Katy A., ed. *African Women Playwrights.* Urbana: University of Illinois Press, 2009.

Perro, Ebony L. "Thee Megan Movement: Defining and Exploring Hot Girl Rhetoric." *NANO: New American Notes Online,* no. 16 (June 2022). https://nanocrit.com/index.php/issues/issue16/Thee-Megan-Movement-Defining-and-Exploring-Hot-Girl-Rhetoric.

Perry, Imani. *Prophets of the Hood: Politics and Poetics in Hip Hop.* Durham, NC: Duke University Press, 2004.

Philbin, Morgan, Elizabeth Kinnard, Amanda Tanner, Samuella Ware, Brittany Chambers, Alice Ma, and Dennis Fortenberry. "The Association between Incarceration and Transactional Sex among HIV-Infected Young Men Who Have Sex with Men in the United States." *Journal of Urban Health* 95, no. 4 (August 2018): 576–83.

BIBLIOGRAPHY • 153

Phillips, Kenneth, Richard Sowell, Charles Rush, and Carolyn Murdaugh. "Psychosocial and Physiologic Correlates of Perceived Health among HIV-Infected Women." *Southern Online Journal of Nursing Research* 3, no. 2 (2001). https://snrs.org/wp-content/uploads/2022/02/isso3vol02.pdf.

Pizzi, Michael. "Women, HIV Infection, and AIDS: Tapestries of Life, Death, and Empowerment." *American Journal of Occupational Therapy* 46, no. 11 (November 1992): 1021–27.

Polacsek, Michele, David Celentano, Patricia O'Campo, and John Santelli. "Correlates of Condom Use Stage of Change: Implications for Intervention." *AIDS Education and Prevention* 11, no. 1 (1999): 38–52.

Pollard, Cherise. "The P-Word Exchange: Representing Black Female Sexuality in Contemporary Urban Fiction." In *Black Female Sexualities,* edited by Trimiko Melancon and Joanne M. Braxton, 113–28. New Brunswick, NJ: Rutgers University Press, 2015.

Pomeroy, Claire. "Virtual Mentor." *AMA Journal of Ethics* 10, no 7 (July 2008): 457–64. https://journalofethics.ama-assn.org/sites/journalofethics.ama-assn.org/files/2018-06/pfor1-0807.pdf.

Pough, Gwendolyn. *Check It While I Wreck It: Black Womanhood, Hip-Hop Culture, and the Public Sphere.* Boston: Northeast University Press, 2004.

———. "What It Do, Shorty? Women, Hip-Hop, and a Feminist Agenda." *Black Women, Gender, and Families* 1, no. 2 (2007): 78–99.

Price, Gwendolyn, Marissa Ogren, and Catherine Sandhofer. "Sorting Out Emotions: How Labels Influence Emotion Categorization." *Developmental Psychology* 58, no. 9 (2022): 1665–75.

Price, Kimala. "Hip Hop Feminism at the Political Crossroads: Organizing for Reproductive Justice and Beyond." In *Home Girls Make Some Noise: Hip Hop Feminism Anthology,* edited by Gwendolyn D. Pough, Elaine Richardson, Aisha Durham, and Rachel Raimist, 389–407. Mira Loma, CA: Parker Publishing, 2007.

Rangel, Maria, Loretta Gavin, Christie Reed, Mary Fowler, and Lisa Lee. "Epidemiology of HIV and AIDS among Adolescents and Young Adults in the United States." *Journal of Adolescent Health* 39, no. 2 (August 2006): 156–63.

Rao, Sharanya, Tashuna Albritton, Paulo Pina, Yilin Liang, and Tamara Taggart. "'You Don't Want Your Parents Knowing That You're Taking Pre-Exposure Prophylaxis': Pre-Exposure Prophylaxis Stigma among Black and Latinx Adolescents." *Journal of the Association of Nurses in AIDS Care* 33, no. 4 (July–August 2022): 395–405.

Rasmussen, Hannah, Jessica Borelli, Patricia Smiley, Chloe Cohen, Ryan Cheuk Ming Cheung, Schuyler Fox, Matthew Marvin, and Betsey Blackard. "Mother-Child Language Style Matching Predicts Children's and Mother's Emotion Reactivity." *Behavioral Brain Research* 325 (2017): 203–13.

Rehak, Melanie. "The Way We Live Now: 5:30:99: Questions for Sister Souljah; The Drama of the Ghetto Child." *New York Times Magazine,* May 30, 1999. See https://go.gale.com/ps/i.do?p=BIC&u=tulane&id=GALE|A150002414&v=2.1&it=r&sid=bookmark-BIC&asid=d074e647.

Reid, Rachelle, and Sannisha Dale. "Moderating Effects of Social Support on the Relationship between Substance Abuse Disorders and HIV Viral Load and Medication Adherence among Black Women Living with HIV in the United States." *AIDS Care* 34 (October 1, 2022): 1219–28.

Ren, Kexin, Yiqiao Wang, Marsha Weinraub, Nora Newcombe, and Elizabeth Gunderson. "Fathers' and Mothers' Praise and Spatial Language during Play with First Graders: Patterns of Interactions and Relations to Math Achievement." *Developmental Psychology* 58, no. 10 (2022): 1931–46.

Rice, Lynette. "Is the Black Situation Comedy Dying?" *Entertainment Weekly* 871 (April 2006): 9–10.

Richardson, Nicole Marie. "Top 50 Power Brokers in Hollywood." *Black Enterprise*, March 1, 2007.

Rissman, Nathan, dir. *I Am Because We Are*. Written and produced by Madonna. Simtex Films, 2008.

Roberts, Amelia C., Wendee M. Wechsberg, William Zule, and Angela R. Burroughs. "Contextual Factors and Other Correlates of Sexual Risk of HIV among African American Crack-Abusing Women." *Addictive Behavior* 28, no. 3 (2003): 523–36.

Roberts, Dorothy. *Killing the Black Body: Race Reproduction, and the Meaning of Liberty*. New York: Vintage, 1997.

Robinson, Gayle. "Qualitative Study of African American Women's Intergenerational Dialogue for HIV Prevention." *Western Journal of Nursing Research* 43, no. 5 (2021): 409–15.

Rose, Tricia. *Black Noise: Rap Music and Black Culture in Contemporary America*. Middletown, CT: Wesleyan University Press, 1994.

———. *The Hip Hop Wars: What We Talk about When We Talk about Hip Hop—and Why It Matters*. New York: Basic Books, 2008.

———. *Longing to Tell: Black Women Talk about Sexuality and Intimacy*. New York: Farrar, Straus, and Giroux, 2003.

Rosenberg, Philip S. "Scope of the AIDS Epidemic in the United States." *Science* 27 (November 24, 1995): 1372–75.

Rosenthal, Lila, Deborah Scott, Zeman Kelleta, Astatkie Zikarge, Matthew Momoh, Judith Lahai-Momoh, Michael Ross, and Andy Baker. "Assessing the HIV/AIDS Health Services Needs of African Immigrants to Houston." *AIDS Education and Prevention* 15, no. 6 (December 2003): 570–80.

Rousseau, Nicole. "Social Rhetoric and the Construction of Black Motherhood." *Journal of Black Studies* 44, no. 5 (July 2013): 451–71.

Royles, Dan. *To Make the Wounded Whole: The African American Struggle against HIV/AIDS*. Chapel Hill: University of North Carolina Press, 2020.

———. "Why Black AIDS History Matters." *Black Perspectives*, February 7, 2022. https://www.aaihs.org/why-black-aids-history-matters/.

Rutledge, Jaleah, Kaston Anderson-Carpenter, and Jae Puckett. "HIV Testing and Associated Characteristics among Black Cisgender and Transgender Women in the United States." *Journal of Healthcare, Science, and Humanities* 11, no. 1 (2021): 149–62.

Sangaramoorthy, Thurka, Amelia Jamison, and Typhanye Dyer. "Intersectional Stigma among Midlife and Older Black Women Living with HIV." *Culture Health Sexuality* 19, no. 12 (December 2017): 1329–43.

Sapphire. "For Colored Girls: The Sapphire Interview." Interview by Ernest Hardy. *LA Weekly*, November 11, 2009. https://www.laweekly.com/for-colored-girls-the-sapphire-interview/.

———. *PUSH: A Novel*. 25th anniversary ed. Vintage: New York, 2021.

———. "'A *PUSH* out of Chaos': An Interview with Sapphire." Interview by Marq Wilson. *MELUS* 37, no. 4 (2012): 31–39.

———. "Sapphire." Interview by Kelvin Christopher James. *Bomb* 57 (October 1, 1996): 42–45.

Schalk, Sami. *Black Disability Politics*. Durham, NC: Duke University Press, 2022.

Schoepf, Brook Grundfest. "Women at Risk: Case Studies from Zaire." In *The Times of AIDS: Social Analysis, Theory, and Method,* edited by Gilbert Herdt and Shirley Lindenbaum, 259–86. Newbury Park, CA: Sage Publications, 1992.

Schulman, Sarah. *Let the Record Show: A Political History of ACT UP New York, 1987–1993.* New York: Farrah, Straus, and Giroux, 2021.

Shangase, Nisopho, Jess Edwards, Brian Pence, Allison Aiello, Andrea Hussong, Xavier Goméz-Olivé, Kathleen Kahn, Marie Stoner, and Audrey Pettifor. "Effect of Quality of Caregiver-Adolescent Relationship on Sexual Debut, Transactional Sex, and on Age-Disparate Relationships among Young Women in Rural South Africa Enrolled in HPTN-68." *Journal of Acquired Immune Deficiency Syndrome* 89, no. 4 (April 1, 2022): 366–73.

Sharpe, Tanya. *Behind the Eight Ball: Crack Cocaine Exchange and Poor Black Women.* New York: Routledge, 2005.

Sharpley-Whiting, T. Denean. *Pimps Up, Ho's Down: Hip Hop's Hold on Young Black Women.* New York: New York University Press, 2007.

Shotwell, Alexis. "'Women Don't Get AIDS, They Just Die from It': Memory, Classification, and the Campaign to Change the Definition of AIDS." *Hypatia* 29, no. 2 (Spring 2014): 509–25.

Siegel, Tatiana. "*Girlfriends'* 100th Episode." *Hollywood Reporter,* November 8, 2004.

Sikkema, Kathleen J., Timothy G. Heckman, Jeffrey A. Kelly, and the Community Housing AIDS Prevention Study Group. "HIV Risk Behaviors among Inner-City African American Women." *Women's Health: Research on Gender, Behavior, and Policy* 3, no. 3–4 (1997): 349–66.

Sister Souljah. "Ask the Author: Top Ten Questions." In *The Coldest Winter Ever: Special Collector's Edition,* 293. New York: Atria, 1999.

———. *The Coldest Winter Ever.* New York: Simon and Schuster, 1999.

———. "Sister Souljah Releases Sequel to 'Coldest Winter Ever,' Talks Survival, Cancel Culture, + More." Interview by Angela Yee, Charlamagne Tha God, and DJ Envy. *The Breakfast Club,* March 3, 2021. YouTube video, 40:46. https://www.youtube.com/watch?v=_qk32bHUovE.

———. "A State of War: Sister Souljah." 1991 speech. YouTube video, 1:09:57. https://www.youtube.com/watch?v=HNEZcjMItuE.

Smith, Beverly. "Black Women's Health: Notes for a Course." In *All the Women Are White, All the Blacks Are Men, but Some of Us Are Brave,* edited by Gloria T. Hull, Patricia Bell Scott, and Barbara Smith, 103–15. New York: Feminist Press, 1982.

Smith, Jodie, Penny Levickis, Tricia Eadie, Lesley Bretherton, Laura Conway, and Sharon Goldfeld. "Association between Maternal Behavior at 1 Year and Child Language at 2 Years in a Cohort of Women Experiencing Adversity." *Infancy* 23, no 1 (2018): 74–102.

Smith, Valerie. "The Documentary Impulse in Contemporary African American Film." In *Black Popular Culture,* edited by Michelle Wallace and Gina Dent, 56–64. New York: New Press, 1998.

Smitherman, Geneva. "'The Chain Remain the Same': Communicative Practices in the Hip Hop Nation." *Journal of Black Studies* 28, no. 1 (September 1997): 3–25.

Smith-Shomade, Beretta. *Shaded Lives: African American Women and Television.* New Brunswick, NJ: Rutgers University Press, 2018.

Snorton, C. Riley. *Black on Both Sides: A Racial History of Trans Identity.* Minneapolis: University of Minnesota Press, 2017.

Spillers, Hortense. "Mama's Baby, Papa's Maybe: An American Grammar Book." *Diacritics* 17, no. 2 (Summer 1987): 64–81.

156 • BIBLIOGRAPHY

Staiano, Amanda, and Anisha Abraham. "Competitive v. Cooperative Exergame Play for African American Adolescents' Executive Function Skills: Short-Term Effects in a Long-Term Training Intervention." *Developmental Psychology* 48, no. 2 (2012): 336–42.

Stallings, L. H. "Erotic Literacy and Black Girl Sexual Agency." In *Sapphire'sLiterary Breakthrough: Erotic Literacies, Feminist Pedagogies, Environmental Justice Perspectives*, edited by Elizabeth McNeil, Neal A. Lester, DoVeanna S. Fulton, and Lynette D. Myles, 113–40. New York: Palgrave, 2012.

———. *Mutha' Is Half a Word: Intersections of Folklore, Vernacular, Myth, and Queerness in Black Female Culture*. Columbus: Ohio State University Press, 2007.

Stapleton, Laurie. "Toward a New Learning System: A Freirean Reading of Sapphire's *PUSH*." *Women's Studies Quarterly* 32, no. 1/2 (Summer 2004): 213–33.

State of Louisiana v. Ricky Fugler. 737 So.2d 894 (La. Ct. App. 1st Cir. 1998).

Stebbins, Michael, Erica Davis, Lucas Royland, and Gartrell White. "Public Access Failure at PubMed." *Science* 313 (July 7, 2006): 43.

Steinberg, Sybil. "[Review of] *The Coldest Winter Ever*." *Publisher's Weekly* 246, no. 8 (February 22, 1999): 63.

Stephens, Dionne. "The Effects of Images of African American Women in Hip Hop on Early Adolescents' Attitudes toward Physical Attractiveness and Interpersonal Relationships." *Sex Roles* 56 (2007): 251–64.

Stoner, Marie, Katherine Rucinski, Carrie Lyons, and Sue Napierala. "Differentiating the Incidence and Burden of HIV by Age among Women Who Sell Sex: A Systematic Review and Meta-Analysis." *Journal of International AIDS Society* 25, no. 10 (October 2022): e26028.

Stuntzner-Gibson, Denise. "Women and HIV Disease: An Emerging Crisis." *Social Work* 36, no. 1 (January 1991): 22–28.

Taylor, Ula. "The Historical Evolution of Black Feminist Theory and Praxis." *Journal of Black Studies* 29, no. 2 (November 1998): 234–53.

Thompson, Danielle. "Why We Need to Understand Intersectional Changes in Midwifery to Reclaim Home Birth." *Columbia Journal of Race and Law* 6, no. 1 (2016), 27–46. https://doi.org/10.7916/cjrl.v6i1.2312.

Thompson, Lisa B. *Beyond the Black Lady: Sexuality and the New African American Middle Class*. Urbana: University of Illinois Press, 2009.

Thompson, Mary. "Third Wave Feminism and the Politics of Motherhood." *Genders* 43 (2006). https://web.archive.org/web/20130513000812/http://www.genders.org/g43/g43_marythompson.html.

Tillerson, Kristin. "Explaining Racial Disparities in HIV/AIDS Incidence among Women in the U.S.: A Systematic Review." *Statistics in Medicine* 27, no. 20 (September 10, 2008): 4132–43.

Tillet, Salamishah, and Scheherazade Tillet. "'You Want to Be Well?': Self-Care as a Black Feminist Intervention in Art Therapy." In *Art Therapy for Social Justice: Radical Intersections*, edited by Savneet K. Talwar, 123–43. New York: Routledge, 2019.

Tillman, Shaquita, Thema Bryant-Davis, Kimberly Smith, and Alison Marks. "Shattering Silence." *Trauma, Violence, and Abuse* 11, no. 2 (April 2010): 59–70.

Tobin, Courtney Thomas, Millicent Robinson, and Kiara Stanifer. "Does Marriage Matter? Racial Differences in Allostatic Loads among Women." *Prevention Medicine Reports* 15 (2019): 1–6.

"Transcript: Vice Presidential Debate, Case Western Reserve University, Cleveland, Ohio, October 5, 2004." Debate between Vice President Dick Cheney and Senator John Edwards. *Washington Post*, October 5, 2004. https://www.washingtonpost.com/wp-srv/politics/debatereferee/debate_1005.html.

BIBLIOGRAPHY • 157

Treichler, Paula. *How to Have Theory in an Epidemic: Cultural Chronicles of AIDS*. Durham, NC: Duke University Press, 1999.

Tsuyuki, Kiyomi, Erica Chan, Marguerite Lucea, Andrea Cimino, Abby Rudolph, Yordanos Tesfai, Jacquelyn Campbell, Christina Catabay, and Jamila Stockman. "Characterising a Syndemic among Black Women at Risk for HIV: The Role of Sociostructural Inequity and Adverse Childhood Experiences." *Sexually Transmitted Infections* 99 (2023): 7–13.

UNAIDS. *Final Report: The Status and Trends of the Global HIV/AIDS Pandemic*. Geneva: Joint United Nations Programme on HIV/AIDS, July 5–6, 1996. https://pdf.usaid.gov/pdf_docs/pnabz128.pdf.

———. "Forty Years into the HIV Epidemic, AIDS Remains the Leading Cause of Death of Women of Reproductive Age—UNAIDS Calls for Bold Action." March 5, 2020. https://www.unaids.org/sites/default/files/20200305_PR_weve-got-the-power_en.pdf.

———. "HIV Estimates with Uncertainty Bounds: 1990–Present." July 13, 2023. https://www.unaids.org/en/resources/documents/2023/HIV_estimates_with_uncertainty_bounds_1990-present.

———. *The Path That Ends AIDS: 2023 UNAIDS Global AIDS Update 2023*. Geneva: Joint United Nations Programme on HIV/AIDS, 2023.

———. *Report on the Global HIV/AIDS Epidemic*. Geneva: Joint United Nations Programme on HIV/AIDS, 2000.

———. "World AIDS Day 2023: Fact Sheet." Accessed January 24, 2024. https://www.unaids.org/sites/default/files/media_asset/UNAIDS_FactSheet_en.pdf.

US Census Bureau. "HIV/AIDS Surveillance Data Base." Accessed January 29, 2024. https://www.census.gov/data-tools/demo/hiv/#/map?s_datacode=I.

Venable, Malcolm, Tayannah McQuillar, and Yvette Mingo. "It's Urban, It's Real, but Is This Literature?" *Black Issues Book Review* 6, no. 5 (September–October 2004): 24–27.

Venkatasan, Sathyaraj. "'Telling Your Story Git You Over That River': AIDS and Scenes of Reading and Writing in Sapphire's PUSH." *Journal of Language, Literature, and Culture* 60, no. 2 (August 2013): 109–17.

Vernon-Feagans, Lynn, Mary Bratsch-Hines, and Elizabeth Reynolds. "How Early Maternal Input Varies by Race and Education and Predicts Later Child Development." *Child Development* 91, no. 4 (July/August 2020): 1098–1115.

Vicari, Stephanie, Barbara Caravale, Giovanni Augusto Carlesimo, Anna Maria Casadei and Federico Allemand. "Spatial Working Memory Deficits in Children at Ages 3–4 Who Were Low Birth Weight, Preterm Infants." *Neuropsychology* 18, no. 4 (2004): 673–78.

Wagner, Rachel. "Race, (In)Justice, and the Prison Industrial Complex in Sister Souljah's *The Coldest Winter Ever*." *Harvard Journal of African American Public Policy* (2018): 33–38.

Wall, Cheryl. "On Dolls, Presidents, and Little Black Girls." In *Still Brave: The Evolution of Black Women's Studies*, edited by Stanlie James, Frances Smith Foster, and Beverly Guy-Sheftall, 435–39. New York: Feminist Press, 2009.

Wallace, Maeve, Joia Crear-Perry, Lisa Richardson, Meshawn Tarver, and Katherine Theall. "Separate and Unequal: Structural Racism and Infant Mortality in the US." *Health and Place* 45 (May 2017): 140–44.

Wallace, Michele. *Black Macho and the Myth of the Superwoman*. New York: Dial Press, 1979.

———. "Boyz N the Hood and Jungle Fever." In *Black Popular Culture: A Project by Michele Wallace*, edited by Gina Dent, 123–31. Seattle: Bay Press, 1992.

———. *Dark Designs and Visual Culture*. Durham, NC: Duke University Press, 2004.

158 • BIBLIOGRAPHY

Walter, Heather, Roger Vaughan, Deborah Ragin, Alwyn Cohall, and Stephanie Kasen. "Prevalence and Correlates of AIDS-Related Behavioral Intentions among Urban Minority High School Students." *AIDS Education and Prevention* 6, no. 4 (1994): 339–50.

Wamoyi, Joyce, Lori Heise, Rebecca Meiksin, Nambusi Kyegombe, Daniel Nyato, and Ana Maria Buller. "Is Transactional Sex Exploitative? A Social Norms Perspective, with Implications for Interventions with Adolescent Girls and Young Women in Tanzania." *PLoS One* 14, no. 4 (April 2, 2019): e0214366.

Ward, Jesmyn. *Men We Reaped.* New York: Bloomsbury, 2013.

Watkins-Hayes, Celeste. *Remaking a Life: How Women Living with HIV/AIDS Confront Inequality.* Berkeley: University of California Press, 2019.

Wells-Barnett, Ida B. *Crusade for Justice: The Autobiography of Ida B. Wells.* Edited by Alfreda M. Duster. Chicago: University of Chicago Press, 1970.

West, Carolyn, Linda Williams, and Jane Siegel. "Adult Sexual Revictimization among Black Women Sexually Abused in Childhood: A Prospective Examination of Series Consequences of Abuse." *Child Maltreatment* 5, no. 1 (2000): 49–57.

White, Deborah Gray. *Ar'n't I a Woman? Female Slaves in the Plantation South.* 2nd ed. New York: W. W. Norton, 1999.

White, Evelyn, ed. *The Black Women's Health Book: Speaking for Ourselves.* Seattle: Seal Press, 1990.

Wild, David, and Jon Wiederhorn. "Eazy-E: 1963–1995." *Rolling Stone* 701 (May 4, 1995).

Williams, Angela. "Danai Gurira Thought Her Manager Was Pranking Her about 'Black Panther' Role." *Good Morning America,* February 21, 2018. https://www.goodmorningamerica.com/culture/story/danai-gurira-thought-manager-pranking-black-panther-role-53246670.

Willoughby, Michael, Kesha Hudson, Yihua Hong, and Amanda Wylie. "Improvements in Motor Competence Skills are Associated with Improvements in Executive Function and Math Problem-Solving Skills in Early Childhood." *Developmental Psychology* 57, no. 9 (2021): 1463–70.

Wingood, Gina, and Ralph DiClemente. "Child Sexual Abuse, HIV Sexual Risk, and Gender Relations of African-American Women." *American Journal of Prevention Medicine* 13, no. 5 (September–October 1997): 380–84.

———. "The Influence of Psychosocial Factors, Alcohol, Drug Use on African American Women's High-Risk Sexual Behavior." *American Journal of Preventive Medicine* 15, no. 1 (July 1998): 54–59.

Wohl, David, David Rosen, and Andrew Kaplan. "HIV and Incarceration: Duel Epidemics." *AIDS Read* 16, no 5 (2006): 247–50.

Women with a Vision. https://wwav-no.org/.

World Health Organization. "Adolescent Health." Accessed January 29, 2024. https://www.who.int/health-topics/adolescent-health#tab=tab_1.

———. "The Global Burden of Disease: 2004 Update." Accessed January 29, 2024. https://apps.who.int/iris/bitstream/handle/10665/43942/9789241563710_eng.pdf.

Wyatt, Gail. *Stolen Women: Reclaiming Our Sexuality, Taking Back Our Lives.* Hoboken, NJ: John Wiley and Sons, 1998.

Wyatt, Gail, Jennifer Vargas Carmona, Tamra Loeb, and John Williams. "HIV-Positive Black Women with Histories of Childhood Sexual Abuse: Patterns of Substance Abuse and Barriers to Health Care." *Journal of Health Care for the Poor and Underserved* 16, no. 4 (November 2005): 9–23.

Wyatt, Gail, Nell Forge, and Donald Guthrie. "Family Constellation and Ethnicity: Current and Lifetime HIV-Related Risk-Taking." *Journal of Family Psychology* 12, no. 1 (1998): 93–101.

Yan, Haiping. "Staging Modern Vagrancy: Female Figures of Border-Crossing in Ama Ata Aidoo and Caryl Churchill." *Theater Journal* 54, no. 2 (May 2002): 245–62.

Zembe, Yanga, Loraine Townsend, Anna Thorson, and Anna Mia Ekström. "'Money Talks, Bullshit Walks': Interrogating Notions of Consumption and Survival Sex among Young Women Engaging in Transactional Sex in Post-Apartheid South Africa: A Qualitative Inquiry." *Globalization and Health* 9 (July 18, 2013): article no. 28. https://doi.org/10.1186/1744-8603-9-28.

Ziesenheim, Sherry, and Matthew Darling. "Writing, Mothering, and Traumatic Subjectivity in Sapphire's *PUSH*." In *Disjointed Perspectives on Motherhood,* edited by Catalina Florina Florescu, 171–83. New York: Lexington Books, 2013.

INDEX

access: health care, 4n12, 9–10, 13, 23n31, 77, 81, 83, 86, 100, 127n16, 128; information, 72–73, 72n21, 72nn24–25, 73n26, 128. *See also* HIV/AIDS: awareness and education

activism, 4, 7–8, 20, 23n31, 25n41, 26, 33, 65, 75n33, 81, 83, 124

ACT-UP (AIDS Coalition to Unleash Power), 7–8

advertising, 13, 126–27, 126n12, 127nn13–14

Africa, sub-Saharan, 4, 4n12, 5n21, 8, 12n51, 18, 22, 23n31, 40n56, 66–91, 70n10

Aguayo-Romero, Rodrigo, 8–9

Ahmad, 70

AIDSCAP (AIDS Control and Prevention Project), 5n19

Akil, Salim, 94n7

Allen, Anita, 93, 101–2

Allen, Debbie, 117–18. See also *Different World, A*

Angelou, Maya, 25, 32, 88

antiretroviral therapy, 4, 13n54, 77, 77n44, 86–87; AZT, 22, 22n28; viral suppression, 13, 77, 129n20

Armstrong, Linda, 69

Asante, M. K., Jr., 95

Avery, Byllye, 1, 15, 24, 73

awareness, HIV/AIDS. *See* education; HIV/AIDS: awareness and education

AZT, 22, 22n28. *See also* antiretroviral therapy

Bailey, Marlon, 8, 60, 100

Balkin, Sarah, 127

Bambara, Toni Cade, 23–24

Bank, Nina, 23n31

Barris, Kenya, 22, 22n26, 98

birth control, 35, 40, 65. *See also* safer sex practices

Black Women's Health Conference Task Force, 124

Black Women's Health Imperative. *See* Avery, Byllye

Boone, Eunetta, 98

Borrego, Silvia Pilar Castro, 30n9

Bowser, Yvette Lee, 98, 118

Boykin, Keith, 109n29

Boyz n the Hood (film), 45, 48–49, 49n97

161

162 • INDEX

Brock Akil, Mara, 1, 2, 4, 6, 9–10, 12–13, 17–19, 21–23, 26, 91–122, 94n6

Brown, Ruth Nicole, 26

Bush, George W., 6n26

Butler, Octavia, 25

call-and-response, 68, 73–74, 77–78, 77n46, 89–90

cascade of care, 13, 13n54, 87

CDC (Centers for Disease Control and Prevention), 2n3, 3n11, 4n12, 5, 36, 42n65, 71, 87n62, 109

Chapola-Chimombo, Callista, 67–68

Chappelle, Dave, 125–28

Cheney, Dick, 5–6

child sexual abuse. *See under* sexual violence

Childress, Alice, 25

Clair, Brittany, 17

Cleage, Pearl, 18

Clifton, Lucille, 25

Closer, The (TV special), 125–28

Cohen, Cathy, 36n44, 108

Cokal, Susann, 50n100

Coldest Winter Ever, The (Sister Souljah), 10–11, 22, 27–66, 29n4, 38n53, 39nn54–55, 69, 76n41

Collins, Patricia Hill, 31, 38, 48n91

Color Purple, The (Walker), 24

Combs, Sean, 98, 106n25

comorbidities, HIV/AIDS, 21, 54n115, 128

condom use. *See under* safer sex practices

Congressional Black Caucus, 6n26

consent, 41n60, 76n41

controlling images, 31, 38, 48n91

Cooper, Anna Julia, 123–24

Cooper, Brittney, 19, 20n16, 23, 30n10, 54, 94

Cosby Show, The (TV series), 117–18, 120

COVID-19, 3, 3n6, 4nn12–13, 125

crack cocaine. *See under* substance use

Crenshaw, Kimberle, 76, 82. *See also* intersectionality

criminal justice system, 32, 76, 50, 51n103. *See also* incarceration

Cross, Tracy, 25

CW, The (broadcast network), 12, 93, 93n1, 94n4, 99, 119–21

Da Brat. *See* MCs, female

DaBaby, 12–13, 125–26, 126n11

Dagbovie, Sika, 31n14

Daniels, Lee, 99

Darling, Matthew, 37, 37n48, 50n100

David, Marlo, 30n9

Davis, Angela Michaela, 116

Davis, Dana Ain, 16

Diallo, Dazón Dixon, 83–84, 83n56

diaspora, African, 11–12, 20n16, 66–91

DiClemente, Ralph, 60n122, 76, 76n42

Different World, A (TV series), 117–18, 117nn38–39, 118n40

disparities, health, 3, 6–10, 13, 17, 19–21, 23, 31, 34–36, 87, 91, 100, 116, 124, 129n20

domestic violence, 10, 13, 15, 19, 24, 30n9, 47, 50, 76, 82–84, 94n7, 99, 128

down low, 78, 108–9, 109n29, 116n37

Dugger, Celia W., 36

Dunn, Stephanie, 45n76

Durham, Aisha, 20n16, 23

Duvernay, Ava, 95

Eazy-E, 2

education, 7, 16, 29, 31–32, 32n21, 43, 93, 98, 106, 118, 126

Edwards, John, 5–6

Elliot, Missy, 95–96, 98

environmental factors, HIV/AIDS, 3, 7, 18, 43–44

epidemiology, 3n11, 10, 36, 42, 87, 87n62

Espinosa, Mariola, 23n31

Evans-Winters, Venus, 46

Eve, 95, 98

Eve (TV series), 120

Farrakhan, Louis, 52, 54

Finamore, Adrianna, 51n105

Forge, Nell, 111–12

Foster, Pamela, 80

Foucault, Michel, 6, 6n28

INDEX · 163

Foxxy Brown. *See* MCs, female

Freire, Paolo, 30n9

Fullilove, Mindy Thompson and Robert, 6, 57

Fuqua, Antoine, 99

Game, The (TV series), 12, 22, 22n26, 93–122, 93n1, 94n3; legacy, 119–22; predecessors, 94n6, 116–18; viewership, 94, 94n4

Gates, Henry Louis, 79

Gaunt, Kyra D., 26, 67, 78–79

gay men, 7, 20n16, 34, 40n56, 60, 72, 79–80, 94n6, 95, 108–10, 109n29, 116n37, 127

gender identity and expression, 12n57, 38, 46, 71, 111–12, 127–29, 127n11

Gentry, Quinn, 100n17

George, Nelson, 98

Gilbert, Dorie, 6–7, 46

Gilroy, Paul, 68

Giovanni, Nikki, 25

Girlfriends (TV series), 12, 22, 22n26, 93–122, 93n1; legacy, 119–22; predecessors, 94n6, 116–18; viewership, 94, 94n4

GLAAD (Gay and Lesbian Alliance Against Defamation), 126

Global Coalition on Women and AIDS, 72. *See also* UNAIDS

Goldberg, Whoopi, 117

Gourdine, Angeletta K. M., 52n108

Gray, Anissa, 25

Gurira, Danai, 1, 2, 4, 6, 9–10, 11–13, 17–19, 21–23, 26, 66–91, 68n5, 70n10, 77n46

Guthrie, Donald, 111–12

Hammonds, Evelynn, 65, 81

Hansberry, Lorainne, 25

Harris, E. Lynn, 109n29

Harris, Trudier, 90

Harris-Perry, Melissa, 75n32

Haskins, Susan, 68n5, 74

health care access. *See* access: health care

health disparities. *See* disparities, health

Henderson, Aneeka Ayanna, 50n100

Higginbotham, Evelyn Brooks, 75n33. *See also* respectability

Highberg, Nels, 30n9

Hill, Lauryn. *See* MCs, female

Hillsburg, Heather, 48n90

Hinton, Elizabeth, 51n103

HIV/AIDS

—awareness and education, 3–4, 20–21, 20n16, 35, 42n65, 46, 55, 70, 83, 100, 124, 126

—diagnosis, 3–5, 7, 13n54, 20–21, 30n9, 34, 34n31, 42n65, 69–70, 74, 79–87, 99, 108

—HIV+ status, 2, 13n54, 37, 41, 54–56, 56n116, 62, 70, 77, 82–87, 90, 100, 110, 117, 120

—incidence, 3–5, 5n21, 8, 18–21, 24, 29, 36, 40–42, 40n56, 42n65, 71–72, 95, 99–100, 108; in infants, 36n46, 87, 87n62

—mortality. *See* mortality

—political context, 22–23, 30n9, 31–32, 75nn32–33, 81, 94–95, 117–19; political responses, 3–7, 6n26, 108–9, 124

—prevalence, 4, 8, 15, 29, 33–34, 36n46, 41–42, 42n65, 71–72, 99

—prevention, 5n19, 33–36, 36n43, 40n56, 42–45, 60, 65–66, 71, 73n20, 83, 86, 100, 124

—risk, 6–13, 21, 29, 33–46, 51–62, 65–66, 71–89, 91, 101–4, 112–15, 122; and risk reduction, 35, 61, 65, 71, 82, 86, 89, 106

—risk factors, psychological, 18, 23–24, 35–38, 50, 55–56, 75, 75n32, 81, 101, 104, 102, 109n29

—risk factors, structural, 8, 10, 43–44, 51, 78, 99–100

—surveillance research, 4–5, 4nn12–13, 33–36, 71–72, 87n62, 99–100, 129n20

—testing, 4n12, 79–80, 82, 87, 120, 124, 128–29

—transmission, 2n3, 36, 76, 99; heterosexual, 59, 79, 81; perinatal, 37, 83, 86–87, 87n62; risk factors, 41, 79, 101

Hogan, Katie, 18

Holloway, Karla, 25

homophobia, 13, 94n6, 99, 101, 125–27

Hunt, Darnell, 117–18, 118n40

Hurston, Zora Neale, 24–25

I Am Because We Are (documentary), 67–68

Ifill, Gwen, 5–6

IMARA (Informed, Motivated, Aware, and Responsible about AIDS), 46

164 • INDEX

In the Continuum (Gurira and Salter), 11, 67–91, 68nn4–5

incarceration, 19, 39n55, 47, 50–51, 51nn103–4, 62, 65, 78, 106, 117, 117n39

infant mortality, 7, 17, 31, 87

information access. *See* access: information

Institute of Women and Ethnic Studies (IWES), 40

intersectionality, 6–9

Isherwood, Charles, 69

Jay-Z, 98

Jemisin, N. K., 25

Jemmott, John, 36

Jemmott, Loretta Sweet, 36

Johnson, Earvin "Magic," 2, 117, 125

Joint United Nations Programme on HIV/AIDS. *See* UNAIDS

Jones, Gayl, 33n22

Jordan-Zachery, Julie, 76–77

Juvenile, 28–29, 45

Kelley, Robin D. G., 27–28

King, J. L., 29n109

Kokkola, Lydia, 30, 43n74

Kramer, Larry, 7–8

Ladner, Joyce, 31–32, 43

laws and policies, 8, 17–18, 20, 32, 40, 51n103, 127n16

Lee, Barbara, 6n26

Leigh, Wilhemina, 81

Lewis, Marva, 38

Lil' Kim. *See* MCs, female

Lindsey, Treva, 20n16

Living Single (TV series), 118

Lorde, Audre, 25, 123–24

Mandela, Winnie, 88

marriage, 7, 20, 108–10, 113–14, 116n37

Marshall, Paule, 33n22

maternal mortality. *See under* mortality

MC Lyte, 95, 98

McNeil, Elizabeth, 42n65, 48n91

MCs, female, 95–98, 118n42, 120–21

Megan Thee Stallion, 29n4

Melton, Monica, 77

mental health, 6–7, 10, 25, 47, 50n100, 62–63, 68, 76–77, 99, 104, 128; depression, 25, 31, 128

Menzies, Alisha, 56n116

Mitchell, W. J. T., 121

morbidity, 7, 23n31

Morgan, Joan, 15, 19, 106–7

Morgan, Marcyliena, 98

Morris, Susana M., 20n16, 23, 32n18, 50n100

Morrison, Toni, 27–29, 32, 45; *The Bluest Eye,* 24; *Tar Baby,* 123

mortality, 3, 5, 7, 18–21, 23n31, 30, 34, 42, 71–72, 95; infant, 7, 17, 31, 87; maternal, 7, 17, 24, 87

motherhood, 11, 28–32, 30n9, 35n38, 36–66, 70, 84–88, 90, 105–6, 112, 114–15, 117

MSM (men who have sex with men), 4, 40n56, 109–11, 109n29

Müller, Claudia, 48n90

National Black Women's Health Project. *See* Avery, Byllye

National Black Women's Justice Institute (NBWJI), 40

Naylor, Gloria, 33n22

Nehanda, Mbuya, 88

NO/AIDS Task Force, 124, 124n1

nonbinary people, 12n51, 127

O'Daniel, Alyson, 7

Ogur, Barbara, 19n9

Oprah Winfrey Show, The (TV series), 109n29

organizing. *See* activism

Osaka, Naomi, 25

Pappas, Christine, 32n21

Parrish, Man, 15–16

Patterson, Saladin K., 98

Peoples, Whitney, 5n24, 98, 98n13

Perkins, Kathy, 70n10

INDEX · 165

Perro, Ebony L., 29n4

Perry, Tyler, 99

Pinkett Smith, Jada, 98

Polk, Patrik-Ian, 98

Pollard, Cherise, 29n4, 30n10

Pough, Gwendolyn, 9, 49, 75, 98

poverty, 25, 28n90, 78, 81, 84, 100, 106

pregnancy, 7, 10, 17, 24n36, 31, 35, 38, 40–41, 46, 52, 55–57, 90; drug use during, 52, 56–57; HIV+, 83–85, 90; on screen, 105, 105n24, 117–18

President's Emergency Plan for AIDS Relief (PEPFAR), 6n26

Price, Kimala, 19–20

public health, 4, 7, 8, 12, 16–17, 23–25, 40, 51n104, 65, 71, 74, 108

PUSH (Sapphire), 10–11, 18–19, 22, 27–66, 29n4, 30nn9–10, 32n18, 32n21, 33n22, 42n65, 43n74, 76n41

Queen Latifah, 98–99, 118, 118n42

racism, 8–10, 16–17, 20–21, 32, 48, 75–84, 119

Rae, Issa, 99

Rah Digga. *See* MCs, female

rape. *See under* sexual violence

Reagan, Ronald, 23, 23n31, 32

religion, 43, 75n33, 103

respectability, 18, 32n18, 44, 75n33, 94, 109

Rhimes, Shonda, 99

Riedel, Michael, 68n5, 74

Roberts, Dorothy, 18, 74n31, 75

Robinson, Gayle, 85

Rose, Tricia, 19, 19n9, 43, 112

Ryalls, Emily, 56n116

safer sex practices: condom use, 35–36, 40–41, 49, 79–80, 86–87, 117, 117n38; condomless sex, 35–36, 41, 59–60, 60n122, 76, 79, 110

Salter, Nikkole, 1–13, 17–23, 26, 66–91, 68n5, 70n10

Salt-N-Pepa. *See* MCs, female

Sapphire, 1–13, 17–23, 26–66, 30n9, 76n41

Schalk, Sami, 9

Schoepf, Brooke Grundfest, 71

Schulman, Sarah, 7

sex workers, 77, 80, 84, 86–87; stereotypes, 77, 80

sexual and reproductive health, 18, 20, 24, 41, 83

sexual desire, 11, 33, 35, 59–60, 85, 101, 109n29

sexual violence, 24, 30n9, 128; child sexual abuse, 30n9, 36–37, 50–51, 50n100, 54–56, 55n115, 62, 76, 76nn41–42; rape, 10, 11, 30n9, 50, 76n41, 118

Shange, Ntozake, 25

Sherman, Charlotte Watson, 18

Sister Souljah, 1–13, 17–23, 26–66, 43n70, 53n113, 63n127, 73, 76n41

Smith, Beverly, 15, 23

Smith, Will, 98

Smitherman, Geneva, 68

Smith-Shomade, Beretta, 118n42

Snorton, C. Riley, 12n51

social norms, 8, 35, 38, 40n56, 100

socioeconomic factors, 7, 10–11, 22, 31–32, 40, 43, 47–50, 77, 77n44, 81, 88, 98, 100, 106, 109

Spillers, Hortense, 27, 29–30

Stallings, L. H., 12n51, 33, 42

Stapleton, Laurie, 30n9

Stephens, Dionne, 35

stereotypes of black women, 32, 35, 35n38, 48–50, 48nn90–91, 75n32, 74–77, 101, 107, 112–13

stigma, 3, 8, 11–12, 21–22, 54–55, 67–91, 100–101, 126

STIs/STDs (sexually transmitted infections/diseases), 18, 21, 41, 46, 81, 101–2, 117, 128

substance use, 15, 19, 25, 51, 54, 57–60, 77, 84, 99, 128; addiction, 24, 51n102, 77; crack cocaine, 19n9, 49–54, 56–58, 60n122, 61–64, 117

Tar Baby (Morrison). *See under* Morrison, Toni

Taylor, Ula, 23n31

Thomas, Rozonda "Chili," 120

Thompson, Mary, 30n9

166 • INDEX

Thornton, Rae Lewis, 2

Tillet, Salamishah and Scheherazade, 25, 25n41

transactional sex, 38, 40, 40n56, 52–53, 101

transgender women, 12–13, 84–86, 128–29, 128n16

transphobia, 13, 94, 127

Treichler, Paula, 7

Trina. *See* MCs, female

Turner, Kriss, 98

UNAIDS, 4–5, 18, 72, 72n21

UPN (broadcast network), 12, 93, 93n1, 94n4, 99, 119–20

Venkatasan, Sathyaraj, 30n9

viral suppression, 13, 77, 129n20. *See also* antiretroviral therapy

Wagner, Rachel, 39, 39n55

Walker, Alice, 16, 25, 32; *The Color Purple,* 24

Wall, Cheryl, 32–33, 33n22

Wallace, Michelle, 48n91, 49, 49n95

War on Crime/Drugs. *See* criminal justice system; incarceration

Ward, Jesmyn, 25

Watkins-Hayes, Celeste, 67, 76n42, 87–88

WB (broadcast network), 119–20

welfare, 32, 48n90, 49, 78. *See also* stereotypes of black women

Wells-Barnett, Ida B., 1

When Chickenheads Come Home to Roost (Morgan). *See* Morgan, Joan

White, Deborah Gray, 11–12

White, Evelyn, 25

Williams, Larry, 98

Wingood, Gina, 60n122, 76, 76n42

Women with a Vision (WWAV), 40

World Health Organization, 5n29

Wright, Ednita, 6–7, 46

Wyatt, David, 120

Wyatt, Gail, 75–76, 111–12

Yo-Yo. *See* MCs, female

Ziesenheim, Sherry, 37, 37n48, 50n100

Zimbabwe, 22, 69, 70, 78, 86